Geraint Williams was born in 1942 and was educated in Flintshire and University College, Swansea. From 1966-8 he was lecturer in Political Theory at University College, Swansea, and since 1968 he has been Lecturer in the Department of Political Theory and Institutions at the University of Sheffield. In 1971-2 he was visiting professor at the University of Calgary, Canada.

JOHN STUART MILL
On Politics and Society

Selected and edited by
GERAINT L. WILLIAMS

International Publications Service

Published in the U.S.A. 1976 by
International Publications Service
114 East 32nd Street
New York, N.Y. 10016
By agreement with Fontana

John Stuart Mill on Politics and Society
This edition first published in 1976
by The Harvester Press Limited
By agreement with Fontana

Library of Congress Cataloging in Publication Data

Mill, John Stuart, 1806–1873.
John Stuart Mill on politics and society.

Bibliography: p.
Includes index
1. Political science–Collected works. I. Title.
JC223.M6585 1976 320.5 75–45159
ISBN 0–8002–0169–8

Printed in Great Britain by Redwood Burn Limited
Trowbridge, Wiltshire

Er cof am fy nhad

Contents

Preface

In presenting a selection of Mill's writings on politics and society my aim has been to reveal both the structure and the development of his thought. In such an enterprise and in such a limited space it is clear that certain gaps will appear. Mill wrote extensively for fifty years; where I have omitted whole areas of his concern, as with the detail of nineteenth-century politics and parliamentary reform, I have tried to include sufficient material to reveal the manner and the principles of his approach to these questions.

Generally I have included complete articles and chapters; in two or three cases, where space would not permit the inclusion of the complete article, I have printed short extracts. Again, I have generally used the original versions of Mill's works and, where Mill republished in his own lifetime, I have noted substantial changes which appeared in the later editions in the textual notes.

My general thanks go to Mr John Rees for inspiring my lasting interest in J. S. Mill; my special thanks to Professor Bernard Crick for his necessary encouragement and kind help in this venture. I am very grateful to Mrs Maureen Parrett for her careful and patient typing, and to Mrs Elizabeth Dawson for her help in preparing the manuscript; also to the University of Sheffield Research Fund for financial help.

GERAINT WILLIAMS

Sheffield.
April 1975

Introduction

John Stuart Mill (1806-1873) has had many reputations; both in his lifetime and since. He has been seen and thus praised or criticized variously as a logician, an economist, a moral philosopher, a political theorist, and a campaigning reformer. There has been controversy both as to the nature of his particular talent and as to his success in exercising it. Within the field of politics his writings were controversial while he was alive, and have continued to be so since his death. Common to the host of interpretations of Mill's political thought is the centrality given to the essay *On Liberty*. Whether Mill is seen as a brave, noble spirit championing freedom in the face of a hostile environment, or as a mere representative thinker of mid-Victorian England, or as a crude individualist, or as a secret and intolerant dogmatist; in all cases *On Liberty* is crucial to the argument. As well as this work, his *Representative Government* has also been widely read, and *Utilitarianism* has made up the conventional trio of works by which to understand Mill. His general reputation today as the philosopher of liberalism is based on these three works, and while they do offer a necessary and clear picture of Mill at a certain stage in his life, they tend to offer too settled a view. Without some attention to his earlier and later work in the context of his life and his intellectual development we tend to forget the restless and questioning approach which was part of Mill's political thinking. Furthermore, it is important not to divorce Mill's political theory from the rest of his work; he did not see politics as an area of study totally separate from logic, history, or ethics; his intention was to bring to the study of politics and society the lessons gained from the study of related fields. So that Mill as a political thinker has often been interpreted too narrowly and his political thought itself has been wrongly divorced from his larger concern with the nature of social, historical and ethical understanding. The aim of this book is to correct both these traditional imbalances.

His Life

The year 1808 saw the first meeting between James Mill, a young Scottish writer and editor, and Jeremy Bentham, a philosopher who had been promoting and planning reform for over thirty years. The intimacy which soon developed affected both their lives, as it did the life of James's young son, John Stuart, born two years previously.

'James Mill was born on the 6th of April, 1773, at Northwater Bridge, parish of Logie Pert, county of Forfar or Angus.'[1] His father was a shoemaker, his mother a proud, somewhat superior woman determined that young James should rise above their fairly modest circumstances. Thanks to the patronage of Sir John Stuart, James Mill proceeded to Edinburgh University and subsequently entered the ministry. He did not, however, obtain a living of his own and so as well as taking the occasional service here and there he became private tutor for various noble families. It was hardly a regular or successful way of life for a man of James Mill's exceptional ability, and in 1802 he determined to move to London, to earn a living as a writer. Within six months he had achieved success, and soon had a good income as writer and editor. In 1805 he married, and a year later, on 20 May 1806 a son was born. James Mill soon abandoned regular journalism and began his *History of India,* meanwhile writing the odd article and developing his interest in politics, reading amongst other things the works of that leading reformer, Jeremy Bentham.

Bentham was born in 1748, the son of a lawyer. He attended Oxford University, and looked destined for a legal career. As it turned out, however, Bentham saw his future as a critic and a reformer rather than as a practitioner of the law, and for the rest of his long life he pursued this objective with tremendous industry and enthusiasm, moving also into the fields of politics, economics and morality. If there was one thing that Bentham lacked in 1808 it was a group of publicists, reformers, disciples, who would convey his radical message to the public at large. Bentham had the complete view, the intellectual force, and the creativity, but not the political sense; indeed he was reluctant to publish at all, and up to this time was regarded as a theorist rather than a real force in English politics. Who better to provide this extra punch than a vigorous and brilliant journalist? While Bentham provided a unified intellectual scheme, Mill gave it a sharper and more realistic political dimension. He also introduced Bentham to a number of people actually engaged on the radical side in the political life of the country. From now on their relationship grew closer, and their influence on politics much greater.

Bentham and Mill were agreed that formal education was generally of a low standard, and they determined to educate the young boy, John, in the more reliable environment of his own home. Between the age of three and fourteen he was taught Greek, Arithmetic, History, Latin, Algebra, Geometry, and Political Economy. As his father supervised his education, so he in turn tutored his younger brothers and sisters. This intensive system of learning lasted until 1820, when John was sent for an extended visit to France to stay with Bentham's brother Samuel and his family. His year there taught him the value of leisure and variety of interest and developed in him a keen and abiding interest in French intellectual and political life. His education was now almost complete; on his return to England his father gave him to read Bentham's *Traité de Législation*. The effect was momentous:

> My previous education had been, in a certain sense, already a course in Benthamism. The Benthamic stan-

dard of 'the greatest happiness' was that which I had always been taught to apply . . . Yet in the first pages of Bentham it burst upon me with all the force of novelty, What thus impressed me was the chapter in which Bentham passed judgment on the common modes of reasoning in morals and legislation, deduced from phrases like 'law of nature', 'right reason', 'the moral sense', 'natural rectitude', and the like, and characterised them as dogmatism in disguise, imposing its sentiments upon others under cover of sounding expressions which convey no reason for the sentiment, but set up the sentiment as its own reason. It had not struck me before, that Bentham's principle put an end to all this. The feeling rushed upon me, that all previous moralists were superseded, and that here indeed was the commencement of a new era in thought. This impression was strengthened by the manner in which Bentham put into scientific form the application of the happiness principle to the morality of actions, by analysing the various classes and orders of their consequences.

When I laid down the last volume of the *Traité,* I had become a different being. The 'principle of utility', understood as Bentham understood it, and applied in the manner in which he applied it through these volumes, fell exactly into its place as the keystone which held together the detached and fragmentary component parts of my knowledge and beliefs. It gave unity to my conceptions of things. I now had opinions; a creed, a doctrine, a philosophy; in one among the best senses of the word, a religion; the inculcation and diffusion of which could be made the principal outward purpose of a life.[2]

In 1823 he joined his father at the East India Company, beginning as a junior clerk. (Thirty-five years later he was to become Chief Examiner.) Fortunately for him his official duties allowed him enough time to pursue his private intellectual interests through discussion and by writing books and articles. Mill was never a man of independent means – at least until he retired – and yet, as he recognized, his particular profession gave him both a certain means of livelihood and the leisure to pursue his own philosophical and political activities. His early commitment to the utilitarian cause took the form of discussions and letters, reviews, and articles in the newspapers, mainly in the *Morning Chronicle*. At this time the place for lengthy and weighty articles on politics was generally in one of the two great *Reviews*, the *Edinburgh* and the *Quarterly*, one Whig, the other Tory. In January 1824 the *Westminster Review* was launched, financed by Bentham, and intended as a Radical alternative. Over the next four years, Mill wrote for it regularly, his articles ranging from literature to history to contemporary politics. At the same time he was discussing and debating, editing Bentham's *Rationale of Judicial Evidence,* as well as working at the India Office. His object in life – 'to be a reformer of the world' was pursued with intense energy and enthusiasm. In 1826, however, it struck him with terrifying force that the success of these early objectives would not in fact bring him personal joy and happiness. This severe depression Mill attributed to the 'habit of analysis' which 'has a tendency to wear away the feelings'.

> My education, I thought, had failed to create the feelings [of sympathy] in sufficient strength to resist the dissolving influence of analysis, while the whole course of my intellectual cultivation had made precocious and premature analysis the inveterate habit of my mind.[8]

This mental crisis had two important consequences for Mill's approach to moral and political thought. Firstly, he no longer believed that happiness should be pursued as a personal goal, but was something to be attained by not making it the direct end. Aiming at something else – the good of others, the improvement of mankind – we find happiness on the way. Secondly, he now came to believe that for human happiness, the internal culture of the individual was essential. The Benthamite stress on the ordering of outward circumstances, and the calculation of means toward pleasurable consequences was now considerably modified.

Such doubts as Mill had during this period rendered him both susceptible to and eager for new influences. Wordsworth offered him a view of happiness in inward joy and tranquil contemplation, the Coleridgians, Maurice and Sterling, gave him close and friendly contact with individuals at the opposite intellectual pole. New ideas flooded in:

> I found the fabric of my old and taught opinions giving way in many fresh places, and I never allowed it to fall to pieces, but was incessantly occupied in weaving it anew.[4]

This period of adjustment and renewal continued for many years – indeed in one sense it lasted all his life – and in 1829 it received a new and disturbing challenge. In that year Macaulay published his attack on James Mill's *Essay on Government* in the *Edinburgh Review*.[5] While Mill rejected what he saw as Macaulay's empirical mode, he could also see that several of the criticisms of his father were correct:

> . . . my father's premises were really too narrow, and included but a small number of the general truths on which, in politics, the important consequences depend . . . This made me think that there was really something more fundamentally erroneous in my father's conception of philosophical method, as applicable to politics, than I had hitherto supposed there was.[6]

It was Mill's attempt to cope with this problem that finally led to his own position as outlined in Book VI of the *System of Logic*.

The other major influence of this period was that of the Saint-Simonians, with their division of history into organic and critical periods. At the very least this taught Mill not to assume that the characteristics of any one era were necessarily the normal qualities of humanity generally. Moral views, religious beliefs, economic assumptions all needed to be seen not as indefeasible facts but as ideas to be periodically thrown off during an age of transition. In 1831 Mill attempted to convey this general approach in a series of articles headed 'The Spirit of the Age'.[7]

The mental depression, then, gave way to a new period of activity, a new outlook on the world. Mill sums it up in this way:

> If I am asked, what system of political philosophy I substituted for that which, as a philosophy, I had abandoned, I answer No system: only a conviction that the true system was something much more complex and many-sided than I had previously had any idea of, and that its office was to supply, not a set of model institutions, but principles from which the institutions suitable to any given circumstances might be deduced.[8]

In 1830 Mill met Harriet Taylor, the woman who was eventually, after the death of her husband, to be his wife. It is difficult to assess the importance of her influence. Mill lavished on her the very highest praise; others have been more sceptical. Probably the most balanced view comes from Mill himself, who whilst painting a picture of a most perfect, most wise, most noble, most sensitive creature, adds that her influence 'even after it became, I may truly say, the presiding principle of my mental progress, it did not alter the path, but only made me move forward more boldly, and, at the same time, more cautiously, in the same course.'[9] Where substantial changes did occur in Mill's views – especially in politics – Harriet was by no means the only influence. Mill's changing views on democracy, for example, probably owed most to his reading of Tocqueville's *Democracy in America,* which he reviewed in 1835 (vol. I) and 1840 (vol. II). The discussions of popular government and of centralization, the care to see their weaknesses as well as their strengths, convinced Mill to take a moderate line on both questions. His first review appeared in the new

London Review, established in 1835 to promote and discuss the Radical cause. The Mills had in 1828 forsaken the *Westminster Review,* and the new review was meant to give the philosophical radicals a fresh outlet for their ideas, as well as to introduce new ideas. Molesworth was the proprietor and ostensible editor, Mill the real editor, who from 1834 to 1840 spent most of his spare time on the running of the review. As well as editing, he wrote extensively in the new review, on philosophy, politics, poetry, and history.[10] His approach to it is perhaps best summed up by the quotation from Locke which appeared on the title page:

> Those who have not thoroughly examined to the bottom all their own tenets, must confess they are unfit to prescribe to others; and are unreasonable in imposing that as truth on other men's beliefs which they themselves have not searched into, nor weighed the arguments of probability on which they should receive or reject it.

Meanwhile, the health of James Mill had been declining, and in 1836 he died. John Stuart Mill was already suffering from the first stages of a general physical collapse, and over the next few years he was compelled to take considerable time off from his official duties. In 1836 for three months and again in 1839 for six months he went to the Continent in the hope of improving his health. There, he and Harriet, accompanied by various children of their respective families, sought release from overwork and poor health. However, despite these prolonged stays abroad, and despite his official, family, and editorial responsibilities in London, Mill still managed to write long articles for the *Review* (it was during this period that he wrote his two most impressive essays – on Bentham, and on Coleridge) as well as resuming his work on the *Logic*. In 1840 he gave up control of the *Review* and concentrated more fully on the *Logic,* which was completed the following year and published in 1843, some thirteen years after Macaulay's article had first prompted him to consider the nature and structure of human knowledge. The other major stimulus was the work of Auguste Comte, whose book on Positive Philosophy reached England in 1837.

The next decade of Mill's life was spent in relative isolation. Being released from his literary and editorial responsibilities, he more and more sought the company only of those few worthy of being friends. General society he thought to be insipid and unattractive. His main intellectual and emotional companion was Harriet Taylor. In what Mill calls the third period of his mental progress, he concentrated less on government and more on poverty and injustice. He considered himself to be less of a democrat and more of a socialist than he had been. This movement can be seen by comparing the first three editions of his *Principles of Political Economy,* where between 1848 and 1852 his opposition to socialism is replaced by sympathetic discussion.

In 1849 John Taylor died, and two years later Mill and Harriet were married. Three years after that, Mill's illness was finally diagnosed as consumption. Harriet herself was also in poor health, and faced with the fact that death might come sooner rather than later, they resolved to get down on paper their thoughts on those topics most important to them. Apart from religion and logic, their list of priorities included the need to write on liberty, socialism, morality, government, and the family. On all of these topics Mill did finally publish, all after the death of Harriet, and all based on their joint discussions. Alongside this intense intellectual effort, Mill continued his work at the East India Company, and they still managed to travel extensively on the Continent. At last, in 1858 Mill was freed from the need to work and the need to live in London. The East India Company was taken over by the government, and Mill, now its Chief Examiner, retired on a generous pension. He resolved to leave immediately for Europe; they travelled as far as Avignon where, suddenly, after a few days' illness, Harriet died. Mill buried her there and bought a small house near the cemetery for his retirement.

Soon after, Mill began to publish the works which he and Harriet had spent so long discussing. *On Liberty* appeared in 1859, and *Utilitarianism* and *Representative Government* two years later. He also wrote extensively on the principles and details of parliamentary reform, on philosophy, on international affairs, and on the American Civil War. So that though his wife's death was a grievous loss, Mill still felt the need, indeed the obligation, to carry on his life's work. During this period he spent most of his time in Avignon with his work, his thoughts, his memories, and his step-daughter Helen. However, in 1865 he was tempted to return to London for longer than his usual fairly brief visits. He was invited to stand as parliamentary candidate for Westminster:

> I wrote, in reply to the offer, a letter for publication, saying that I had no personal wish to be a member of Parliament, that I thought a candidate ought neither to canvass nor to incur any expense, and that I could not consent to do either. I said further, that if elected, I could not undertake to give any of my time and labour to their local interests. With respect to general politics, I told them without reserve, what I thought on a number of important subjects on which they had asked an opinion: and one of these being the suffrage, I made known to them, among other things, my conviction (as I was bound to do, since I intended, if elected, to act on it), that women were entitled to representation in Parliament, on the same terms with men.[11]

His conditions were accepted, he stood, and was elected to Parliament, where he spoke on reform, on Ireland, on the position of the working classes, on land reform, on brutality in the West Indies, and on various problems about which he felt deeply. Inside and outside parliament, the most dramatic of these issues broke to the surface in 1866. Mill, amongst others, proposed that the Governor of Jamaica, for his savage and senseless violence and killing, should be brought to justice. In 1865, in the course of dealing with a relatively small rebellion, Governor Eyre and those under his command had managed to hang or shoot over five hundred of the non-white population, and flog and brutalize a great many more. In its reaction to the news, English opinion was sharply and bitterly divided. Carlyle, Tennyson, Kingsley, Ruskin, and Dickens to a lesser degree, supported Eyre; Mill, Huxley, Spencer, Bright, Fitzjames Stephen and many others condemned him. Although Eyre was never actually punished Mill wanted him hanged – the controversy did arouse public indignation, did limit the operation of martial law, and, Mill believed, would act as a deterrent to future colonial authorities.

In 1868 Mill stood again for Parliament but was defeated, and returned to Avignon, where he once more had the time to think at leisure and to continue writing; as well as producing many articles, he wrote on religion, on the position of women, on socialism, and revised and brought up to date his *Autobiography*. His life during his last years, in Avignon and in London, was active and amiable. In 1873, he died at Avignon, and was buried there next to his wife, leaving Helen as his literary executor.

The understanding of politics

Until his mental crisis in 1826, Mill's approach to the study of politics was that provided for him by Benthamism; the belief that human nature can be analysed in terms of pleasure and pain. All motives, desires, and therefore actions are capable of being understood in terms of the pursuit of pleasure and the avoidance of pain. This simple psychological theory is paralleled in the moral sphere by an equally crude account; not only does pain and pleasure explain cause and effect, it also operates as the standard of right and wrong. In politics, virtues and good institutions are regarded as such because they promote human happiness, i.e. they produce more pleasure than pain. Mill accepted all this in general as well as in its application to the study of politics. The method was clear – its basis was an analysis of human nature in terms of pleasure and pain, its goal was the maximization of the happiness of the members of the political community. From the first principles to the required conclusion the argument proceeded deductively. In the best and most well-known application of the method to the study of government, James Mill attempted to demonstrate that democracy is a necessary conclusion based on the facts of human nature.

His essay begins with a summary of the utilitarian analysis of human nature and the utilitarian view of the proper end of government. The problem facing James Mill is how to attain the latter in a manner consistent with the former. If government is necessary, how can it be made good? Mill formulates the problem in this way:

> All the difficult questions of government relate to the means of restraining those in whose hands are lodged the powers necessary for the protection of all from making bad use of it.[12]

If it is true that we can trust no one who is in a position of power lest he be tempted to pursue his pleasure at our expense, then we must look for securities against the abuse of power. Those cannot be found, James Mill believed, in any but a representative system of government. In all other forms the ruling group will tend to pursue its own sinister interests. Only in a representative democracy can sufficient checks be found to prevent abuse. The community checks its representatives by regular election, and the representatives in turn check those in government. Though the tendency of this argument would seem to point to universal suffrage – how else identify the interest of the rulers with that of the community? – Mill believes that some individuals or classes of individuals (e.g. women) can be excluded from the vote 'without inconvenience,' as their interests are included in those of others.

This then was the utilitarian orthodoxy to which John

Stuart Mill gave his early allegiance. The conclusion was radical, the method deductive. It was not until 1829 that Macaulay launched his biting attack. By this time the younger Mill was already open to new influences as a result of the doubts thrown up by his mental crisis, and Macaulay's article made a great impact, offering as it did a rival view of the study of politics.[13] His criticisms went to the heart of the dispute:

> We have here an elaborate treatise on Government, from which, but for two or three passing allusions, it would not appear that the author was aware that any governments actually existed among men. Certain propensities of human nature are assumed; and from these premises the whole science of politics is synthetically deduced.

James Mill's reason for pursuing the *a priori* method – that experience is divided – is for Macaulay a reason for *not* pursuing it, but for proceeding by induction.

> Experience can never be divided, or even appear to be divided, except with reference to some hypothesis. When we say that one fact is inconsistent with another fact, we mean only that it is inconsistent with the *theory* which we have founded on that other fact. But if the fact be certain, the unavoidable conclusion is that our theory is false; and in order to correct it, we must reason back from an enlarged collection of facts to principles.

Not only is deduction a false method applied to politics, but the principles of human nature which are to act as its starting point are also false. That men always act from self-interest is true only to the extent that it is identical:

> If the doctrine, that men always act from self-interest, be laid down in any other sense than this – if the meaning of the word self-interest be narrowed so as to exclude

> any one of the motives which may by possibility act on any human being, the proposition ceases to be identical: but at the same time it ceases to be true.

The general statements which the utilitarians see as the fundamentals of their theory are either unverifiable or false. Macaulay believes that such general propositions about human nature are valueless, because

> Man differs from man; generation from generation; nation from nation. Education, station, sex, age, accidental associations, produce infinite shades of variety.

If the first principles are useless and the method inadequate, what does Macaulay offer as an alternative? How can we extend our knowledge of the world of politics?

> How then, are we to arrive at just conclusions on a subject so important to the happiness of mankind? Surely by that method which, in every experimental science to which it has been applied, has signally increased the power and knowledge of our species, . . . by the method of Induction; by observing the present state of the world, by assiduously studying the history of past ages, by sifting the evidence of facts, by carefully combining and contrasting those which are authentic, by generalising with judgment and diffidence, by perpetually bringing the theory which we have constructed to the test of new facts, by correcting, or altogether abandoning it, according as those new facts prove it to be partially or fundamentally unsound.

John Stuart Mill found it impossible to dismiss this argument in the way in which his father did – simply to treat it as an attack on reason. He was sympathetic to at least some of Macaulay's criticisms, with regard both to the inadequacy of the premises, and to the philsophical method. At this stage, however, he could not see the nature of the philosophical error. The logic of politics used by his father and by Macaulay both seemed to be erroneous. The latter's stress on history seemed to be important, but in what way should it be utilized? At this time, his movement towards the recognition of a philosophy of history as central to a study of politics was given added force by the influence on Mill of the Saint-Simonians. Though he was always critical of some aspects of this school, he was impressed by their analysis of history in terms of the alternation of critical and organic periods. Organic periods, which are characterized by positive belief, accepted institutions, and general unity, give way in time to critical periods in which scepticism, social unrest, and division tend to dominate. As this process works on in history, progress occurs as the old and dated are replaced by new, more vigorous institutions. If this is so then our study of politics must be related to a particular historical context, to a particular stage of development. In 1831 Mill wrote a series of articles exploring this notion as applied to the England of his day. In 'The Spirit of the Age' he describes England as being in a transitional period, where beliefs and institutions are seen as old and useless, but where no new ones have yet replaced them.

Still, a recognition of the importance of history and a view of it as progressive did not solve the problem left to him by Macaulay: what is the relationship between this historical attitude and the theorizing about human nature which Bentham and his father engaged in? Deductive theory alone may be inadequate, but so is mere history. In a review article in 1835 he remarks, with regard to history and travel, that they are

> . . . useful in aid of a more searching and accurate experience, not *in lieu* of it. No one learns any thing very valuable either from history or from travelling, who does not come prepared with much that history and travelling can never teach. No one can know other people so well as he may know himself, nor other ages and countries so well as he may know his own age and country:

and the wisdom acquired by the study of ourselves, and of the circumstances which surround us, can alone teach us to interpret the comparatively little which we know of other persons and other modes of existence; to make a faithful picture of them in our own minds, and to assign effects to their right causes. Even to the philosopher, the value both of history and of travelling is not so much positive as negative; they teach little, but they are a protection against much error. Nations, as well as individuals, until they have compared themselves with others, are apt to mistake their own idiosyncracies for laws of our common being, and the accidents of their position, for a part of the destiny of our race. The type of human nature and of human life with which they are familiar, is the only one which presents itself to their imagination; and their expectations and endeavours continually presupposes, as an immutable law something which, perhaps belongs only to the age and state of society through which they are rapidly passing.

The correction of narrowness is the main benefit derived from the study of various ages and nations: of narrowness, not only in our conception of what is, but in our standard of what ought to be. The individualities of nations are serviceable to the general improvement, in the same manner as the individualities of persons: since none is perfect, it is a beneficial arrangement that all are not imperfect in the same way.[14]

But while theory needs to be informed by an historical sense, so in turn the historical mode needs to begin with theory:

Without a hypothesis to commence with, we do not even know what end to begin at, what points to enquire into. Nearly every thing that has ever been ascertained by scientific observers, was brought to light in the attempt to test and verify some theory. To start from a theory, but not to see the object through the theory; to bring light from whencesoever it comes; such is the part of the philosopher, of the true practical seer or person of insight.[15]

The need to balance history and theory – induction and deduction – is accepted, but the nature of the balance is not fully established by Mill until he produces his *System of Logic* in 1843.

His solution to the problem first posed by Macaulay thirteen years before is 'the inverse deductive or historical method', where the study of history and reasoning about human nature is each given its appropriate and limited place. Historical observation may lead to generalizations which, however true, include no explanation as to why they are true. They are unreliable beyond the limits of the circumstances in which they are made; even if they were universally true they would not be ultimate explanations because 'they are not the principles of human nature, but results of those principles under the circumstances in which mankind have happened to be placed'.[16] The most that history can do is to afford Empirical Laws, which consist in discovering certain general tendencies in society. This is a useful exercise, but limited in that these laws must then be connected with the more fundamental laws of human nature, 'by deductions showing that such were the derivative laws naturally to be expected as the consequences of those ultimate ones'.[17] However, though deduction plays this crucial role it is a mistake to take geometry as its model; geometry can not deal with the conflict of causes, the modification of one on another; the results of one geometrical principle cannot be changed or made no longer true by reason of some other principle. On a geometrical theory of society it is wrongly assumed that all social phenomena result always from a single force, or single property of human nature. Both Bentham and James Mill adopted an unscientific method which forced on them too narrow a view of human nature. Once the geometrical method is discarded as unscientific, a broader foundation can be established for a study of society:

> The phenomena of society do not depend, in essentials, on some one agency or law of human nature, with only inconsiderable modifications from others. The whole of the qualities of human nature influence those phenomena, and there is not one which influences them in a small degree. There is not one, the removal or any great alteration of which would not materially affect the whole aspect of society, and change more or less the sequences of social phenomena generally.[18]

The appropriate method, then, is modelled instead on the complex physical sciences which consider 'all the causes which conjunctly influence the effect, and (compound) their laws with one another'. This complex method of reasoning, though an improvement on the geometrical, is in its own way as limited as the method of history:

> The ground of confidence in any concrete deductive science is not the *a priori* reasoning itself, but the accordance between its results and those of observation *a posteriori*. Either of these processes, apart from the other, diminishes in value as the subject increases in complication, and this in so rapid a ratio as soon to become entirely worthless; but the reliance to be placed in the concurrence of the two sorts of evidence not only does not diminish in anything like the same proportion, but is not necessarily much diminished at all. Nothing more results than a disturbance in the order of precedency of the two processes, sometimes amounting to its actual inversion: insomuch that, instead of deducing our conclusions by reasoning, and verifying them by observation, we in some cases begin by obtaining them provisionally from specific experience, and afterwards connect them with the principles of human nature by *a priori* reasoning, which reasonings are thus a real Verification.[19]

Into this scientific method, involving a comparison between the conclusions of reasoning and the results of observation, fit the various departments of the general science of society. Even the most important of these – political ethology, dealing with national character – is a branch only not a separate science, and the study of politics especially is bound up, 'both as cause and effect, with the qualities of the particular people or of the particular age'.[20] In other words there is an intimate and necessary connection between a particular state of civilization and the form of government existing in it. This science, beginning with history, Mill calls, after Comte, Social Statics, the study of stability, and this is to be distinguished from Social Dynamics, the study of progress. The eventual aim is to discover the laws both of social life and of social change, and the primary investigation is historical.

Mill explores the development and possibilities of history at more length in an article published soon after the *Logic*.[21] In order to understand the use and study of history, Mill distinguishes three stages in historical enquiry. The characteristic error in the first stage is

> to transport present feelings and notions back into the past, and refer all ages and forms of human life to the standard of that in which the writer himself lives. Whatever cannot be translated into the language of their own time, whatever they cannot represent to themselves by some fancied modern equivalent, is nothing to them, calls up no ideas in their own mind at all. They cannot imagine any thing different from their own everyday experience.

Because of this they are essentially unhistorical – 'they antedate not only modern ideas, but the essential character of the modern mind'. The second stage sets out to remedy this defect by regarding the past 'not with the eye of a modern, but, as far as possible, with that of a contemporary'. This essentially imaginative enterprise while being useful falls short of the third stage 'in which the aim is not simply to compose histories, but to construct a science of history'. This third stage must clearly follow the second; once we understand the particular ages separately, we can see that these states 'are regarded as a series of phenomena, produced by causes, and susceptible of explanation'. The sequence of causes and effects in each period, in turn causing those of the next, must follow some law; 'how to read that law, is deemed the fundamental problem of the science of history'.[22]

History, of course, has to correspond to human nature, and Mill believed that the two types of evidence in fact combine to show that there is one predominant agent of social change, which is the state of the speculative faculties; not that this is the motive for change, but that it is the condition which determines the present and limits the future. The physical or material as well as the political and moral state of a community is determined by it, just as every considerable advance in these areas is preceded by an advance in knowledge. Human progress depends above all on intellectual progress; to establish this beyond question is firstly the task of the historian in drawing up the empirical law, and then of the scientist in deducing it *a priori* from the principles of human nature.[23]

Such knowledge would, once established, have a practical purpose. The explanation of social order and social change would give us an insight into the future and thus help

> in determining what artificial means may be used, and to what extent, to accelerate the natural progress in so far as it is beneficial; to compensate for whatever may be its inherent inconveniences or disadvantages, and to guard against the accidents to which our species is exposed from the necessary incidents of its progression. Such practical instructions, founded on the highest branch of speculative sociology, will form the noblest and most beneficial portion of the Political Art.[24]

If this is so, if science can be useful in this way, then a major problem remains: what is the relationship between the scientist and his kind of knowledge on the one hand, and the demands and duties of Politics and Morality on the other? The one is science properly so called, the other is Art. The purposes to be pursued in a community can be decided only by Art, or Practice; Science however useful is a servant. The first deals with the desirable, the second with the practicable. Mill expresses the relationship in this way:

> The art proposes to itself an end to be attained, defines the end, and hands it over to the science. The science receives it, considers it as a phenomenon to be studied, and having investigated its causes and conditions, sends it back to art with a theorem of the combination of circumstances by which it could be produced.[25]

If the end defined by Art as desirable is found by Science to be attainable by means of certain actions, then the performance of these actions is given the status of a rule or precept. Inevitably, due to the imperfection of Science and the almost infinite combinations of circumstances, these rules of conduct will be considered as provisional, but still they provide us with a general, reliable guide. In cases of genuine doubt or conflict regarding the rules of Art we must, of course, refer back to the theorems of Science.

The relationship therefore appears relatively simple and straightforward; the ends and the ultimate standard by which to judge the ends are a matter of Art, and the means and the basis for them are a matter of Science. What these ends should be and whether these ends can be distinguished from means, and further whether Mill himself maintains and uses this distinction between ends and means are questions we shall explore in the following sections.

The purpose of politics

As with his original approach to the understanding of politics so with his early view of its overall purpose – he followed orthodox Benthamism. Happiness was the ultimate goal, and this could be calculated in terms of the balance of pleasure over pain. The greatest happiness of the community was the proper and quantifiable purpose of law and politics. As we have seen in the brief sketch of Mill's life, the Benthamic standard of 'the greatest happiness', applied to the morality of actions by analysing their consequences, gave Mill 'a creed, a doctrine, a philosophy; in one among the best senses of the word, a religion.' His mental crisis, beginning in 1826, shattered this simple confidence; the end which he had been pursuing so vigorously 'had ceased to charm', and the 'habit of analysis' by which he had dissected the end and the possible means had weakened his feelings and his spirit. The general good and its calculation no longer attracted him, and (as we have seen) this led him to two important modifications of his previous view of happiness. Firstly, happiness is not something to be sought after directly, but something which is found in the pursuit of some other object followed itself as an ideal end; and secondly, happiness is not achieved simply by changes in the external circumstances of man, but demands the internal cultivation of the individual.

The Benthamic view that men's actions are always determined by their own interests (and that this was as it should be), and the use of this as the single major premise in politics, was therefore for Mill in need of some modification. Macaulay's attack on James Mill put the matter sharply and concisely; the fundamental utilitarian premise was either unverifiable, or false. If the former, then no moral or political principle could be based on an empty tautology; if the latter, then history and practice would soon contradict it. Mill agrees that his father's basic premise is too narrow, and in his eventual assessment of the dispute between James Mill and Macaulay, he puts the matter in terms very similar to those used by Macaulay:

> . . . that men's actions are always determined by their interests. There is an ambiguity in this last expression; for, as the same philosophers, especially Bentham, gave the name of interest to anything which a person likes, the

> proposition may be understood to mean only this, that men's actions are always determined by their wishes. In this sense, however, it would not bear out any of the consequences which these writers drew from it; and the word, therefore, in their political reasonings, must be understood to mean (which is also the explanation they themselves, on such occasions gave of it) what is commonly termed private or worldly interest.[26]

However, this is by no means universally true, and it is by no means a firm enough foundation for a deductive science of politics.

Mill, then, at this period was beginning to see what happiness was not, and this represents a fairly radical departure from his early Benthamism. Happiness was not an object to be pursued directly, nor to be defined externally, nor to be identified with a notion of interest in the wide or narrow sense. He was at odds with orthodox utilitarianism on all these points, and his early reaction to the utilitarian view of happiness was expressed by him in a review of Bentham published anonymously in 1833.[27]

Although Mill writes favourably of Bentham's philosophical and practical contribution in the field of law, he finds his view of human nature, and the concept of happiness derived from it, to be confused and limited. Bentham's great fault is that he had limited the judgement of an action simply to an evaluation of its consequences, and in doing so had ignored the relationship between the act performed and the character of the agent. The moral being of a person and his internal character are in practice largely ignored. In law this emphasis on the direct consequences of an act may work well enough, but in morality and politics it denies us complete understanding. Allied to this narrow view of a moral or political act is Bentham's equally partial view of men's motives in performing them. In practice the notion of the happiness or interest which men strive for is interpreted in a narrow, selfish manner, and the motive of conscience or moral obligation is generally dismissed. This tendency to ignore internal character, its education and improvement, occurs too in the political realm, in a manner equally damaging to 'all rational hope of good for the human species'.

So much for the errors and half-truth in the Benthamic view of the nature and purpose of moral and political life; what of the true view of happiness, that ultimate end of human life? What is the correct picture which the Artist needs to draw before demanding from the Scientist the correct means? Mill's preliminary definition is on the surface very little different to Bentham's. Happiness is pleasure and the absence of pain and such things are the only ends to human action. However, for Mill pleasures are not all of a kind; man is a human being not a mere animal and the notion of pleasure must take account of this distinction. On two grounds we are able to elevate some pleasures above others: firstly, that they are more lasting and secondly that they are more valuable in kind. The pleasures belonging to the higher faculties are superior on both these grounds, so that the exercise of this faculty leads to more happiness even if not to more contentment. This last distinction does, of course, represent a significant shift away from Bentham, and Mill's final definition hardly mentions pleasure in the Benthamic sense at all:

> Utilitarianism, therefore, could only attain its end by the general cultivation of nobleness of character, even if each individual were only benefited by the nobleness of others, and his own, so far as happiness is concerned, were a sheer deduction from the benefit.[28]

So the pursuit of happiness is a pursuit of the higher pleasures – personal affection, social feeling, art, poetry, history, and mental culture generally, and the standard of morality is the happiness of all concerned. Duty, sacrifice, truth, beauty, the public good are all a part of happiness as something elevating and improving. Thus the existence of happiness as a first principle does not exclude the recognition of secondary ones; indeed these moral rules of conduct are, except in cases of conflict, our main guide.

There are, I think, two points to notice here. Firstly, the rules of conduct which Mill supports seem to be justified by him in moral terms, not in scientific. Though in theory the grounds of every rule of Art 'are to be found in theorems of Science' Mill does not in fact define the end and look to Science for knowledge as to the suitable means. The 'means' are for Mill dictated entirely by the 'end'.

The explanation of this lies in the second point; that the language of ends and means hardly represents Mill's position adequately. Can we view his notion of happiness as a separate end with various secondary values as means? Can we even understand the notion of happiness apart from those supposedly instrumental means? Mill himself makes this very point:

> The ingredients of happiness are very various, and each of them is desirable in itself, and not merely when considered as swelling the aggregate. The principle of utility does not mean that any given pleasure, as music for instance, or any given exemption from pain, as for example health, is to be looked upon as a means to a collective something termed happiness, and to be desired on that account. They are desired and desirable in and for themselves; besides being means, they are a part of the end.[29]

If these various ingredients, like truth and virtue, are a part of the end, then clearly they are the business of the Artist and not of the Scientist, but if happiness is made up of such a variety of parts it becomes difficult to see it as an ultimate end, as something recognizably separate which can act as the fundamental basis for moral and political action. Mill makes his position clearer, though I think the problem remains, when he almost dispenses with the language of ends and means:

> I do not mean to assert that the promotion of happiness should be itself the end of all actions, or even of all rules of action. It is the justification, and ought to be the controller, of all ends, but is not itself the sole end.[80]

Whether 'happiness' as Mill describes it, made up of such a variety of parts, can fulfil this arbitrating and controlling role we shall consider when we look at his political thought in more detail. For the moment it would appear that the Artist has performed his task – the ends have been described. Presumably now the major task will be the discovery in politics of the proper means to the desired ends, for according to Mill, the proper theoretical approach is that:

> The Art proposes to itself an end to be attained, defines the end, and hands it over to the Science.

Democracy and Freedom

Mill's early views on democracy and freedom were generally similar to those of his father. James Mill, as well as promoting the cause of democratic reform saw freedom of discussion – in speech and in the press – as essential to this end, both as a means of discovering truth and as a check on rulers. As early as the 1820s John Stuart Mill was arguing in favour of toleration as a means of enabling truth to triumph and as the crucial safeguard against abuse of power by the rulers. In an article written in 1825 he concentrates on these points.[31] Censorship, he believes, is an evil because by it the rulers choose opinions for the people and whoever does this 'possesses absolute control over their actions, and may wield them for his own purposes with perfect security'. Restraint on the press, that great vehicle of criticism and discussion, is always determined by the need to protect the interests of the ruling group; it is, in other words, always despotic. The alternative to restraint is freedom, and its great value is that in such a climate 'truth never fails, in the long run, to prevail over error'. This for

Mill has the status of what he later called a scientific theorem:

> That truth, if it has fair play, always in the end triumphs over error, and becomes the opinion of the world, is a proposition which rests upon the broadest principles of human nature, and to which it would be easy to accumulate testimonials from almost every author, whatever may be his political leanings who has distinguished himself in any branch of politics, morals, or theology.[32]

If freedom of discussion is the essential path to truth then it is especially necessary in the field of politics where a people's whole happiness is involved. And yet, apart from religion, this is the area where such freedom is most restricted, where criticism is most suppressed. Despotism distrusts the truth as it distrusts the people, and thus must act through fear not reason; opinions must be dictated to ensure their 'correctness', and keep the people passive. Although some arguments for a limitation of freedom of expression appear plausible, they all fail by leaving it to the rulers to decide what is and is not allowable, and once this happens rulers will abuse this power as they tend to abuse all power. The power to suppress opinions is the nearest thing to absolute power; 'there is no medium between perfect freedom of expressing opinions, and absolute despotism'.

The argument Mill employs here is that freedom is, on the basis of practical and logical evidence, a necessary *means* to truth and good government, and while he never abandons this belief he does gradually add to it and modify it. The most important early influence which qualifies his approach to freedom is that of the Saint-Simonians with their stress on the relativity of time, place, and circumstances. In the series of articles written in 1831 under the heading 'The Spirit of the Age'[33] Mill writes of freedom not in general but in terms specifically related to his own time and place. The age, he believes, is an age of transition, marked by the discredit of old institutions and doctrines but as yet having found no permanent replacement. The old wisdom has been abandoned not as yet for a newer version, but for the '*diffusion* of superficial *knowledge*'. Discussion has weakened prejudice and attacked error, but this falls short of discovering truth. The agents of discovery are the wisest and best in a generation; discussion and criticism play an important rolé but one that is necessarily limited, not because the 'powers' of most people are limited, but because their 'acquirements' fall short of what is needed for 'enlarging the stock of positive truth'.

The spirit of criticism and discussion in such a period of transition is of most value if allied with respect for the authority of the wise, which should replace that of worldly power or religion. The problem in such a doubting and changing age is that such wisdom may not emerge, but it is essential that it does if real progress is to be made.

Mill's view of freedom here is less optimistic than it was. Where before it was a sure means to truth and good government, now its role is much more limited – to the destruction of error and to providing a climate in which the few influence the many. This more sceptical approach to freedom is paralleled in Mill's attitude to democracy. His father's argument that good government depends on creating an identity of interest between the rulers and the ruled is qualified by the recognition that good government also depends on the qualities of those few who do rule. Where James Mill had turned away from serious consideration of the character of the rulers in favour of emphasizing the need to distrust and therefore constantly check them, John Stuart Mill believes that democracy must combine the wisdom of the few with their responsibility to the many. 'The people ought to be the masters, but they are masters who must employ servants more skilful than themselves.'[34]

This movement from early confidence to gradual caution regarding the virtues of freedom and democracy can be explained very much in terms of the appropriate means to the desired end. Mill does seem to be influenced by the kind of results – however elementary – which the 'Scientist', as historian and logician, appears to have discovered. Thus his change of view is consistent with his belief expressed in the *Logic* that politics must be seen in relation to the circumstances of a particular age. It appears that the Scientist is indeed carrying out his function of analysing means under the general direction of the ends outlined by the Artist. However, these are not Mill's final views on freedom and democracy, and whether the further changes in his position can also be seen in terms of the means proper to the end is, as I shall try to show, open to serious doubt.

Possibly the most important influence on Mill in this area was Tocqueville's work *Democracy in America*.[35] Mill also praises it as an example of the method which he is later to recommend in the *Logic*:

> His method is, as that of a philosopher on such a subject must be – a combination of deduction with induction: his evidences are laws of human nature, on the one hand; the example of America and France, and other modern nations, as far as applicable, on the other.[36]

The first part of the work applied this combined method to an analysis of the political effects of the democratic tendency in modern societies – the trend towards equality of conditions. Such a movement is best accompanied by democratic institutions at the central and local level, with popular participation in all branches of public life. The advantages of such a system are that it releases the energy and intelligence of a people and that it favours the interests of the greater part of the community. Its disadvantages are that it tends to be indifferent to the quality of its public officials who are chosen and changed with little regard to their merits. Thus the standard of politicians is usually poor and law generally lacks consistency. But the greatest danger is the threat from 'the despotism of the majority', not principally over the body – though this is a danger – but over the mind. In the second part of the book Tocqueville shows how individuality and independence of thought are restricted by public opinion which demands deference not dissent. Art and Literature will multiply but not improve; the dominant taste will always favour the second-rate. The danger is not freedom but servility and a loss of moral courage and independence.

Tocqueville's response to his own analysis is not to reject democracy which he sees as inevitable and potentially beneficial but to suggest that for its improvement two things are necessary – popular education and an increased love for and spirit of liberty. Mill, though he has some serious criticisms of Tocqueville's analysis, especially what he takes to be Tocqueville's confusion between democracy and civilization, and between democracy and its particular American form, nevertheless generally agrees both that a danger exists and that freedom is the main remedy. If individuality, spontaneity, and quality on the one hand, and minorities on the other, are to be protected in a democratic or any other system, then education and freedom are the proper means. The 'means' are now, however, becoming somewhat inextricably bound up with the purposes they serve. The weight of Tocqueville's evidence and argument suggests not just that individuality and spontaneity *need* a free climate, but that it is difficult if not impossible to envisage them in theory or in reality without such a spirit of liberty. At the least, freedom is a precondition for the existence of these other values. The relationship is now more intimate than the ends/means category suggests, and indeed Mill's final position moves even further away from this. In his essay *On Liberty* Mill has finally reached the position where freedom is not just a means to progress, not just a precondition of improvement but constitutive of them.

The essay, published in 1859, represents Mill's mature position on a problem that had concerned him for around thirty years – how to balance the value of democracy with that of freedom. Once he had abandoned the view that identity of interest between ruler and ruled could provide the final solution for the happiness of mankind, once he had seen the problem of the majority tyrannizing over the individual or a minority of individuals, he was left with the question of how 'to make the fitting adjustment between individual independence and social control'.[37] His ultimate criterion, he states, is to be 'utility in the largest sense, grounded on the permanent interests of a man as a progressive being'.[38] Before exploring the proper dividing line between the individual and society, Mill attempts to establish his view that freedom is connected with man's interests as a progressive being. In chapter two he shows that intellectual freedom is a necessary means to the triumph of truth over error, but more than this, he shows that only truth freely gained and freely held is of any value:

> . . . assuming that the true opinion abides in the mind, but abides as a prejudice, a belief independent of, and proof against, argument – this is not the way in which truth ought to be held by a rational being. This is not knowing the truth. Truth, thus held, is but one superstition the more, accidentally clinging to the words which enunciate a truth.[39]

So that intellectual freedom is not simply a means to truth, it is what distinguishes it from 'dead dogma'; it is a *characterising quality* of 'living truth'. Without it, 'truth' has very little meaning and very little effect on character.

In practice the most common situation for Mill is not the conflict of truth with error, but the conflict of two opinions, both of which share the truth between them. If these half-truths are not allowed to clash freely, development towards the truth is impossible, but, what is just as bad, will give rise to similarly one-sided characters. Narrow theory, with its suppression of the other half of truth, creates 'low, abject, servile' individuals. So that while freedom and truth are inextricably linked, they are also intimately connected with the moral courage and independent quality of individual character.

If the manner in which we obtain and hold truth is crucial, so is the manner in which we act out our lives

Individuality of character is indeed the 'chief ingredient of individual and social progress'. It is a 'co-ordinate element', 'a necessary part and condition', 'one of the leading essentials' of civilization, well-being, and education. 'But the evil is, that individual spontaneity is hardly recognized by the common models of thinking as having any intrinsic worse or deserving any regard on its own account.'[40] That the free development of individuality is part of Mill's notion of goodness and humanity is clear:

> It really is of importance, not only what men do, but also what manner of men they are that do it. Among the works of man, which human life is rightly employed in perfecting and beautifying, the first in importance surely is man himself. Supposing it were possible to get houses built, corn grown, battles fought, causes tried, and even churches erected and prayers said, by machinery – by automatons in human form – it would be a considerable loss to exchange for these automatons even the men and women who at present inhabit the more civilized parts of the world, and who assuredly are but starved specimens of what nature can and will produce. Human nature is not a machine to be built after a model, and set to do exactly the work prescribed for it, but a tree, which requires to grow and develop itself on all sides, according to the tendency of the inward forces which make it a living thing.[41]

Though Mill believes that this argument can stand on its own, he also holds that something good in itself can in addition be of use to others. Individuality is valued for itself but also because through it new truths, practices, and discoveries are made which benefit the whole community. Indeed, liberty is the only sure and lasting source of such improvement, 'since by it there are as many possible independent sources of improvement as there are individuals'.

Mill's arguments in defence of freedom are thus not simply of its utility to progress, but dominantly in terms of its being a part of what is meant by progress, goodness, improvement, or whatever. The Artist/Scientist distinction seems to be abandoned, though the fruits of that distinction are used and transformed into something very different. However, establishing freedom as a primary virtue does not in itself answer the question as to the proper balance between the individual and society. The social feelings and the desire for unity are also crucial to mankind:

> The social state is at once so natural, so necessary, and so habitual to man, that, except in some unusual circumstances or by an effort of voluntary abstraction, he never conceives himself otherwise than as a member of a body; and this association is riveted more and more, as mankind are further removed from the state of savage independence.[42]

Between the legitimate claims of society and the proper independence of the individual, Mill believes a clear line can be drawn. Society should not compel or control, by physical or moral force, unless the actions of an individual harm the interests of others. Neither happiness nor morality can justify interference unless injury is done to the interests of another person. Where no injury is proven the individual should be left free. This did not mean for Mill that the alternative to control was indifference; indeed he encourages benevolence while emphasizing the need to limit it to disinterested exertion.

Clearly this 'very simple principle' of Mill's rests on the possibility of giving a clear meaning to the notion of 'interests', injury to which is to act as the criterion for justifying interference. The closest Mill gets to this in chapter III of *On Liberty* is when he writes briefly of 'interests' in terms of 'rights'. A fuller elaboration of his notion of rights is found in chapter V of *Utilitarianism,* where Mill analyses justice in terms of rights, and talks of injury to rights as the justifying criterion for interference.[43] Whether Mill's principle can be adequately clarified is open to much controversy; what should not be forgotten is that the reasons for the principle – the crucial importance of freedom – are in some ways more important than the principle itself:

> To the judge, the rule, once positively ascertained is final; but the legislator, or other practitioner, who goes by rules rather than by their reasons, like the old-fashioned German tacticians who were vanquished by Napoleon, or the physician who preferred that his patients should die by rule rather than recover contrary to it, is rightly judged to be a mere pedant, and the slave of his formulas.[44]

This is Mill's solution to one of the major problems in a democracy – the protection of the individual; there remains another important question – the quality of leadership possible in a representative system. Mill's answer is to so arrange the electoral system that the intelligent are helped and the uninstructed are restrained. The many are still the masters, but the system is so devised that they can make use of those more morally and intellectually gifted. By protecting the role of minorities in the political process, Mill hopes to raise the general standard of public life, while still retaining the democratic base. In this way, Mill believes, both despotism and mediocrity can be avoided. While his fear of the dominance of the many over the few is well-known, it should also be noted that he disliked as intensely the tyranny of the few over the many. Although he gives the few certain protections and advantages, these should never amount to unrestricted rule. Mill is fearful of power in whoever's hands it resides:

> If there be an ethical doctrine which more than all others requires to be taught, and has been taught with deepest conviction by the great moral teachers, it is, that the love of power is the most evil passion of human nature; that power over others, power of coercion and compulsion, any power other than that of moral and intellectual

> influence, even in the cases where it is indispensable, is a snare, and in all others a curse, both to the possessor and to those over whom it is possessed; a burthen which no rightly constituted moral nature consents to take upon itself, but by one of the greatest sacrifices which inclination ever makes to duty. With the love of liberty it is wholly the reverse. The love of liberty, in the only proper sense of that word, is unselfish; it places no one in a position of hostility to the good of his fellow-creatures; all alike may be free, and the freedom of one has no solid security but in the equal freedom of the rest; the appetite for power is, on the contrary, essentially selfish; for all cannot have power; the power of one is power over others, who not only do not share in his elevation, but whose depression is the foundation on which it is raised.[45]

So that while Mill devised various detailed schemes for the advantage of excellence over mere numbers, these were all motivated by a desire to protect minorities and benefit the mass, rather than to give the few power over the many.[46] Democracy is a value but one which must co-exist with the other values of freedom, individuality and diversity.

The Working Classes

Although from the 1820s onwards Mill had written fairly regularly on questions of political economy, his first major comment on labour appears in a review published in 1840.[47] By this time, as we have seen, his general approach to political questions had departed from the orthodox position inherited from his father and Bentham; the purpose of politics was now no longer such a clear thing, and the apparent 'means' discovered by the Scientist were now more like values in their own right. His attitude to the position and future development of the working classes while it still retains something of the ends/means distinction is essentially in terms of the manner rather than the mere fact of improvement. Thus his attack on paternalism is not that it will not work but that it depends for its working on the servility of those who might benefit. A situation in which the employers of labour and the owners of land are responsible for the well-being of the labouring classes is certainly possible, as is shown in the example of the Russian serfs and West Indian slaves, but the necessary accompaniment of such paternal care is paternal authority:

> . . . this obligation never has existed, and never will nor can exist, without, as a countervailing element, absolute power, or something approaching to it, in those who are bound to afford this support, over those entitled to receive it. Such a relation has never existed between human beings, without ultimate degradation to the character of the dependent class.[48]

The working classes cannot be given 'the immunities of slaves' without depriving them at the same time of the freedom of 'independent citizens'.

If the poor are not to be cared *for,* they must care for themselves, and the greatest obstacle to this is ignorance. A well-educated working class will not be content to be servile or destitute. In the long run Mill believes that 'cash payment' must cease to be the major relationship between man and man; society must be united on some other basis:

> . . . if we might point to the principle on which, at some distant date, we place our chief hope for healing the widening breach between those who toil and those who live on the produce of former toil; it would be that of raising the labourer from a receiver of hire – a mere bought instrument in the work of production, having no residuary interest in the work itself – to the position of being, in some sort, a partner in it.[49]

In the short run, however, an increasingly educated working class will demand justice, not the sort of kindness offered by the supporters of paternalism:

> Will the poor thank you for giving them money in alms; for subscribing to build baths and lay out parks for them, or, as Lord John Manners proposes, playing at cricket with them, if you are at the same time taxing their bread to swell your rents?[50]

Mill's attack on paternalism and his belief that the labouring classes must forward their own improvement was again expressed in his *Principles of Political Economy*, first published in 1848. In this work he also discusses the socialist alternative, in a manner, at least by the time of the second edition, sympathetic if critical. However his faith at this time still lies in competition and education to solve the problems of poverty without destroying individual integrity.

How the working classes should actually proceed in their progress towards economic improvement is not adequately explored, except in vague terms, until 1869. In a review of Thornton's book *On Labour,* Mill discusses the role of trade unions as the instruments of working-class advance. What made a serious discussion of this possible was Mill's abandonment, in response to Thornton's argument, of the theory that there is at any one time a fixed sum of wealth that can be devoted to the payment of wages. According to the theory, wages depended solely on the number of workers sharing the total amount. A consequence of denying this theory was to see that trade unions could now play an important role; if the wage fund was not fixed, then trade unions could help to raise wages just as employers could act to keep them down.

> The power of Trades Unions may therefore be so exercised as to obtain for the labouring classes collectively, both a larger share and a larger positive amount of the produce of labour.

Mill then goes on, in a second article[51] to examine the position of labour and the role of trade unions. There are two opposing approaches to the cause of labour; firstly, that labour has certain rights, e.g. to a fair wage, and secondly, that the only right it has is to get as much as it can from society. Mill denies any intrinsic virtue or rights in labour, and accepts that the labourer must get what he can though subject to the general interest. No *a priori* doctrines with regard to property or labour are adequate; utility must still be the guiding principle. Practices and forbearances if necessary to the general well-being, must be compulsory; otherwise society should leave the individual free, however much his actions may give rise to dislike, distaste, or hostility. There is a standard by which to judge the activities of employer and labourer, and that is the interests of society as an instrument of civilization and improvement. Subject to this limitation, operative over the whole field of human conduct, the individual must strive as best he can.

Mill, however, recognized that the individual as labourer is in an isolated and vulnerable position, unless he combines with others in unions. As workmen in combination they must be free to do what they would be free to do individually. Physical violence and injury to property would be criminal whether done by one or by many; unions should suffer no more restrictions than do ordinary citizens. The activities of unions raise certain new problems, but not ones that need new laws. On the question of the pressure that may be exerted on men to join the union, or to take part in a strike, Mill sees few problems:

> . . . it must be admitted that the members of Unions may reasonably feel a genuine moral disapprobation of those who profit by the higher wages or other advantages that the Unions procure for non-Unionists as well as for their own members, but refuse to take their share of the payments, and submit to restrictions, by which those advantages are obtained. It is vain to say that if a strike is really for the good of the workmen, the whole body will join in it from a mere sense of the common interest. There is always a considerable number who will hope to share the benefit without submitting to the sacrifices; and to

> say that these are not to have it brought before them, in an impressive manner, what their fellow-workmen think of their conduct, is equivalent to saying that social pressure ought not to be put upon anyone to consider the interests of others as well as his own.

That pressure must stop short of an infringement of person or property Mill upholds in this case as he does in other cases like picketing.

One problem which does arise for Mill as a result of unionization is the relationship between unionists and the rest of the working classes. Mill believes that a *general* rise in wages can come from only one source, profit, and not from prices. In the limited case a wage rise may also come from the loss of wages to another sector of the labouring class. Thus the success of the unionized may mean a loss to workers in non-unionized occupations. While unionists owe no obligations to the employers, they do towards the rest of their class, and towards the community in general. Thus restrictive practices, closed shops, high wages in one sector but not in another, all have to be justified; otherwise one section is sacrificed to another, one group dominates at the expense of others. Mill offers two considerations by which to justify unionism, despite these possible objections:

> The first is, by considering the Unions of particular trades as a mere step towards an universal Union, including all labour, and as a means of educating the elite of the working classes for such a future.[52]

The second is that, towards the lowest and most miserable,

> We do them no wrong by intrenching ourselves behind a barrier, to exclude those whose competition would bring down our wages, without more than momentarily raising theirs, but only adding to the total numbers in existence.[53]

An enlightened body of unionists will not be indifferent to others, or to society generally; it will promote efficient and co-operative enterprises. In the long run industrial partnership is the most beneficial solution to the present state of the working class and society generally. Meanwhile the role of the trade unions is educational: to combine in mutual dependence is to promote moral development by increasing fellow-feeling and the sense of human dignity.

At the time that these views were being published, Mill was becoming increasingly aware of the spread of socialist ideas, and began to examine seriously the view that society had to be transformed rather than merely improved. His unrevised thoughts on this were published in 1879[54] after his death. Socialist theory contains two elements – its analysis of the evils of the present, and its proposals for a better future. The various types of socialism tend to be united on the first, but not on the second. As to the injustices of the existing social arrangements, socialists point to the increasing poverty and misery of labour resulting from competition. Individualism is seen as an economic and a moral evil; selfishness, envy, hatred and conflict all result from the belief that each must be for himself and against the rest. While labourers become slaves or serfs, a few great capitalists form a new feudality. The consequences of individualism are not freedom and equality, but poverty and oppression leading to absolute power and absolute dependence.

Mill's general response to socialist criticisms is to state that though they see the evils clearly they present them in an exaggerated form. The present system is certainly riddled with injustices, but Mill believes that these are diminishing not increasing. The existing state of affairs is not doomed, and socialism is not the only path to happiness. However, on intellectual and moral grounds socialist principles might be desirable even if the economic analysis fails to prove them necessary.

When socialism looks to the future it loses the unity which it had in its examination of the past and present. Mill believes there are two major divisions based, in the first instance, on a disagreement about scale. In order to abolish private property, competition, and their resultant vices, some socialists concentrate on the small self-acting unit, a village or town, whilst others propose that the whole country should be managed from the centre. The virtue of the first approach is that it can be introduced gradually, and prove itself in comparison with the old; the second, or revolutionary, approach gambles all at a single throw, confident in an idea, but reckless of human suffering. Mill believes this second form would bring disaster to all, with the resulting chaos leading not to speedy improvement but to the violent and tyrannical oppression of the weak by the strong. However, the more cautious and reasonable form deserves a fair trial. If the experiment shows that improvement demands a change in the existing ideas of property, then so be it. The possibility of such success depends, however, not only on economic factors; education and social sympathy are essential elements in making such self-acting units possible. At the same time the actual working of such units has a beneficial effect on the higher qualities of human character. If the social side of man can be strengthened in this way, then socialism may prove to be the most desirable context for the development of the human personality.

Conclusion

I have tried to show how Mill attempts in two ways to provide his thoughts on politics with a unified structure. In the moral field he draws the distinction between ends and means and in the logical field between art and science. However, I have also tried to reveal how, as his thought develops, these two distinctions fail to account for the variety and complexity of his views on political life. The interest in Mill is not that he fails to maintain these distinctions, but that he succeeds in escaping from them. His political thought, reflecting as it does the variety of values, the conflict of ends, and the problematic nature of social progress, would perhaps be more consistent but certainly more narrow had he kept faithfully within the ordered schemes of utility and logic.

Probably the single constant theme in Mill's writings is his concern with the quality of individual life; this reveals itself in his early reaction to Benthamite utilitarianism as it does also in his interest in socialism. While this concern with the integrity and development of character is constant, the conditions for its realization change; Mill does not identify his ideal with any particular system or any unchanging political structure. Indeed, generally, this commitment to liberation from custom, tyranny, and oppression is what leads him to take up the cause of reform in Ireland and to support nationalism, women's suffrage, and anti-slavery; his was a state of 'habitual rebellion' and whilst injustice is various, so must the assertion of freedom be constant. It was Mill's refusal to identify the values he held with any particular system that has given him a lasting appeal. He is concerned in various contexts and in the face of differing obstacles – intellectual, economic, and political – to encourage independence, vigour, individuality, creativity, and the exercise of choice against the dominance of tyranny and servility.

As a result it is difficult to label Mill precisely as one kind of thinker or another. The selection of his writings reprinted below is intended to provide the reader with some account of his views on politics, but also to show how, on the basis of an original unity, Mill is in practice constantly and restlessly challenging the validity of his own assumptions.

1. *James Mill* by Alexander Bain, London, 1882.
2. *Autobiography,* chapter III.
3. ibid., chapter V.
4. ibid.
5. *Edinburgh Review,* XLIX, 1829. This is reprinted as the Appendix to the present volume.
6. *Autobiography,* chapter V.
7. *Examiner,* 6 January—29 May 1831. See below for extracts, pp. 170-9.

8. *Autobiography,* chapter V.
9. ibid., chapter VI.
10. In 1836 the *Westminster* was bought, and the two reviews merged into one, the *London and Westminster.* Later, in 1840, the title became the *Westminster* again.
11. *Autobiography,* chapter VII.
12. James Mill, *An Essay on Government,* ed. C. V. Shields, Liberal Arts Press, New York, 1955; reprinted from the supplement to the fifth edition of the *Encyclopaedia Britannica,* 1820.
13. Macaulay, op. cit. (see note 5).
14. 'The State of Society in America', *London Review,* vol. II, 1836, pp. 365-6.
15. From the review of Carlyle's *French Revolution, London and Westminster Review,* V and XXVII, 1837, p. 48.
16. *System of Logic, Collected Works,* vol. VIII, p. 861.
17. ibid., p. 916.
18. ibid., p. 894.
19. ibid., p. 896.
20. ibid.
21. 'Michelet's History of France', *Edinburgh Review,* LXXIX, 1844; reprinted in *Dissertations and Discussions,* vol. II. See below, pp. 90-3.
22. These quotations are from ibid.
23. *System of Logic,* op. cit. See below, p. 74.
24. ibid. See below, p. 77.
25. ibid. See below, p. 80.
26. *System of Logic,* op. cit. p. 890.
27. Appendix B in Bulwer's *England and the English,* London, 1833. See below, pp. 97-116 for the full text.
28. *Utilitarianism,* See below, p. 123.
29. *Utilitarianism* in *Collected Works,* vol. X, p. 235.
30. *System of Logic,* op. cit. See below, p. 88.
31. 'Law of Libel and Liberty of the Press', *Westminster Review,* III, 1825. See below, pp. 143-70.
32. ibid. See below, p. 150.
33. op. cit. (see note 7).
34. See below, p. 182.
35. Mill reviewed the first volume for the *London Review,* vol. II, 1835, and the whole work on the appearance of the second volume in *Edinburgh Review,* LXXII, 1840. See below, pp. 186-248, for the full text of the 1840 article.
36. See below, p. 189.
37. *On Liberty,* in *Utilitarianism,* ed. M. Warnock, Fontana, 1962, p. 130.
38. ibid., p. 136.

39. ibid., p. 162.
40. All these quotations are from chapter III. See below, pp. 248-69.
41. See below, p. 252.
42. *Utilitarianism,* op. cit., p. 284.
43. For an indication of the possible interpretation of Mill's principle in terms of rights, see J. C. Rees, 'A Re-reading of Mill on Liberty', especially the Postscript, in *Limits of Liberty,* ed. P. Radcliff, Wadsworth, California, 1966.
44. *System of Logic,* op. cit. See below, pp. 79.
45. 'Centralisation', *Edinburgh Review,* CXV, 1862.
46. For a detailed account of Mill's views on democracy, see J. H. Burns, 'J. S. Mill and Democracy', *Political Studies,* 5 1957.
47. 'Claims of Labour', *Edinburgh Review,* LXXXI, 1845. See below, pp. 273-303.
48. ibid. See below, p. 284.
49. ibid. See below, p. 295.
50. ibid. See below, p. 297.
51. 'Thornton on Labour and its Claims', *Fortnightly Review,* n.s. V, 1869. In two parts, the second of which is reprinted below, pp. 303-35.
52. ibid. See below, p. 326.
53. ibid. See below, pp. 328-9.
54. 'Chapters on Socialism', *Fortnightly Review,* n.s. XXV, 1879. In three parts, the last of which is reprinted below, pp. 335-58.

PART I METHOD

1 *Of the Inverse Deductive, or Historical Method*

(Bk VI, chapter X of *System of Logic,* first published 1843. This version from the Eighth Edition, London 1872.[1])

1. There are two kinds of sociological inquiry. In the first kind, the question proposed is, what effect will follow from a given cause, a certain general condition of social circumstances being presupposed. As, for example, what would be the effect of imposing or of repealing Corn Laws, of abolishing monarchy or introducing universal suffrage, in the present condition of society and civilisation in any European country, or under any other given supposition with regard to the circumstances of society in general, without reference to the changes which might take place, or which may already be in progress, in those circumstances. But there is also a second inquiry, namely, what are the laws which determine those general circumstances themselves. In this last the question is, not what will be the effect of a given cause in a certain state of society, but what are the causes which produce, and the phenomena which characterise, States of Society generally. In the solution of this question consists the general Science of Society, by which the conclusions of the other and more special kind of inquiry must be limited and controlled.

2. In order to conceive correctly the scope of this general science, and distinguish it from the subordinate departments of sociological speculation, it is necessary to fix the ideas attached to the phrase 'a State of Society'. What is called a state of society is the simultaneous state of all the greater social facts or phenomena. Such are the degree of knowledge,

and of intellectual and moral culture, existing in the community, and of every class of it; the state of industry, of wealth and its distribution; the habitual occupations of the community; their division into classes, and the relations of those classes to one another; the common beliefs which they entertain on all the subjects most important to mankind, and the degree of assurance with which those beliefs are held; their tastes, and the character and degree of their aesthetic development; their form of government, and the more important of their laws and customs. The condition of all these things, and of many more which will readily suggest themselves, constitute the state of society or the state of civilisation at any given time.

When states of society, and the causes which produce them, are spoken of as a subject of science, it is implied that there exists a natural correlation among these different elements; that not every variety of combination of these general social facts is possible, but only certain combinations; that, in short, there exist Uniformities of Co-existence between the states of the various social phenomena. And such is the truth; as is indeed a necessary consequence of the influence exercised by every one of those phenomena over every other. It is a fact implied in the *consensus* of the various parts of the social body.

States of society are like different constitutions or different ages in the physical frame; they are conditions not of one or a few organs or functions, but of the whole organism. Accordingly, the information which we possess respecting past ages, and respecting the various states of society now existing in different regions of the earth, does, when duly analysed, exhibit uniformities. It is found that when one of the features of society is in a particular state, a state of many other features, more or less precisely determinate, always or usually coexists with it.

But the uniformities of coexistence obtaining among phenomena which are effects of causes must (as we have so often observed) be corollaries from the laws of causation by which these phenomena are really determined. The mutual correlation between the different elements of each state of society is therefore a derivative law, resulting from the laws which regulate the succession between one state of society and another; for the proximate cause of every state of society is the state of society immediately preceding it. The fundamental problem, therefore, of the social science, is to find the laws according to which any state of society produces the state which succeeds it and takes its place. This opens the great and vexed question of the progressiveness of man and society; an idea involved in every just conception of social phenomena as the subject of a science.

3. It is one of the characters, not absolutely peculiar to the sciences of human nature and society, but belonging to them in a peculiar degree, to be conversant with a subject-matter whose properties are changeable. I do not mean changeable from day to day, but from age to age; so that not only the qualities of individuals vary, but those of the majority are not the same in one age as in another.

The principal cause of this peculiarity is the extensive and constant reaction of the effects upon their causes. The circumstances in which mankind are placed, operating according to their own laws and to the laws of human nature, form the characters of the human beings; but the human beings, in their turn, mould and shape the circumstances for themselves and for those who come after them. From this reciprocal action there must necessarily result either a cycle or a progress. In astronomy also, every fact is at once effect and cause; the successive positions of the various heavenly bodies produce changes both in the direction and in the intensity of the forces by which those positions are determined. But in the case of the solar system, these mutual actions bring round again, after a certain number of changes, the former state of circumstances; which of course leads to the perpetual recurrence of the same series in an unvarying order. Those bodies, in short, revolve in orbits: but there are (or, conformably to the laws of astronomy, there might be) others which, instead of an orbit, describe a trajectory a course not returning into itself. One or other of these must be the type to which human affairs must conform.

One of the thinkers who earliest conceived the succession of historical events as subject to fixed laws, and endeavoured to discover these laws by an analytical survey of history, Vico, the celebrated author of *Scienza Nuova,* adopted the former of these opinions. He conceived the phenomena of human society as revolving in an orbit; as going through periodically the same series of changes. Though there were not wanting circumstances tending to give some plausibility to this view, it would not bear a close scrutiny and those who have succeeded Vico in this kind of speculations have universally adopted the idea of a trajectory or progress, in lieu of an orbit or cycle.

The words Progress and Progressiveness are not here to be understood as synonymous with improvement and tendency to improvement. It is conceivable that the laws of human nature might determine, and even necessitate, a certain series of changes in man and society, which might not in every case, or which might not on the whole, be improvements. It is my belief indeed that the general tendency is, and will continue to be, saving occasional and temporary exceptions, one of improvement – a tendency towards a better and happier state. This, however, is not a question of the method of the social science, but a theorem of the science itself. For our purpose it is sufficient that there is a progressive change, both in the character of the human race and in their outward circumstances so far as moulded by themselves; that in each successive age the principal phenomena of society are different from what they were in the age preceding, and still more different from any previous age: the periods which most distinctly mark these successive changes being intervals of one generation, during which a new set of human beings have been educated, have grown up from childhood, and taken possession of society.

The progressiveness of the human race is the foundation on which a method of philosophising in the social science has been of late years erected, far superior to either of the two modes which had previously been prevalent, the chemical or experimental, and the geometrical modes. This method, which is now generally adopted by the most advanced thinkers on the Continent, consists in attempting, by a study and analysis of the general facts of history, to discover (what these philosophers term) the law of progress; which law, once ascertained, must according to them enable us to predict future events, just as after a few terms of an infinite series in algebra we are able to detect the principle of regularity in their formation, and to predict the rest of the series to any number of terms we please. The principal aim of historical speculation in France, of late years, has been to ascertain this law. But while I gladly acknowledge the great services which have been rendered to historical knowledge by this school, I cannot but deem them to be mostly chargeable with a fundamental misconception of the true method of social philosophy. The misconception consists in supposing that the order of succession which we may be able to trace among the different states of society and civilisation which history presents to us, even if that order were more rigidly uniform than it has yet been proved to be, could ever amount to a law of nature. It can only be an empirical law. The succession of states of the human mind and of human society cannot have an independent law of its own; it must depend on the psychological and ethological laws which govern the action of circumstances on men and of men on circumstances. It is conceivable that those laws might be such, and the general circumstances of the human race such, as to determine the successive transformations of man and society to one given and unvarying order. But even if the case were so, it cannot be the ultimate aim of science to discover an empirical law. Until that law could be connected with the psychological and ethological laws on which it must depend, and, by the consilience of deduction *a priori* with historical evidence, could be converted from an empirical law into a scientific one, it could not be relied on for the prediction of future events, beyond, at most, strictly adjacent cases. M. Comte alone, among the new historical school, has seen the necessity of thus connecting all our generalisations from history with the laws of human nature.

4. But while it is an imperative rule never to introduce any generalisations from history into the social science unless sufficient grounds can be pointed out for it in human nature, I do not think any one will contend that it would have been possible, setting out from the principles of human nature and from the general circumstances of the position of our species, to determine *a priori* the order in which human development must take place, and to predict, consequently, the general facts of history up to the present time. After the first few terms of the series, the influence exercised over each generation by the generations which preceded it becomes (as is well observed by the writer last referred to) more and more preponderant over all other influences; until at length what we now are and do is in a very small degree the result of the universal circumstances of the human race, or even of our own circumstances acting through the original qualities of our species, but mainly of the qualities produced in us by the whole previous history of humanity. So long a series of actions and reactions between Circumstances and Man, each successive term being composed of an ever greater number and variety of parts, could not possibly be computed by human faculties from the elementary laws which produce it. The mere length of the series would be a sufficient obstacle, since a slight error in any one of the terms would augment in rapid progression at every subsequent step.

If, therefore, the series of the effects themselves did not, when examined as a whole, manifest any regularity, we should in vain attempt to construct a general science of society. We must in that case have contented ourselves with that subordinate order of sociological speculation formerly noticed, namely, with endeavouring to ascertain what would be the effect of the introduction of any new cause, in a state of society supposed to be fixed; a knowledge sufficient for the more common exigencies of daily political practice, but liable to fail in all cases in which the progressive movement of society is one of the influencing elements; and therefore more precarious in proportion as the case is more important. But since both the natural varieties of mankind, and the original diversities of local circumstances are much less considerable than the points of agreement, there will naturally be a certain degree of uniformity in the progressive development of the species and of its works. And this uniformity tends to become greater, not less, as society advances; since the evolution of each people, which is at first determined exclusively by the nature and circumstances of that people, is gradually brought under the influence (which becomes stronger as civilisation advances) of the other nations of the earth, and of the circumstances by which they have been influenced. History accordingly does, when judiciously examined, afford Empirical Laws of Society. And the problem of general sociology is to ascertain these, and connect them with the laws of human nature, by deductions showing that such were the derivative laws naturally to be expected as the consequences of those ultimate ones.

It is, indeed, hardly ever possible, even after history has suggested the derivative law, to demonstrate *a priori* that such was the only order of succession or of co-existence in which the effects could, consistently with the laws of human nature, have been produced. We can at most make out that there were strong *a priori* reasons for expecting it, and that no other order of succession or co-existence would have been so likely to result from the nature of man and the general circumstances of his position. Often we cannot do even this; we cannot even show that what did take place was probably *a priori,* but only that it was possible. This, however – which, in the Inverse Deductive Method that we are now characterising, is a real process of verification – is as indispensable as verification by specific experience has been shown to be, where the conclusion is originally obtained by the direct way of deduction. The empirical laws must be the result of but a few instances, since few nations have ever attained at all and still fewer by their own independent development, a high stage of social progress. If, therefore, even one or two of these few instances be insufficiently known, or imperfectly analysed into their elements, and therefore not adequately compared with other instances, nothing is more probable than that a wrong empirical law will emerge instead of the right one. Accordingly, the most erroneous generalisations are continually made from the course of history: not only in this country, where history cannot yet be said to be at all cultivated as a science, but in other countries where it is so cultivated, and by persons well versed in it. The only check or corrective is constant verification by psychological and ethological laws. We may add to this, that no one but a person competently skilled in those laws is capable of preparing the materials for historical generalisation by analysing the facts of history, or even by observing the social phenomena of his own time. No other will be aware of the comparative importance of different facts, nor consequently know what facts to look for or to observe; still less will he be capable of estimating the evidence of facts which, as is the case with most, cannot be ascertained by direct observation or learnt from testimony, but must be inferred from marks.

5. The Empirical Laws of Society are of two kinds; some are uniformities of co-existence, some of succession. According as the science is occupied in ascertaining and verifying the former sort of uniformities or the latter, M. Comte gives it the title of Social Statics or of Social Dynamics, comformably to the distinction in mechanics between the conditions of equilibrium and those of movement, or in biology between the laws of organisation and those of life. The first branch of the science ascertains the conditions of stability in the social union; the second, the laws of progress. Social Dynamics is the theory of society considered in a state of progressive movement; while Social Statics is the theory of the *consensus* already spoken of as existing among the different parts of the social organism; in other words, the

theory of the mutual actions and reactions of contemporaneous social phenomena; 'making* provisionally, as far as possible, abstraction, for scientific purposes, of the fundamental movement which is at all times gradually modifying the whole of them.

'In this first point of view, the provisions of sociology will enable us to infer one from another (subject to ulterior verification by direct observation) the various characteristic marks of each distinct mode of social existence; in a manner essentially analogous to what is now habitually practised in the anatomy of the physical body. This preliminary aspect, therefore, of political science, of necessity supposes that (contrary to the existing habits of philosophers) each of the numerous elements of the social state, ceasing to be looked at independently and absolutely, shall be always and exclusively considered relatively to all the other elements, with the whole of which it is united by mutual interdependence. It would be superfluous to insist here upon the great and constant utility of this branch of sociological speculation. It is, in the first place, the indispensable basis of the theory of social progress. It may, moreover, be employed, immediately and of itself, to supply the place, provisionally at least, of direct observation, which in many cases is not always practicable for some of the elements of society, the real condition of which may, however, be sufficiently judged of by means of the relations which connect them with others previously known. The history of the sciences may give us some notion of the habitual importance of this auxiliary resource, by reminding us, for example, how the vulgar errors of mere erudition concerning the pretended acquirements of the ancient Egyptians in the higher astronomy, were irrevocably dissipated (even before sentence had been passed on them by a sounder erudition) from the single consideration of the inevitable connexion between the general state of astronomy and that of abstract geometry, then evidently in its infancy. It would be easy to cite a multitude of analogous cases, the character of which could admit of no dispute.

* *Cours de Philosophie Positive,* iv, 325-9.

In order to avoid exaggeration, however, it should be remarked that these necessary relations among the different aspects of society cannot, from their very nature, be so simple and precise that the results observed could only have arisen from some one mode of mutual co-ordination. Such a notion, already too narrow in the science of life, would be completely at variance with the still more complex nature of sociological speculations. But the exact estimation of these limits of variation, both in the healthy and in the morbid state, constitutes, at least as much as in the anatomy of the natural body, an indispensable complement to every theory of Sociological Statics, without which the indirect exploration above spoken of would often lead into error.

'This is not the place for methodically demonstrating the existence of a necessary relation among all the possible aspects of the same social organism; a point on which, in principle at least, there is now little difference of opinion among sound thinkers. From whichever of the social elements we choose to set out, we may easily recognise that it has always a connexion, more or less immediate, with all the other elements, even with those which at first sight appear the most independent of it. The dynamical consideration of the progressive development of civilised humanity, affords, no doubt, a still more efficacious means of effecting this interesting verification of the *consensus* of the social phenomena, by displaying the manner in which every change in any one part operates immediately, or very speedily, upon all the rest. But this indication may be preceded, or at all events followed, by a confirmation of a purely statical kind; for, in politics as in mechanics, the communication of motion from one object to another proves a connexion between them. Without descending to the minute interdependence of the different branches of any one science or art, is it not evident that among the different sciences, as well as among most of the arts, there exists such a connexion, that if the state of any one well-marked division of them is sufficiently known to us, we can with real scientific assurance infer, from their necessary correlation, the contemporaneous state of every one of the others? By a further extension of this consideration, we may conceive the necessary relation which exists between the condition of the sciences in general and that of the arts in general, except that the mutual dependence is less intense in proportion as it is more indirect. The same is the case when, instead of considering the aggregate of the social phenomena in some one people, we examine it simultaneously in different contemporaneous nations, between which the perpetual reciprocity of influence, especially in modern times, cannot be contested, though the *consensus* must in this case be ordinarily of a less decided character, and must decrease gradually with the affinity of the cases and the multiplicity of the points of contact, so as at last, in some cases, to disappear almost entirely; as, for example, between Western Europe and Eastern Asia, of which the various general states of society appear to have been hitherto almost independent of one another.'

These remarks are followed by illustrations of one of the most important, and, until lately, most neglected, of the general principles which, in this division of the social science, may be considered as established; namely, the necessary correlation between the form of government existing in any society and the contemporaneous state of civilisation: a natural law which stamps the endless discussions and innumerable theories respecting forms of government in the abstract as fruitless and worthless for any other purpose than as a preparatory treatment of materials to be afterwards used for the construction of a better philosophy.

As already remarked, one of the main results of the science of social statistics would be to ascertain the requisites of stable political union. There are some circumstances which, being found in all societies without exception, and in the greatest degree where the social union is most complete, may be considered (when psychological and ethological laws confirm the indication) as conditions of the existence of the complex phenomenon called a State. For example, no numerous society has ever been held together without laws, or usages equivalent to them; without tribunals, and an organised force of some sort to execute their decisions. There have always been public authorities whom, with more or less strictness, and in cases more or less accurately defined, the rest of the community obeyed, or according to general opinion were bound to obey. By following out this course of inquiry we shall find a number of requisites which have been present in every society that has maintained a collective existence, and on the cessation of which it has either merged in some other society, or reconstructed itself on some new basis, in which the conditions were conformed to. Although these results, obtained by comparing different forms and states of society, amount in themselves only to empirical laws, some of them, when once suggested, are found to follow with so much probability from general laws of human nature, that the consilience of the two processes raises the evidence to proof, and the generalisations to the rank of scientific truths.

This seems to be affirmable (for instance) of the conclusions arrived at in the following passage, extracted, with some alterations from a criticism on the negative philosophy of the eighteenth century,* and which I quote, though (as in some former instances) from myself, because I have no better way of illustrating the conception I have formed of the kind of theorems of which sociological statics would consist:

'The very first element of the social union, obedience to a government of some sort, has not been found so easy a thing to establish in the world. Among a timid and spiritless race like the inhabitants of the vast plains of tropical countries, passive obedience may be of natural growth; though even there we doubt whether it has ever been found among any people with whom fatalism, or, in other words, submission to the pressure of circumstances as a divine decree, did not prevail as a religious doctrine. But the difficulty of inducing a brave and warlike race to submit their individual *arbitrium* to any common umpire has always been felt to be so great, that nothing short of supernatural power has been deemed adequate to overcome it; and such tribes have always assigned to the first institution of civil society a divine origin. So

* Since reprinted entire in *Dissertations and Discussions,* as the concluding paper of the first volume.

differently did those judge who knew savage men by actual experience, from those who had no acquaintance with them except in the civilised state. In modern Europe itself, after the fall of the Roman Empire, to subdue the feudal anarchy and bring the whole people of any European nation into subjection to government (though Christianity in the most concentrated form of its influence was co-operating in the work) required thrice as many centuries as have elapsed since that time.

'Now if these philosophers had known human nature under any other type than that of their own age, and of the particular classes of society among whom they lived, it would have occurred to them, that wherever this habitual submission to law and government had been firmly and durably established, and yet the vigour and manliness of character which resisted its establishment have been in any degree preserved, certain requisites have existed, certain conditions have been fulfilled, of which the following may be regarded as the principal:

'First, there has existed, for all who were accounted citizens, – for all who were not slaves, kept down by brute force, – a system of *education,* beginning with infancy and continued through life, of which, whatever else it might include, one main and incessant ingredient was *restraining discipline*. To train the human being in the habit, and thence the power, of subordinating his personal impulses and aims to what were considered the ends of society; of adhering, against all temptation, to the course of conduct which those ends prescribed; of controlling in himself all feelings which were liable to militate against those ends, and encouraging all such as tended towards them; this was the purpose to which every outward motive that the authority directing the system could command, and every inward power or principle which its knowledge of human nature enabled it to evoke, were endeavoured to be rendered instrumental. The entire civil and military policy of the ancient commonwealths was such a system of training; in modern nations its place has been attempted to be supplied, principally, by religious teaching. And whenever and in proportion as the strictness of the restraining discipline was relaxed, the natural tendency of mankind to anarchy reasserted itself; the state became disorganised from within; mutual conflict for selfish ends neutralised the energies which were required to keep up the contest against natural causes of evil; and the nation, after a longer or briefer interval of progressive decline, became either the slave of a despotism, or the prey of a foreign invader.

'The second condition of permanent political society has been found to be the existence, in some form or other, of the feeling of allegiance or loyalty. This feeling may vary in its objects, and is not confined to any particular form of government; but whether in a democracy or in a monarchy, its essence is always the same, viz. that there be in the constitution of the state *something* which is settled, something permanent, and not to be called in question; something which, by general agreement, has a right to be where it is, and to be secure against disturbance, whatever else may change. This feeling may attach itself, as among the Jews (and in most of the commonwealths of antiquity), to a common God or gods, the protectors and guardians of their state. Or it may attach itself to certain persons, who are deemed to be, whether by divine appointment, by long prescription, or by the general recognition of their superior capacity and worthiness, the rightful guides and guardians of the rest. Or it may connect itself with laws; with ancient liberties or ordinances. Or, finally (and this is the only shape in which the feeling is likely to exist hereafter), it may attach itself to the principles of individual freedom and political and social equality, as realised in institutions which as yet exist nowhere, or exist only in a rudimentary state. But in all political societies which have had a durable existence there has been some fixed point, something which people agree in holding sacred; which, wherever freedom of discussion was a recognised principle, it was of course lawful to contest in theory, but which no one could either fear or hope to see shaken in practice; which, in short (except perhaps during some temporary crisis) was in the common estimation placed beyond discussion. And the necessity of this may easily be made evident. A state never is, nor, until mankind are vastly improved, can hope to be, for any long time exempt from internal dissension; for there neither is nor ever has been any state of society in which collisions did not occur between the immediate interests and passions of powerful sections of the people. What, then, enables nations to weather these storms, and pass through turbulent times without any permanent weakening of the securities for peaceable existence? Precisely this – that however important the interests about which men fall out, the conflict did not affect the fundamental principle of the system of social union which happened to exist, nor threaten large portions of the community with the subversion of that on which they had built their calculations, and with which their hopes and aims had become identified. But when the questioning of these fundamental principles is (not the occasional disease or salutary medicine, but) the habitual condition of the body politic, and when all the violent animosities are called forth which spring naturally from such a situation, the state is virtually in a position of civil war, and can never long remain free from it in act and fact.

'The third essential condition of stability in political society is a strong and active principle of cohesion among the members of the same community or state. We need scarcely say that we do not mean nationality, in the vulgar sense of the term; a senseless antipathy to foreigners; indifference to the general welfare of the human race, or an unjust preference of the supposed interest of our own country; a cherishing of bad peculiarities because they are national, or a refusal to adopt what has been found good by other countries. We mean a principle of sympathy, not of hostility; of union, not of separation. We mean a feeling of common interest among those who live under the same government, and are contained within the same natural or historical boundaries. We mean, that one part of the community do not consider themselves as foreigners with regard to another part; that they set a value on their connexion – feel that they are one people, that their lot is cast together, that evil to any of their fellow-countrymen is evil to themselves, and do not desire selfishly to free themselves from their share of any common inconvenience by severing the connexion. How strong this feeling was in those ancient commonwealths which attained any durable greatness everyone knows. How happily Rome, in spite of all her tyranny, succeeded in establishing the feeling of a common country among the provinces of her vast and divided empire, will appear when anyone who has given due attention to the subject shall take the trouble to point it out. In modern times the countries which have had that feeling in the strongest degree have been the most powerful countries; England, France, and in proportion to their territory and resources, Holland and Switzerland; while England in her connexion with Ireland is one of the most signal examples of the consequences of its absence. Every Italian knows why Italy is under a foreign yoke; every German knows what maintains despotism in the Austrian empire;* the evils of Spain flow as much from the absence of nationality among the Spaniards themselves as from the presence of it in their relations with foreigners: while the completest illustration of all is afforded by the republics of South America, where the parts of one and the same state adhere so slightly together, that no sooner does any province think itself aggrieved by the general government than it proclaims itself a separate nation.'

6. While the derivative laws of social statics are ascertained by analysing different states of society, and comparing them with one another, without regard to the order of their succession, the consideration of the successive order is, on the contrary, predominant in the study of social dynamics, of which the aim is to observe and explain the sequences of social conditions. This branch of the social science would be as complete as it can be made if every one of the leading general circumstances of each generation were traced to

* Written and first published in 1840.

its causes in the generation immediately preceding. But the *consensus* is so complete (especially in modern history) that, in the filiation of one generation and another, it is the whole which produces the whole, rather than any part a part. Little progress, therefore, can be made in establishing the filiation directly from laws of human nature, without having first ascertained the immediate or derivative laws according to which social states generate one another as society advances – the *axiomata media* of General Sociology.

The empirical laws which are most readily obtained by generalisation from history do not amount to this. They are not the 'middle principles' themselves, but only evidence towards the establishment of such principles. They consist of certain general tendencies which may be perceived in society; a progressive increase of some social elements and diminution of others, or a gradual change in the general character of certain elements. It is easily seen, for instance, that as society advances, mental tend more and more to prevail over bodily qualities, and masses over individuals; that the occupation of all that portion of mankind who are not under external restraint is at first chiefly military, but society becomes progressively more and more engrossed with productive pursuits, and the military spirit gradually gives way to the industrial; to which many similar truths might be added. And with generalisations of this description ordinary inquirers, even of the historical school now predominant on the Continent, are satisfied. But these and all such results are still at too great a distance from the elementary laws of human nature on which they depend, – too many links intervene, and the concurrence of causes at each link is far too complicated – to enable these propositions to be presented as direct corollaries from those elementary principles. They have, therefore, in the minds of most inquirers, remained in the state of empirical laws, applicable only within the bounds of actual observation, without any means of determining their real limits, and of judging whether the changes which have hitherto been in progress are destined to continue indefinitely, or to terminate, or even to be reversed.

7. In order to obtain better empirical laws, we must not rest satisfied with noting the progressive changes which manifest themselves in the separate elements of society, and in which nothing is indicated but the relation of fragments of the effect to corresponding fragments of the cause. It is necessary to combine the statical view of social phenomena with the dynamical, considering not only the progressive changes of the different elements, but the contemporaneous condition of each, and thus obtain empirically the law of correspondence not only between the simultaneous states, but between the simultaneous changes, of those elements. This law of correspondence it is, which duly verified *a priori,* would become the real scientific derivative law of the development of humanity and human affairs.

In the difficult process of observation and comparison which is here required, it would evidently be a great assistance if it should happen to be the fact that some one element in the complex existence of social man is pre-eminent over all others as the prime agent of the social movement. For we could then take the progress of that one element as the central chain, to each successive link of which the corresponding links of all the other progressions being appended, the succession of the facts would by this alone be presented in a kind of spontaneous order, far more nearly approaching to the real order of their filiation than could be obtained by any other merely empirical process.

Now, the evidence of history and that of human nature combine, by a striking instance of consilience, to show that there really is one social element which is thus predominant, and almost paramount, among the agents of the social progression. This is the state of the speculative faculties of mankind, including the nature of the beliefs which by any means they have arrived at concerning themselves and the world by which they are surrounded.

It would be a great error, and one very little likely to be committed, to assert that speculation, intellectual activity, the pursuit of truth, is among the more powerful propensities of human nature, or hold a predominating place in the lives of any, save decidedly exceptional, individuals. But, notwithstanding the relative weakness of this principle among other sociological agents, its influence is the main determining cause of the social progress; all the other dispositions of our nature which contribute to that progress being dependent on it for the means of accomplishing their share of the work. Thus (to take the most obvious case first) the impelling force to most of the improvements effected in the arts of life is the desire of increased material comfort: but as we can only act upon external objects in proportion to our knowledge of them, the state of knowledge at any time is the limit of the industrial improvements possible at that time; and the progress of industry must follow, and depend on, the progress of knowledge. The same thing may be shown to be true, though it is not quite so obvious, of the progress of the fine arts. Further, as the strongest propensities of uncultivated or half-cultivated human nature (being the purely selfish ones, and those of a sympathetic character which partake most of the nature of selfishness) evidently tend in themselves to disunite mankind, not to unite them – to make them rivals, not confederates; social existence is only possible by a disciplining of those more powerful propensities, which consists in subordinating them to a common system of opinions. The degree of this subordination is the measure of the completeness of the social union, and the nature of the common opinions determines its kind. But in order that mankind should conform their actions to any set of opinions, these opinions must exist, must be believed by them. And thus the state of the speculative faculties, the character of the propositions assented to by the intellect, essentially determines the moral and political state of the community, as we have already seen that it determines the physical.

These conclusions, deduced from the laws of human nature, are in entire accordance with the general facts of history. Every considerable change historically known to us in the condition of any portion of mankind, when not brought about by external force, has been preceded by a change of proportional extent in the state of their knowledge or in their prevalent beliefs. As between any given state of speculation and the correlative state of everything else, it was almost always the former which first showed itself; though the effects, no doubt, reacted potently upon the cause. Every considerable advance in material civilisation has been preceded by an advance in knowledge; and when any great social change has come to pass, either in the way of gradual development or of sudden conflict, it has had for its precursor a great change in opinions and modes of thinking of society. Polytheism, Judaism, Christianity, Protestantism, the critical philosophy of modern Europe, and its positive science – each of these has been a primary agent in making society what it was at each successive period, while society was but secondarily instrumental in making *them,* each of them (so far as causes can be assigned for its existence) being mainly an emanation not from the practical life of the period, but from the previous state of belief and thought. The weakness of the speculative propensity in mankind generally has not, therefore, prevented the progress of speculation from governing that of society at large; it has only, and too often, prevented progress altogether, where the intellectual progression has come to an early stand for want of sufficiently favourable circumstances.

From this accumulated evidence, we are justified in concluding that the order of human progression in all respects will mainly depend on the order of progression in the intellectual convictions of mankind, that is, on the law of the successive transformations of human opinions. The question remains, whether this law can be determined, at first from history as an empirical law, then converted into a scientific theorem by deducing it *a priori* from the principles of human nature. As the progress of knowledge and the changes in the opinions of mankind are very slow, and manifest themselves in a well-defined manner only at long intervals, it cannot be expected that the general order of sequence should be discoverable from the examination of less than a very considerable part of the duration of the social progress. It is necessary to take into consideration the whole of past time, from the first recorded condition of the human race, to the memorable phenomena of the last and present generations.

8. The investigation which I have thus endeavoured to characterise has been systematically attempted, up to the present time, by M. Comte alone. His work is hitherto the only known example of the study of social phenomena according to this conception of the Historical Method. Without discussing here the worth of his conclusions, and especially of his predictions and recommendations with respect to the Future of society, which appear to me greatly inferior in value to his appreciation of the Past, I shall confine myself to mentioning one important generalisation, which M. Comte regards as the fundamental law of the progress of human knowledge. Speculation he conceives to have, on every subject of human inquiry, three successive stages; in the first of which it tends to explain the phenomena by supernatural agencies, in the second by metaphysical abstractions, and in the third or final state confines itself to ascertaining their laws of succession and similitude. This generalisation appears to me to have that high degree of scientific evidence which is derived from the concurrence of the indications of history with the probabilities derived from the constitution of the human mind. Nor could it be easily conceived, from the mere enunciation of such a proposition, what a flood of light it lets in upon the whole course of history, when its consequences are traced, by connecting with each of the three states of human intellect which it distinguishes, and with each successive modification of those three states, the correlative condition of other social phenomena.*

* This great generalisation is often unfavourably criticised (as by Dr Whewell, for instance) under a misapprehension of its real import. The doctrine that the theological explanation of phenomena belongs only to the infancy of our knowledge of them, ought not to be construed as if it was equivalent to the assertion that mankind, as their knowledge advances, will necessarily cease to believe in any kind of theology. This was M.

But whatever decision competent judges may pronounce on the results arrived at by any individual inquirer, the method now characterised is that by which the derivative laws of

Comte's opinion; but it is by no means implied in his fundamental theorem. All that is implied is, that in an advanced state of human knowledge, no other Ruler of the World will be acknowledged than one who rules by universal laws, and does not at all, or does not unless in very peculiar cases, produce events by special interpositions. Originally all natural events were ascribed to such interpositions. At present every educated person rejects this explanation in regard to all classes of phenomena of which the laws have been fully ascertained; though some have not yet reached the point of referring all phenomena to the idea of Law, but believe that rain and sunshine, famine and pestilence, victory and defeat, death and life, are issues which the Creator does not leave to the operation of his general laws, but reserves to be decided by express acts of volition. M. Comte's theory is the negation of this doctrine.

Dr Whewell equally misunderstands M. Comte's doctrine respecting the second or metaphysical stage of speculation. M. Comte did not mean that 'discussions concerning ideas' are limited to an early stage of inquiry, and cease when science enters into the positive stage. (*Philosophy of Discovery,* p. 226 *et seq.*) In all M. Comte's speculations as much stress is laid on the process of clearing up our conceptions as on the ascertainment of facts. When M. Comte speaks of the metaphysical stage of speculation, he means the stage in which men speak of 'Nature' and other abstractions as if they were active forces, producing effects; when Nature is said to do this, or forbid that; when Nature's horror of a vacuum, Nature's non-admission of a break, Nature's *vis medicatrix,* were offered as explanations of phenomena; when the qualities of things were mistaken for real entities dwelling in the things; when the phenomena of living bodies were thought to be accounted for by being referred to a 'vital force'; when, in short, the abstract names of phenomena were mistaken for the causes of their existence. In this sense of the word it cannot be reasonably denied that the metaphysical explanation of phenomena, equally with the theological, gives way before the advance of real science.

That the final, or positive stage, as conceived by M. Comte, has been equally misunderstood, and that, notwithstanding some expressions open to just criticism, M. Comte never dreamed of denying the legitimacy of inquiry into all causes which are accessible to human investigations, I have pointed out in a former place.

social order and of social progress must be sought. By its aid we may hereafter succeed not only in looking far forward into the future history of the human race, but in determining what artificial means may be used, and to what extent, to accelerate the natural progress in so far as it is beneficial; to compensate for whatever may be its inherent inconveniences or disadvantages, and to guard against the dangers or accidents to which our species is exposed from the necessary incidents of its progression. Such practical instructions, founded on the highest branch of speculative sociology, will form the noblest and most beneficial portion of the Political Art.

That of this science and art even the foundations are but beginning to be laid is sufficiently evident. But the superior minds are fairly turning themselves towards that object. It has become the aim of really scientific thinkers to connect by theories the facts of universal history: it is acknowledged to be one of the requisites of a general system of social doctrine that it should explain, so far as the data exist, the main facts of history; and a Philosophy of History is generally admitted to be at once the verification and the initial form of the Philosophy of the Progress of Society.

If the endeavours now making in all the more cultivated nations, and beginning to be made even in England (usually the last to enter into the general movement of the European mind), for the construction of a Philosophy of History, shall be directed and controlled by those views of the nature of sociological evidence which I have (very briefly and imperfectly) attempted to characterise, they cannot fail to give birth to a sociological system widely removed from the vague and conjectural character of all former attempts, and worthy to take its place, at last, among the sciences. When this time shall come, no important branch of human affairs will be any longer abandoned to empiricism and unscientific surmise; the circle of human knowledge will be complete, and it can only thereafter receive further enlargement by perpetual expansion from within.

2 *Of the Logic of Practice or Art*

(Bk VI, chapter XII of *System of Logic,* first published 1843. This version from the Eighth Edition, London 1872.)

1. In the preceding chapters we have endeavoured to characterise the present state of those among the branches of knowledge called Moral which are sciences in the only proper sense of the term, that is, inquiries into the course of nature. It is customary, however, to include under the term Moral Knowledge, and even (though improperly) under that of Moral Science, an inquiry the results of which do not express themselves in the indicative, but in the imperative mood, or in periphrases equivalent to it; what is called the knowledge of duties, practical ethics, or morality.

Now, the imperative mood is the characteristic of art, as distinguished from science. Whatever speaks in rules or precepts, not in assertions respecting matters of fact, is art; and ethics or morality is properly a portion of the art corresponding to the sciences of human nature and society.*

The Method, therefore, of Ethics, can be no other than that of Art, or Practice, in general: and the portion yet uncompleted, of the task which we proposed to ourselves in the concluding Book is to characterise the general Method of Art, as distinguished from Science.

2. In all branches of practical business, there are cases in which individuals are bound to conform their practice to a

* It is almost superfluous to observe, that there is another meaning of the word Art, in which it may be said to denote the poetical department or aspect of things in general, in contradistinction to the scientific. In the text, the word is used in its older, and, I hope, not yet obsolete sense.

pre-established rule, while there are others in which it is part of their task to find or construct the rule by which they are to govern their conduct. The first, for example, is the case of a judge under a definite written code. The judge is not called upon to determine what course would be intrinsically the most advisable in the particular case in hand, but only within what rule of law it falls; what the legislature has ordained to be done in the kind of case, and must therefore be presumed to have intended in the individual case. The method must here be wholly and exclusively one of ratiocination or syllogism; and the process is obviously what in our analysis of the syllogism we showed that all ratiocination is, namely, the interpretation of a formula.

In order that our illustration of the opposite case may be taken from the same class of subjects as the former, we will suppose, in contrast with the situation of the judge, the position of the legislator. As the judge has laws for his guidance, so the legislator has rules and maxims of policy; but it would be a manifest error to suppose that the legislator is bound by these maxims in the same manner as the judge is bound by the laws, and that all he has to do is to argue down from them to the particular case, as the judge does from the laws. The legislator is bound to take into consideration the reasons or grounds of the maxim; the judge has nothing to do with those of the law, except so far as a consideration of them may throw light upon the intention of the lawmaker, where his words have left it doubtful. To the judge, the rule, once positively ascertained, is final; but the legislator, or other practitioner, who goes by rules rather than by their reasons, like the old-fashioned German tacticians who were vanquished by Napoleon, or the physician who preferred that his patients should die by rule rather than recover contrary to it, is rightly judged to be a mere pedant, and the slave of his formulas.

Now, the reasons of a maxim of policy, or of any other rule of art, can be no other than the theorems of the corresponding science.

The relation in which rules of art stand to doctrines of science may be thus characterised. The art proposes to itself an end to be attained, defines the end, and hands it over to the science. The science receives it, considers it as a phenomenon or effect to be studied, and having investigated its causes and conditions, sends it back to art with a theorem of the combination of circumstances by which it could be produced. Art then examines these combinations of circumstances, and according as any of them are or are not in human power, pronounces the end attainable or not. The only one of the premises, therefore, which Art supplies is the original major premise, which asserts that the attainment of the given end is desirable. Science then lends to Art the proposition (obtained by a series of inductions or of deductions) that the performance of certain actions will attain the end. From these premises Art concludes that the performance of these actions is desirable, and finding it also practicable, converts the theorem into a rule or precept.

3. It deserves particular notice that the theorem or speculative truth is not ripe for being turned into a precept until the whole, and not a part merely, of the operation which belongs to science has been performed. Suppose that we have completed the scientific process only up to a certain point; have discovered that a particular cause will produce the desired effect, but have not ascertained all the negative conditions which are necessary, that is, all the circumstances which, if present, would prevent its production. If, in this imperfect state of the scientific theory, we attempt to frame a rule of art, we perform that operation prematurely. Whenever any counteracting cause, overlooked by the theorem, takes place, the rule will be at fault; we shall employ the means, and the end will not follow. No arguing from or about the rule itself will then help us through the difficulty; there is nothing for it but to turn back and finish the scientific process which should have preceded the formation of the rule. We must reopen the investigation to inquire into the remainder of the conditions on which the effect depends; and

only after we have ascertained the whole of these are we prepared to transform the completed law of the effect into a precept, in which those circumstances or combinations of circumstances which the science exhibits as conditions are prescribed as means.

It is true that, for the sake of convenience, rules must be formed from something less than this ideally perfect theory; in the first place, because the theory can seldom be made ideally perfect; and next, because, if all the counteracting contingencies, whether of frequent or of rare occurrence, were included, the rules would be too cumbrous to be apprehended and remembered by ordinary capacities, on the common occasions of life. The rules of art do not attempt to comprise more conditions than require to be attended to in ordinary cases; and are therefore always imperfect. In the manual arts, where the requisite conditions are not numerous, and where those which the rules do not specify are generally either plain to common observation or speedily learnt from practice, rules may often be safely acted on by persons who know nothing more than the rule. But in the complicated affairs of life, and still more in those of states and societies, rules cannot be relied on, without constantly referring back to the scientific laws on which they are founded. To know what are the practical contingencies which require a modification of the rule, or which are altogether exceptions to it, is to know what combinations of circumstances would interfere with, or entirely counteract, the consequences of those laws; and this can only be learnt by a reference to the theoretic grounds of the rule.

By a wise practitioner, therefore, rules of conduct will only be considered as provisional. Being made for the most numerous cases, or for those of most ordinary occurrence, they point out the manner in which it will be least perilous to act, where time or means do not exist for analysing the actual circumstances of the case, or where we cannot trust our judgment in estimating them. But they do not at all supersede the propriety of going through (when circumstances permit) the scientific process requisite for framing a rule from the data of the particular case before us. At the same time, the common rule may very properly serve as an admonition that a certain mode of action has been found by ourselves and others to be well adapted to the cases of most common occurrence; so that if it be unsuitable to the case in hand, the reason of its being so will be likely to arise from some unusual circumstance.

4. The error is therefore apparent of those who would deduce the line of conduct proper to particular cases from supposed universal practical maxims, overlooking the necessity of constantly referring back to the principles of the speculative science, in order to be sure of attaining even the specific end which the rules have in view. How much greater still, then, must the error be of setting up such unbending principles, not merely as universal rules for attaining a given end, but as rules of conduct generally; without regard to the possibility, not only that some modifying cause may prevent the attainment of the given end by the means which the rule prescribes, but that success itself may conflict with some other end, which may possibly chance to be more desirable.

This is the habitual error of many of the political speculators whom I have characterised as the geometrical school; especially in France, where ratiocination from rules of practice forms the staple commodity of journalism and political oratory; a misapprehension of the functions of Deduction which has brought much discredit, in the estimation of other countries, upon the spirit of generalisation, so honourably characteristic of the French mind. The commonplaces of politics, in France, are large and sweeping practical maxims, from which, as ultimate premises, men reason downwards to particular applications, and this they call being logical and consistent. For instance, they are perpetually arguing that such and such a measure ought to be adopted, because it is a consequence of the principle on which the form of government is founded; or the principle of the sovereignty of the people. To which it may be answered, that, if these be really practical principles, they must rest on speculative grounds; the sovereignty of the people (for example) must be a right foundation for government, because a government thus constituted tends to produce certain beneficial effects. Inasmuch, however, as no government produces all possible beneficial effects, but all are attended with more or fewer inconveniences, and since these cannot usually be combated by means drawn from the very causes which produce them, it would be often a much stronger recommendation of some practical arrangement that it does not follow from what is called the general principle of the government, than that it does. Under a government of legitimacy, the presumption is far rather in favour of institutions of popular origin; and in a democracy, in favour of arrangements tending to check the impetus of popular will. The line of argumentation so commonly mistaken in France for political philosophy tends to the practical conclusion that we should exert our utmost efforts to aggravate, instead of alleviating, whatever are the characteristic imperfections of the system of institutions which we prefer, or under which we happen to live.

5. The grounds, then, of every rule of art are to be found in theorems of science. An art, or a body of art, consists of the rules, together with as much of the speculative propositions as comprises the justification of those rules. The complete art of any matter includes a selection of such a portion from the science as is necessary to show on what conditions the effects which the art aims at producing depend. And Art in general consists of the truths of science, arranged in the most convenient order for practice, instead of the order which is the most convenient for thought. Science groups and arranges its truths so as to enable us to take in at one view as much as possible of the general order of the universe. Art, though it must assume the same general laws, follows them only into such of their detailed consequences as have led to the formation of rules of conduct, and brings together from parts of the field of science most remote from one an-

other the truths relating to the production of the different and heterogeneous conditions necessary to each effect which the exigencies of practical life require to be produced.*

Science, therefore, following one cause to its various effects, while art traces one effect to its multiplied and diversified causes and conditions, there is need of a set of intermediate scientific truths, derived from the higher generalities of science, and destined to serve as the generalia or first principles of the various arts. The scientific operation of framing these intermediate principles, M. Comte characterises as one of those results of philosophy which are reserved for futurity. The only complete example which he points out as actually realised, and which can be held up as a type to be imitated in more important matters, is the general theory of the art of Descriptive Geometry, as conceived by M. Monge. It is not, however, difficult to understand what the nature of these intermediate principles must generally be. After framing the most comprehensive possible conception of the end to be aimed at, that is, of the effect to be produced, and determining in the same comprehensive manner the set of conditions on which that effect depends, there remains to be taken a general survey of the resources which can be commanded for realising this set of conditions; and when the result of this survey has been embodied in the fewest and most extensive propositions possible, those propositions will express the general relation between the available means and the end, and will constitute the general scientific theory of the art, from which its practical methods will follow as corollaries.

6. But though the reasonings which connect the end or purpose of every art with its means belong to the domain of Science, the definition of the end itself belongs exclusively to Art, and forms its peculiar province. Every art has one first principle, or general major premise, not borrowed from

* Professor Bain and others call the selection from the truths of science made for the purposes of an art, a Practical Science; and confine the name Art to the actual rules.

science; that which enunciates the object aimed at, and affirms it to be a desirable object. The builder's art assumes that it is desirable to have buildings; architecture (as one of the fine arts), that it is desirable to have them beautiful or imposing. The hygienic and medical arts assume, the one that the preservation of health, the other that the cure of disease, are fitting and desirable ends. These are not propositions of science. Propositions of science assert a matter of fact: an existence, a co-existence, a succession, or a resemblance. The propositions now spoken of do not assert that anything is, but enjoin or recommend that something should be. They are a class by themselves. A proposition of which the predicate is expressed by the words *ought* or *should be,* is generically different from one which is expressed by *is* or *will be*. It is true that, in the largest sense of the words, even these propositions assert something as a matter of fact. The fact affirmed in them is, that the conduct recommended excites in the speaker's mind the feeling of approbation. This, however, does not go to the bottom of the matter, for the speaker's approbation is no sufficient reason why other people should approve; nor ought it to be a conclusive reason even with himself. For the purposes of practice, every one must be required to justify his approbation; and for this there is need of general premises, determining what are the proper objects of approbation, and what the proper order of precedence among those objects.

These general premises, together with the principal conclusions which may be deduced from them, form (or rather might form) a body of doctrine, which is properly the Art of Life, in its three departments, Morality, Prudence or Policy, and Aesthetics; the Right, the Expedient, and the Beautiful or Noble, in human conduct and works. To this art (which, in the main is unfortunately still to be created) all other arts are subordinate; since its principles are those which must determine whether the special aim of any particular art is worthy and desirable, and what is its place in the scale of desirable things. Every art is thus a joint result of laws of nature disclosed by science, and of the general principles of what has been called Teleology, or the Doctrine of Ends;* which, borrowing the language of the German metaphysicians, may also be termed, not improperly, the principles of Practical Reason.

A scientific observer or reasoner, merely as such, is not an adviser for practice. His part is only to show that certain consequences follow from certain causes, and that to obtain certain ends, certain means are the most effectual. Whether the ends themselves are such as ought to be pursued, and if so, in what case and to how great a length, it is no part of his business as a cultivator of science to decide, and science alone will never qualify him for the decision. In purely physical science there is not much temptation to assume this ulterior office; but those who treat of human nature and society invariably claim it; they always undertake to say, not merely what is, but what ought to be. To entitle them to do this, a complete doctrine of Teleology is indispensable. A scientific theory, however perfect, of the subject-matter, considered merely as part of the order of nature, can in no degree serve as a substitute. In this respect the various subordinate arts afford a misleading analogy. In them there is seldom any visible necessity for justifying the end, since in general its desirableness is denied by nobody, and it is only when the question of precedence is to be decided between that end and some other, that the general principles of Teleology have to be called in; but a writer on Morals and Politics requires those principles at every step. The most elaborate and well-digested exposition of the laws of succession and co-existence among mental or social phenomena, and of their relation to one another as causes and effects, will be of no avail towards the art of Life or of Society, if the ends to be aimed at by that art are left to the vague suggestions of the *intellectus sibi permissus,* or are taken for granted without analysis or questioning.

* The word Teleology is also, but inconveniently and improperly, employed by some writers as a name for the attempt to explain the phenomena of the universe from final causes.

7. There is, then, a *Philosophia Prima* peculiar to Art, as there is one which belongs to Science. There are not only first principles of Knowledge, but first principles of Conduct. There must be some standard by which to determine the goodness or badness, absolute and comparative, of ends or objects of desire. And whatever that standard is, there can be but one: for if there were several ultimate principles of conduct, the same conduct might be approved by one of those principles and condemned by another; and there would be needed some more general principle as umpire between them.

Accordingly, writers on moral philosophy have mostly felt the necessity not only of referring all rules of conduct, and all judgments of praise and blame, to principles, but of referring them to some one principle; some rule or standard, with which all other rules of conduct were required to be consistent, and from which by ultimate consequence they could all be deduced. Those who have dispensed with the assumption of such an universal standard have only been enabled to do so by supposing that a moral sense, or instinct, inherent in our constitution, informs us, both what principles of conduct we are bound to observe, and also in what order these should be subordinated to one another.

The theory of the foundations of morality is a subject which it would be out of place, in a work like this, to discuss at large, and which could not to any useful purpose be treated incidentally. I shall content myself therefore with saying, that the doctrine of intuitive moral principles, even if true, would provide only for that portion of the field of conduct which is properly called moral. For the remainder of the practice of life some general principle, or standard, must still be sought, and if that principle be rightly chosen, it will be found, I apprehend, to serve quite as well for the ultimate principle of Morality, as for that of Prudence, Policy, or Taste.

Without attempting in this place to justify my opinion, or even to define the kind of justification which it admits of, I merely declare my conviction, that the general principle to which all rules of practice ought to conform, and the test by which they should be tried, is that of conduciveness to the happiness of mankind, or rather of all sentient beings: in other words, that the promotion of happiness is the ultimate principle of Teleology.*

I do not mean to assert that the promotion of happiness should be itself the end of all actions, or even of all rules of action. It is not itself the sole end. There are many virtuous actions, and even virtuous modes of action (though the cases are, I think, less frequent than is often supposed), by which happiness in the particular instance is sacrificed, more pain being produced than pleasure. But conduct of which this can be truly asserted admits of justification only because it can be shown that on the whole more happiness will exist in the world if feelings are cultivated which will make people, in certain cases, regardless of happiness. I fully admit that this is true: that the cultivation of an ideal nobleness of will and conduct should be to individual human beings an end, to which the specific pursuit either of their own happiness or of that of others (except so far as included in that idea) should, in any case of conflict, give way. But I hold that the very question, what constitutes this elevation of character, is itself to be decided by a reference to happiness as the standard. The character itself should be, to the individual, a paramount end, simply because the existence of this ideal nobleness of character, or of a near approach to it, in any abundance, would go further than all things else towards making human life happy, both in the comparatively humble sense of pleasure and freedom from pain, and in the higher meaning of rendering life, not what it now is almost universally, puerile and insignificant, but such as human beings with highly developed faculties can care to have.

8. With these remarks we must close this summary view of the application of the general logic of scientific inquiry to

* For an express discussion and vindication of this principle, see *Utilitarianism*.

the moral and social departments of science. Notwithstanding the extreme generality of the principles of method which I have laid down (a generality which, I trust, is not in this instance synonymous with vagueness) I have indulged the hope that to some of those on whom the task will devolve of bringing those most important of all sciences into a more satisfactory state these observations may be useful, both in removing erroneous and in clearing up the true conceptions of the means by which, on subjects of so high a degree of complication, truth can be attained. Should this hope be realised, what is probably destined to be the great intellectual achievement of the next two or three generations of European thinkers will have been in some degree forwarded.

3 Michelets' *History of France*

(*Edinburgh Review* LXXXIX, 1844; reprinted in *Dissertations and Discussions*, Vol. II 1859.[2])

. . . we may observe that there are three distinct stages in historical enquiry.

The type of the first stage is Larcher, the translator of Herodotus, who, as remarked by Paul Louis Courier, carries with him to the durbar of Darius the phraseology of the Court of Louis Quatorze;[3] . . .

The character of this school is to transport present feelings and notions back into the past, and refer all ages and forms of human life to the standard of that in which the writer himself lives. Whatever cannot be translated into the language of their own time, whatever they cannot represent to themselves by some fancied modern equivalent, is nothing to them, calls up no ideas in their minds at all. They cannot imagine any thing different from their own everyday experience. They assume that words mean the same thing to a monkish chronicler as to a modern member of parliament. If they find the term *rex* applied to Clovis or Clotaire, they already talk of 'the French monarchy', or 'the kingdom of France'. If among a tribe of savages newly escaped from the woods, they find mention of a council of leading men, or an assembled multitude giving its sanction to some matter of general concernment, their imagination jumps to a system of free institutions, and a wise contrivance of constitutional balances and checks. If, at other times, they find the chief killing and plundering without this sanction, they just as promptly figure to themselves an acknowledged despotism. In this manner they antedate not only modern ideas, but the essential characters of the modern mind; and imagine their ancestors to be very like their next neighbours, saving a few eccentricities, occasioned by being still Pagans or Catholics, by having no *habeas corpus* act, and no Sunday schools. If an historian of this stamp takes a side in controversy, and passes judgment upon actions or personages that have figured in history, he applies to them in the crudest form the canons of some modern party or creed. If he is a Tory, and his subject is Greece, every thing Athenian must be cried down, and Philip and Dionysius must be washed white as snow, lest Pericles and Demosthenes should not be sufficiently black. If he be a Liberal, Caesar and Cromwell, and all usurpers similar to them, are 'damned to everlasting fame'. Is he an unbeliever? a pedantic narrow-minded[4] Julian becomes his pattern of a prince, and the heroes and martyrs of Christianity objects of scornful pity. If he is of the Church of England, Gregory VII, must be an ambitious impostor, because Leo X was a self-indulgent voluptuary; John Knox nothing but a coarse-minded fanatic, because the historian does not like John Wesley. Humble as our estimate must be of this kind of writers, it would be unjust to forget, that even *their* mode of treating history is an improvement upon the unenquiring credulity which contented itself with copying or translating the ancient authorities, without ever bringing the writer's own mind in contact with the subject. It is better to conceive Demosthenes even under the image of Anacharsis Clootz, than not as a living being at all, but a figure in a puppet-show, of which Plutarch is the showman; and Mitford, so far, is a better historian than Rollin. He does give a sort of reality to historical personages: he ascribes to them passions and purposes, which, though not those of their age or position, are still human; and enables us to form a tolerably distinct, though, in general, an exceedingly false notion of their qualities and circumstances. This is a first step; and, that step made, the reader, once in motion, is not likely to stop there.

Accordingly, the second stage of historical study attempts to regard former ages not with the eye of a modern, but, as far as possible, with that of a contemporary; to realize a true and living picture of the past time, clothed in its circumstances and peculiarities. This is not an easy task: the knowledge of any amount of dry generalities, or even of the practical life and business of his own time, go a very little way to qualify a writer for it. He needs some of the characteristics of the poet. He has to 'body forth the forms of things unknown'. He must have the faculty to see, in the ends and fragments which are preserved of some element of the past the consistent whole to which they once belonged; to discern, in the individual fact which some monument hands down, or to which some chronicler testifies, the general, and for that very reason unrecorded, facts which it presupposes. Such gifts of imagination he must possess; and, what is rarer still, he must forbear to abuse them. He must have the conscience and self-command to assert no more than can be vouched for, or reduced by legitimate inference from what is vouched for. With the genius for producing a great historical romance, he must have the virtue to add nothing to what can be proved to be true: What wonder if so rare a combination is not often realized?

Realized, of course, in its ideal perfection, it never is; but many now aim at it, and some approach it, according to the measure of their faculties. Of the sagacity which detects the meaning of small things, and drags to light the forgotten elements of a gone-by state of society, from scattered evidences which the writers themselves who recorded them did not understand, the world has now, in Niebuhr, an imperishable model. The reproduction of past events in the colours of life, and with all the complexity and bustle of a real scene, can hardly be carried to a higher pitch than by Mr Carlyle. But to find a school of writers, and among them several of the first rank, who systematically direct their aims towards this ideal of history, we must look to the French historians of the present day.

There is yet a third and the highest stage of historical investigation, in which the aim is not simply to compose histories, but to construct a science of history. In this view, the whole of the events which have befallen the human race, and the states through which it has passed, are regarded as a series of phenomena, produced by causes, and susceptible of explanation. All history is conceived as a progressive chain of causes and effects; or (by an apter metaphor) as a gradually unfolding web, in which every fresh part that comes to view is a prolongation of the part previously unrolled, whether we can trace the separate threads from the one into the other, or not. The facts of each generation are looked upon as one complex phenomenon, caused by those of the generation preceding, and causing, in its turn, those of the next in order. That these states must follow one another according to some law, is considered certain: how to read that law, is deemed the fundamental problem of the science of history. To find on what principles, derived from the nature of man and the system of the universe,[5] each state of society and of the human mind produced that which came after it; and whether there can be traced any order of production sufficiently definite, to show what future states of society may be expected to emanate from the circumstances which exist at present – is the aim of historical philosophy in its third stage.

This ultimate and highest attempt, must, in the order of nature, follow, not precede, that last described; for before we can trace the filiation of states of society one from another, we must rightly understand and clearly conceive them, each apart from the rest. Accordingly, this greatest achievement is rather a possibility to be one day realized, than an enterprise in which any great progress has yet been made. But of the little yet done in that direction, by far the greater part has hitherto been done by French writers. They have made more hopeful attempts than any one else, and have more clearly pointed out the path: they are the real harbingers of the dawn of historical science.

PART II PURPOSE

4 *Remarks on Bentham's Philosophy*

(Appendix B to Bulwer's
England and the English, London, 1833.[6])

It is no light task to give an abridged view of the philosophical opinions of one, who attempted to place the vast subjects of morals and legislation upon a scientific basis: a mere outline is all that can be attempted.

The first principles of Mr Bentham's philosophy are these; – that happiness, meaning by that term pleasure and exemption from pain, is the only thing desirable in itself; that all other things are desirable solely as means to that end: that the production, therefore, of the greatest possible happiness, is the only fit purpose of all human thought and action, and consequently of all morality and government; and moreover, that pleasure and pain are the sole agencies by which the conduct of mankind is in fact governed, whatever circumstances the individual may be placed in, and whether he is aware of it or not.

Mr Bentham does not appear to have entered very deeply into the metaphysical grounds of these doctrines; he seems to have taken those grounds very much upon the showing of the metaphysicians who preceded him. The principle of utility, or as he afterwards called it 'the greatest-happiness principle,' stands no otherwise demonstrated in his writings, than by an enumeration of the phrases of a different description which have been commonly employed to denote the rule of life, and the rejection of them all, as having no intelligible meaning, further than as they may involve a tacit reference to considerations of utility. Such are the phrases 'law of nature,' 'right reason,' 'natural rights,' 'moral sense.' All these Mr Bentham regarded as mere covers for dogmatism; excuses for setting up one's own *ipse dixit* as a rule to bind other people. 'They consist, all of them,' says he, 'in so many contrivances for avoiding the obligation of appealing to any external standard, and for prevailing upon the reader to accept the author's sentiment or opinion as a reason for itself.'

This, however, is not fair treatment of the believers in other moral principles than that of utility. All modes of speech are employed in an ignorant manner, by ignorant people; but no one who had thought deeply and systematically enough to be entitled to the name of a philosopher, ever supposed that his *own* private sentiments of approbation and disapprobation must necessarily be well-founded, and needed not to be compared with any external standard. The answer of such persons to Mr Bentham would be, that by an inductive and analytical examination of the human mind, they had satisfied themselves, that what we call our moral sentiments, (that is, the feelings of complacency and aversion we experience when we compare actions of our own or of other people with our standard of right and wrong,) are as much part of the original constitution of man's nature as the desire of happiness and the fear of suffering: That those sentiments do not indeed attach themselves to the same actions under all circumstances, but neither do they, in attaching themselves to actions, follow the law of utility, but certain other general laws, which are the same in all mankind naturally; though education or external circumstances may counteract them, by creating artificial associations stronger than they. No proof indeed can be given that we ought to abide by these laws; but neither can any proof be given, that we ought to regulate our conduct by utility. All that can be said is, that the pursuit of happiness is natural to us; and so, it is contended, is the reverence for, and the inclination to square our actions by, certain general laws of morality.

Any one who is acquainted with the ethical doctrines either of the Reid and Stewart school, or of the German metaphysicians (not to go further back), knows that such would be the answer of those philosophers to Mr Bentham; and it is an answer of which Mr Bentham's writings furnish no sufficient refutation. For it is evident, that these views of the origin of moral distinctions are *not,* what he says all such views are, destitute of any precise and tangible meaning; nor chargeable with setting up as a standard the feelings of the particular person. They set up as a standard what are assumed (on grounds which are considered sufficient) to be the instincts of the species, or principles of our common nature as universal and inexplicable as instincts.

To pass judgment on these doctrines, belongs to a profounder and subtler metaphysics than Mr Bentham possessed. I apprehend it will be the judgment of posterity, that in his views of what, in the felicitous expression of Hobbes, may be called the *philosophia prima,* it has for the most part, even when he was most completely in the right, been reserved for others to *prove* him so. The greatest of Mr Bentham's defects, his insufficient knowledge and appreciation of the thoughts of other men, shows itself constantly in his grappling with some delusive shadow of an adversary's opinion, and leaving the actual substance unharmed.

After laying down the principle of Utility, Mr Bentham is occupied through the most voluminous and the most permanently valuable part of his works, in constructing the outlines of practical ethics and legislation, and filling up some portions of the latter science (or rather art) in great detail; by the uniform and unflinching application of his own greatest-happiness principle, from which the eminently consistent and systematic character of his intellect prevented him from ever swerving. In the writings of no philosopher, probably, are to be detected so few contradictions – so few instances of even momentary deviation from the principles he himself has laid down.

It is perhaps fortunate that Mr Bentham devoted a much larger share of his time and labour to the subject of legislation, than to that of morals; for the mode in which he understood and applied the principle of Utility, appears to me far more conducive to the attainment of true and valuable results in the former, than in the latter of these two branches of inquiry. The recognition of happiness as the only thing desirable in itself, and of the production of the state of things most favourable to happiness as the only rational end both of morals and policy, by no means necessarily leads to the doctrine of expediency as professed by Paley; the ethical canon which judges of the morality of an act or a class of actions, solely by the probable *consequences* of that particular kind of act, supposing it to be generally practised. This is a very small part indeed of what a more enlarged understanding of the 'greatest-happiness principle' would require us to take into the account. A certain kind of action, as for example, theft, or lying, would, if commonly practised, occasion certain evil consequences to society: but those evil consequences are far from constituting the entire moral bearing of the vices of theft or lying. We shall have a very imperfect view of the relation of those practices to the general happiness, if we suppose them to exist singly, and insulated. All acts suppose certain dispositions, and habits of mind and heart, which may be in themselves states of enjoyment or of wretchedness, and which must be fruitful in *other* consequences, besides those particular acts. No person can be a thief or a liar without being much else: and if our moral judgments and feelings with respect to a person convicted of either vice, were grounded solely upon the pernicious tendency of thieving and of lying, they would be partial and incomplete many considerations would be omitted, which are at least equally 'germane to the matter,' many which, by leaving them out of our general views, we may indeed teach ourselves a habit of overlooking, but which it is impossible for any of us not to be influenced by, in particular cases, in proportion as they are forced upon our attention.

Now, the great fault I have to find with Mr Bentham as a moral philosopher, and the source of the chief part of the temporary mischief which in that character, along with a vastly greater amount of permanent good, he must be allowed to have produced, is this: that he has practically, to a very great extent, confounded the principle of Utility with the principle of specific consequences, and has habitually made up his estimate of the approbation or blame due to a particular kind of action, from a calculation solely of the consequences to which that very action, if practised generally, would itself lead. He has largely exemplified, and contributed very widely to diffuse, a tone of thinking, according to which any kind of action or any habit, which in its own specific consequences cannot be proved to be necessarily or probably productive of unhappiness to the agent himself or to others, is supposed to be fully justified; and any disapprobation or aversion entertained towards the individual by reason of it, is set down from that time forward as prejudice and superstition. It is not considered (at least, not habitually considered,) whether the act or habit in question, though not in itself necessarily pernicious, may not form part of a *character* essentially pernicious, or at least essentially deficient in some quality eminently conducive to the 'greatest happiness.' To apply such a standard as this, would indeed often require a much deeper insight into the formation of character, and knowledge of the internal workings of human nature, than Mr Bentham possessed. But, in a greater or less degree, he, and every one else, judges by this standard: even those who are warped, by some partial view, into the omission of all such elements from their general speculations.

When the moralist thus overlooks the relation of an act to a certain state of mind as its cause, and its connexion through that common cause with large classes and groups of actions apparently very little resembling itself, his estimation even of the consequences of the very act itself, is rendered imperfect. For it may be affirmed with few exceptions, that any act whatever has a tendency to fix and perpetuate the state or character of mind in which itself has originated. And if that important element in the moral relations of the action be not taken into account by the moralist as a cause, neither probably will it be taken into account as a consequence.

Mr Bentham is far from having altogether overlooked this side of the subject. Indeed, those most original and instructive, though, as I conceive, in their spirit, partially erroneous chapters, on *motives* and on *dispositions,* in his first great work, the Introduction to the *Principles of Morals and Legislation,* open up a direct and broad path to these most important topics. It is not the less true that Mr Bentham, and many others, following his example, when they came to discuss particular questions of ethics, have commonly, in the superior stress which they laid upon the specific consequences of a class of acts, rejected all contemplation of the action in its general bearings upon the entire moral being of the agent; or have, to say the least, thrown those considerations so far into the background, as to be almost out of sight. And by so doing they have not only marred the value of many of their speculations, considered as mere philosophical enquiries, but have always run the risk of incurring, and in many cases have in my opinion actually incurred, serious practical errors.

This incompleteness, however, in Mr Bentham's general views, was not of a nature materially to diminish the value of his speculations through the greater part of the field of legislation. Those of the bearings of an action, upon which Mr Bentham bestowed almost exclusive attention, were also those with which almost alone legislation is conversant. The legislator enjoins or prohibits an action, with very little regard to the general moral excellence or turpitude which it implies; he looks to the consequences to society of the particular kind of action; his object is not to render people incapable of *desiring* a crime, but to deter them from actually *committing* it. Taking human beings as he finds them, he endeavours to supply such inducements as will constrain even persons of the dispositions the most at variance with the general happiness, to practise as great a degree of regard to it in their actual conduct, as can be obtained from them by such means without preponderant inconvenience. A theory, therefore, which considers little in an action besides that action's *own* consequences, will generally be sufficient to serve the purposes of a philosophy of legislation. Such a philosophy will be most apt to fail in the consideration of the greater social questions – the theory of organic institutions and general forms of polity; for those (unlike the details of legislation) to be duly estimated, must be viewed as the great instruments of forming the national character; of carrying forward the members of the community towards perfection, or preserving them from degeneracy. This, as might in some measure be expected, is a point of view in which, except for some partial or limited purpose, Mr Bentham seldom contemplates these questions. And this signal omission is one of the greatest of the deficiencies by which his speculations on the theory of government, though full of valuable ideas, are rendered, in my judgment, altogether inconclusive in their general results.

To these we shall advert more fully hereafter. As yet I have not acquitted myself of the more agreeable task of setting forth some part of the services which the philosophy of legislation owes to Mr Bentham.

The greatest service of all, that for which posterity will award most honour to his name, is one that is his exclusively, and can be shared by no one present or to come; it is the service which can be performed only once for any science, that of pointing out by what method of investigation it may be *made* a science. What Bacon did for physical knowledge, Mr Bentham has done for philosophical legislation. Before Bacon's time, many physical facts had been ascertained; and previously to Mr Bentham, mankind were in possession of many just and valuable detached observations on the making of laws. But he was the first who attempted regularly to deduce all the secondary and intermediate principles of law, by direct and systematic inference from the one great axiom or principle of general utility. In all existing systems of law, those secondary principles or dicta in which the essence of the systems resided, had grown up in detail, and even when founded in views of utility, were not the result of any scientific and comprehensive course of enquiry; but more frequently were purely technical; that is, they had grown out of circumstances purely *historical,* and, not having been altered when those circumstances changed, had nothing left to rest upon but fictions, and unmeaning forms. Take for instance the law of real property; the whole of which continues to this very day to be founded on the doctrine of feudal tenures, when those tenures have long ceased to exist except in the phraseology of Westminster Hall. Nor was the *theory* of law in a better state than the practical systems, speculative jurists having dared little more than to refine somewhat upon the technical maxims of the particular body of jurisprudence which they happened to have studied. Mr Bentham was the first who had the genius and courage to conceive the idea of bringing back the science to first principles. This could not be done, could scarcely even be attempted, without, as a necessary consequence, making obvious the utter worthlessness of many, and the crudity and want of precision of almost all, the maxims which had previously passed everywhere for principles of law.

Mr Bentham, moreover, has warred against the errors of existing systems of jurisprudence, in a more direct manner than by merely presenting the contrary truths. The force of argument with which he rent asunder the fantastic and illogical maxims on which the various technical systems are founded, and exposed the flagrant evils which they practically produce, is only equalled by the pungent sarcasm and exquisite humour with which he has derided their absurdities, and the eloquent declamation which he continually pours forth against them, sometimes in the form of lamentation, and sometimes of invective.

This then was the first, and perhaps the grandest achievement of Mr Bentham; the entire discrediting of all technical systems; and the example which he set of treating law as no peculiar mystery, but a simple piece of practical business, wherein means were to be adapted to ends, as in any of the other arts of life. To have accomplished this, supposing him to have done nothing else, is to have equalled the glory of the greatest scientific benefactors of the human race.

But Mr Bentham, unlike Bacon, did not merely prophesy a science; he made large strides towards the creation of one. He was the first who conceived with anything approaching to precision, the idea of a Code, or complete body of law; and the distinctive characters of its essential parts, – the Civil Law, the Penal Law, and the Law of Procedure. On the first two of these three departments he rendered valuable service; the third he actually created. Conformably to the habits of his mind, he set about investigating *ab initio,* a philosophy or science for each of the three branches. He did with the received principles of each, what a good code would do with the laws themselves; – extirpated the bad, substituting others, re-enacted the good, but in so much clearer and more methodical a form, that those who were most familiar with them before, scarcely recognized them as the same. Even upon old truths, when they pass through his hands, he leaves so many of his marks, that often he almost seems to claim the discovery of what he has only systematized.

In creating the philosophy of Civil Law, he proceeded not much beyond establishing on the proper basis some of its most general principles, and cursorily discussing some of the most interesting of its details. Nearly the whole of what he has published on this branch of law, is contained in the *Traités de Législation,* edited by M. Dumont. To the most difficult part, and that which most needed a master-hand to clear away its difficulties, the nomenclature and arrangement of the Civil Code, he contributed little, except detached observations, and criticisms upon the errors of his predecessors. The 'Vue Générale d'un Corps Complet de Législation,' included in the work just cited, contains almost all which he has given to us on this subject.

In the department of Penal Law, he is the author of the best attempt yet made towards a philosophical classification of offences. The theory of punishments (for which however more had been done by his predecessors, than for any other part of the science of law) he left nearly complete.

The theory of Procedure (including that of the constitution

of the courts of justice) he found in a more utterly barbarous state than even either of the other branches; and he left it incomparably the most perfect. There is scarcely a question of practical importance in this most important department, which he has not settled. He has left next to nothing for his successors.

He has shown with the force of demonstration, and has enforced and illustrated the truth in a hundred ways, that by sweeping away the greater part of the artificial rules and forms which obtain in all the countries called civilized, and adopting the simple and direct modes of investigation, which all men employ in endeavouring to ascertain facts for their own private knowledge, it is possible to get rid of at least nine-tenths of the expense, and ninety-nine hundredths of the delay, of law proceedings; not only with no increase, but with an almost incredible diminution, of the chances of erroneous decision. He has also established irrefragably the principles of a good judicial establishment: a division of the country into districts, with *one* judge in each, appointed only for a limited period, and deciding all sorts of cases; with a deputy under him, appointed and removable by himself: an appeal lying in all cases whatever, but by the transmission of papers only, to a supreme court or courts, consisting each of only *one* judge, and stationed in the metropolis.

It is impossible within the compass of this sketch, to attempt any further statement of Mr Bentham's principles and views on the great science which first became a science in his hands.

As an analyst of human nature (the faculty in which above all it is necessary that an ethical philosopher should excel) I cannot rank Mr Bentham very high. He has done little in this department, beyond introducing what appears to me a very deceptive phraseology, and furnishing a catalogue of the 'springs of action,' from which some of the most important are left out.

That the actions of sentient beings are wholly determined by pleasure and pain, is the fundamental principle from which he starts; and thereupon Mr Bentham creates a *motive,* and an *interest,* corresponding to each pleasure or pain, and affirms that our actions are determined by our *interests,* by the *preponderant* interest, by the *balance* of motives. Now if this only means what was before asserted, that our actions are determined by pleasure and pain, that simple and unambiguous mode of stating the proposition is preferable. But under cover of the obscurer phrase a meaning creeps in, both to the author's mind and the reader's, which goes much farther, and is entirely false: that all our acts are determined by pains and pleasures *in prospect,* pains and pleasures to which we look forward as the *consequences* of our acts. This, as a universal truth, can in no way be maintained. The pain or pleasure which determines our conduct is as frequently one which *precedes* the moment of action as one which follows it. A man *may,* it is true, be deterred, in circumstances of temptation, from perpetrating a crime, by his dread of the punishment, or of the remorse, which he fears he may have to endure *after* the guilty act; and in that case we may say with some kind of propriety, that his conduct is swayed by the balance of motives; or, if you will, of interests. But the case *may* be, and is to the full as likely to be, that he recoils from the very thought of committing the act; the idea of placing himself in such a situation is so painful, that he cannot dwell upon it long enough to have even the physical power of perpetrating the crime. His conduct is determined by pain; but by a pain which precedes the act, not by one which is expected to follow it. Not only *may* this be so, but unless it be so, the man is not really virtuous. The fear of pain *consequent* upon the act, cannot arise, unless there be *deliberation*; and the man as well as 'the woman who deliberates,' is in imminent danger of being lost. With what propriety shrinking from an action without deliberation, can be called yielding to an *interest,* I cannot see. *Interest* surely conveys, and is intended to convey, the idea of an *end,* to which the conduct (whether it be act or forbearance) is designed as the *means.* Nothing of this sort takes place in the above example. It would be more correct to say that conduct is *sometimes* determined by an *interest,* that is, by a deliberate and conscious aim; and sometimes by an *impulse,* that is, by a feeling (call it an association if you think fit) which has no ulterior end, the act or forbearance becoming an end in itself.

The attempt, again, to *enumerate* motives, that is, human desires and aversions, seems to me to be in its very conception an error. Motives are innumerable: there is nothing whatever which may not become an object of desire or of dislike by association. It may be desirable to distinguish by peculiar notice the motives which are strongest and of most frequent operation; but Mr Bentham has not even done this. In his list of motives, though he includes sympathy, he omits conscience, or the feeling of duty: one would never imagine from reading him that any human being ever did an act merely because it is right, or abstained from it merely because it is wrong. In this Mr Bentham differs widely from Hartley, who, although he considers the moral sentiments to be wholly the result of association, does not therefore deny them a place in his system, but includes the feelings of 'the moral sense' as one of the six classes into which he divides pleasures and pains. In Mr Bentham's own mind, deeply imbued as it was with the 'greatest-happiness principle,' this motive was probably so blended with that of sympathy as to be undistinguishable from it; but he should have recollected that those who acknowledge another standard of right and wrong than happiness, or who have never reflected on the subject at all, have often very strong feelings of moral obligation; and whether a person's standard be happiness or anything else, his attachment to his standard is not necessarily in proportion to his benevolence. Persons of weak sympathies have often a strong feeling of justice; and others, again, with the feelings of benevolence in considerable strength, have scarcely any consciousness of moral obligation at all.

It is scarcely necessary to point out that the habitual omission of so important a spring of action in an enumeration professing to be complete, must tend to create a habit of overlooking the same phenomenon, and consequently making no allowance for it, in other moral speculations. It is difficult to imagine any more fruitful source of gross error; though one would be apt to suppose the oversight an impossible one, without this evidence of its having been committed by one of the greatest thinkers our species has produced. How can we suppose him to be alive to the existence and force of the motive in particular cases, who omits it in a deliberate and comprehensive enumeration of all the influences by which human conduct is governed?

In laying down as a philosophical axiom, that men's actions are always obedient to their interests, Mr Bentham did no more than dress up the very trivial proposition that all persons do what they feel themselves most disposed to do, in terms which appeared to him more precise, and better suited to the purposes of philosophy, than those more familiar expressions. He by no means intended by this assertion to impute universal selfishness to mankind, for he reckoned the motive of sympathy as an *interest,* and would have included conscience under the same appellation, if that motive had found any place in his philosophy, as a distinct principle from benevolence. He distinguished two kinds of interests, the self-regarding and the social: in vulgar discourse, the name is restricted to the former kind alone.

But there cannot be a greater mistake than to suppose that, because we may ourselves be perfectly *conscious* of an ambiguity in our language, that ambiguity therefore has no effect in perverting our modes of thought. I am persuaded, from experience, that this habit of speaking of all the feelings which govern mankind under the name of *interests,* is almost always in point of fact connected with a tendency to consider *interest* in the vulgar sense, that is, purely self-regarding interest, as exercising, by the very constitution of human nature, a far more exclusive and paramount control over human actions than it really does exercise. Such, certainly, was the tendency of Mr Bentham's own opinions. Habitually, and throughout his works, the moment he has shown that a man's *selfish* interest would prompt him to a particular course of action, he lays it down without further parley that the man's interest lies that way; and, by sliding insensibly from the vulgar sense of the word into the philosophical, and from the philosophical back into the vulgar, the conclusion which is always brought out is, that the man will act as the selfish interest prompts. The extent to which Mr Bentham was a believer in the predominance of the selfish principle in human nature, may be seen from the sweeping terms in which, in his *Book of Fallacies,* he expressly lays down that predominance as a philosophical axiom.

'In *every* human breast (rare and short-lived ebullitions, the result of some extraordinarily strong stimulus or excitement, excepted) self-regarding interest is predominant over social interest; each person's own individual interest over the interests of all other persons taken together.' (pp. 392-3.)

In another passage of the same work (p. 363) he says, 'Taking the whole of life together, there exists not, *nor ever can exist,* that human being in whose instance any public interest he can have had will not, in so far as depends upon himself, have been sacrificed to his own personal interest. Towards the advancement of the public interest, all that the most public-spirited (which is as much as to say the most virtuous) of men can do, is to do what depends upon himself towards bringing the public interest, that is, his own personal share in the public interest, to a state as nearly approaching to coincidence, and on as few occasions amounting to a state of repugnance, as possible, with his private interests.'

By the promulgation of such views of human nature, and by a general tone of thought and expression perfectly in harmony with them, I conceive Mr Bentham's writings to have done and to be doing very serious evil. It is by such things that the more enthusiastic and generous minds are prejudiced against all his other speculations, and against the very attempt to make ethics and politics a subject of precise and philosophical thinking; which attempt, indeed, if it were necessarily connected with such views, would be still more pernicious than the vague and flashy declamation for which it is proposed as a substitute. The effect is still worse on the minds of those who are not shocked and repelled by this tone of thinking, for on them it must be perverting to their whole moral nature. It is difficult to form the conception of a tendency more inconsistent with all rational hope of good for the human species, than that which must be impressed by such doctrines, upon any mind in which they find acceptance.

There are, there have been, many human beings, in whom the motives of patriotism or of benevolence have been permanent steady principles of action, superior to any ordinary, and in not a few instances, to any possible, temptations of personal interest. There are, and have been, multitudes, in whom the motive of conscience or moral obligation has been thus paramount. There is nothing in the constitution of human nature to forbid its being so in all mankind. Until it is so, the race will never enjoy one-tenth part of the happiness which our nature is susceptible of. I regard any considerable increase of human happiness, through mere changes in outward circumstances, unaccompanied by changes in the state of the desires, as hopeless; not to mention that while the desires are circumscribed in self, there can be no adequate motive for exertions tending to modify to good ends even those external circumstances. No man's individual share of any public good which he can hope to realize by his efforts, is an equivalent for the sacrifice of his ease, and of the personal objects which he might attain by another course of conduct. The balance can be turned in favour of virtuous exertion, only by the interest of *feeling* or by that of *conscience* – those 'social interests,' the necessary subordination of which to 'self-regarding' is so lightly assumed.

But the power of any one to realize in himself the state of mind, without which his own enjoyment of life can be but poor and scanty, and on which all our hopes of happiness or moral perfection to the species must rest, depends entirely upon his having faith in the actual existence of such feelings and dispositions in others, and in their possibility for himself. It is for those in whom the feelings of virtue are weak, that ethical writing is chiefly needful, and its proper office is to strengthen those feelings. But to be qualified for this task, it is necessary, first to have, and next to show, in every sentence and in every line, a firm unwavering confidence in man's capability of virtue. It is by a sort of sympathetic contagion, or inspiration, that a noble mind assimilates other minds to itself; and no one was ever inspired by one whose own inspiration was not sufficient to give him faith in the possibility of making others feel what *he* feels.

Upon those who *need* to be strengthened and upheld by a really inspired moralist – such a moralist as Socrates, or Plato, or (speaking humanly and not theologically) as Christ; the effect of such writings as Mr Bentham's, if they be read and believed and their spirit imbibed, must either be hopeless despondency and gloom, or a reckless giving themselves up to a life of that miserable self-seeking, which they are there taught to regard as inherent in their original and unalterable nature.

Mr Bentham's speculations on politics in the narrow sense, that is, on the theory of government, are distinguished by his usual characteristic, that of beginning at the beginning. He places before himself man in society without a government, and, considering what sort of government it would be advisable to construct, finds that the most expedient would be a representative democracy. Whatever may be the value of this conclusion, the mode in which it is arrived at appears to me to be fallacious; for it assumes that mankind are alike in all times and all places, that they have the same wants and are exposed to the same evils, and that if the same institutions do not suit them, it is only because in the more backward stages of improvement they have not wisdom to see what institutions are most for their good. How to invest certain servants of the people with the power necessary for the protection of person and property, with the greatest possible facility to the people of changing the depositaries of that power, when they think it is abused; such is the only problem in social organization which Mr Bentham has proposed to himself. Yet this is but a part of the real problem. It never seems to have occurred to him to regard political institutions in a higher light, as the principal means of the social education of a people. Had he done so, he would have seen that the same institutions will no more suit two nations in different stages of civilization, then the same lessons will suit children of different ages. As the degree of civilization already attained varies, so does the kind of social influence necessary for carrying the community forward to the next stage of its progress. For a tribe of North American Indians, improvement means, taming down their proud and solitary self-dependence; for a body of emancipated negroes, it means accustoming them to be self-dependent, instead of being merely obedient to orders; for our semi-barbarous ancestors it would have meant, softening them; for a race of enervated Asiatics it would mean hardening them. How can the same social organization be fitted for producing so many contrary effects?

The prevailing error of Mr Bentham's views of human nature appears to me to be this – he supposes mankind to be swayed by only a part of the inducements which really actuate them; but of that part he imagines them to be much cooler and more thoughtful calculators than they really are. He has, I think, been, to a certain extent, misled in the theory of politics, by supposing that the submission of the mass of mankind to an established government is mainly owing to a reasoning perception of the necessity of legal protection, and of the common interest of all in a prompt and zealous obedience to the law. He was not, I am persuaded, aware, how very much of the really wonderful acquiescence of mankind in any government which they find established, is the effect of mere habit and imagination, and, therefore, depends upon the preservation of something like continuity of existence in the institutions, and identity in their outward forms; cannot transfer itself easily to new institutions, even though in themselves preferable; and is greatly shaken when there occurs anything like a break in the line of historical duration – anything which can be termed the end of the old constitution and the beginning of a new one.

The constitutional writers of our own country, anterior to Mr Bentham, had carried feelings of this kind to the height of a superstition; they never considered what was best adapted to their own times, but only what had existed in former times, even in times that had long gone by. It is not very many years since such were the principal grounds on which parliamentary reform itself was defended. Mr Bentham has done much service in discrediting, as he had done completely, this school of politicians, and exposing the absurd sacrifice of present ends to antiquated means; but he has, I think, himself fallen into a contrary error. The very fact that a certain set of political institutions already exist, have long existed, and have become associated with all the historical recollections of a people, is in itself, as far as it goes, a property which adapts them to that people, and gives them a great advantage over any new institutions in obtaining that ready and willing resignation to what has once been decided by lawful authority, which alone renders possible those innumerable compromises between adverse interests and expectations, without which no government could be carried on for a year, and with difficulty even for a week. Of the perception of this important truth, scarcely a trace is visible in Mr Bentham's writings.*

* It is necessary, however, to distinguish between Mr Bentham's practical conclusions, as an English politician of the present day, and his systematic views as a political philosopher. It is to the latter only that the foregoing observations are intended to apply: on the former I am not now called upon to pronounce any opinion. For the just estimation of his merits, the question is not what were his conclusions, but what was his mode of arriving at them. Theoretical views most widely different, may lead to the same practical corollaries: and that part of any system of philosophy which bodies itself forth in directions for immediate practice, must be so small a portion of the whole as to furnish a very insufficient criterion of the degree in which it approximates to scientific and universal truth. Let Mr Bentham's opinions on the political questions of the day be as sound or as mistaken as any one

It is impossible, however, to contest to Mr Bentham, on this subject or on any other which he has touched, the merit, and it is very great, of having brought forward into notice one of the faces of the truth, and a highly important one. Whether on government, on morals, or on any of the other topics on which his speculations are comparatively imperfect, they are still highly instructive and valuable to any one who is capable of supplying the remainder of the truth; they are calculated to mislead only by the pretension which they invariably set up of being the whole truth, a complete theory and philosophy of the subject. Mr Bentham was more a thinker than a reader; he seldom compared his ideas with those of other philosophers, and was by no means aware how many thoughts had existed in other minds, which his doctrines did not afford the means either to refute or to appreciate.

may deem them, the fact which is of importance in judging of Mr Bentham himself is that those opinions rest upon a basis of half-truth. Each enquirer is left to add the other half for himself, and confirm or correct the practical conclusion as the other lights of which he happens to be in possession, allow him.

5 *What Utilitarianism is*

(Chapter II, *Utilitarianism*, first published 1861. This version from the Fourth Edition, London, 1871.)

A passing remark is all that needs be given to the ignorant blunder of supposing that those who stand up for utility as the test of right and wrong, use the terms in that restricted and merely colloquial sense in which utility is opposed to pleasure. An apology is due to the philosophical opponents of utilitarianism, for even the momentary appearance of confounding them with any one capable of so absurd a misconception; which is the more extraordinary, inasmuch as the contrary accusation, of referring everything to pleasure, and that too in its grossest form, is another of the common charges against utilitarianism: and, as has been pointedly remarked by an able writer, the same sort of persons, and often the very same persons, denounce the theory 'as impracticably dry when the word utility precedes the word pleasure, and as too practicably voluptuous when the word pleasure precedes the word utility.' Those who know anything about the matter are aware that every writer, from Epicurus to Bentham, who maintained the theory of utility, meant by it, not something to be contradistinguished from pleasure, but pleasure itself, together with exemption from pain; and instead of opposing the useful to the agreeable or the ornamental, have always declared that the useful means these, among other things. Yet the common herd, including the herd of writers, not only in newspapers and periodicals, but in books of weight and pretension, are perpetually falling into this shallow mistake. Having caught up the word utilitarian, while knowing nothing whatever about it but its sound, they habitually express by it the rejection, or the neglect, of pleasure in some of its forms; of beauty, of ornament, or of amusement. Nor is the term thus ignorantly misapplied solely in disparagement, but occasionally in compliment; as though it implied superiority to frivolity and the mere pleasures of the moment. And this perverted use is the only one in which the word is popularly known, and the one from which the new generation are acquiring their sole notion of its meaning. Those who introduced the word, but who had for many years discontinued it as a distinctive appellation, may well feel themselves called upon to resume it, if by doing so they can hope to contribute anything towards rescuing it from this utter degradation.*

The creed which accepts as the foundation of morals, Utility, or the Greatest Happiness Principle, holds that actions are right in proportion as they tend to promote happiness, wrong as they tend to produce the reverse of happiness. By happiness is intended pleasure, and the absence of pain; by unhappiness, pain, and the privation of pleasure. To give a clear view of the moral standard set up by the theory, much more requires to be said; in particular, what things it includes in the ideas of pain and pleasure; and to what extent this is left an open question. But these supplementary explanations do not affect the theory of life on which this theory of morality is grounded – namely, that pleasure, and freedom from pain, are the only things desirable as ends; and that all desirable things (which are as

* The author of this essay has reason for believing himself to be the first person who brought the word utilitarian into use. He did not invent it, but adopted it from a passing expression in Mr Galt's *Annals of the Parish*. After using it as a designation for several years, he and others abandoned it from a growing dislike to anything resembling a badge or watchword of sectarian distinction. But as a name for one single opinion, not a set of opinions—to denote the recognition of utility as a standard, not any particular way of applying it—the term supplies a want in the language, and offers, in many cases, a convenient mode of avoiding tiresome circumlocution.

numerous in the utilitarian as in any other scheme) are desirable either for the pleasure inherent in themselves, or as means to the promotion of pleasure and the prevention of pain.

Now, such a theory of life excites in many minds, and among them in some of the most estimable in feeling and purpose, inveterate dislike. To suppose that life has (as they express it) no higher end than pleasure – no better and nobler object of desire and pursuit – they designate as utterly mean and grovelling; as a doctrine worthy only of swine, to whom the followers of Epicurus were, at a very early period, contemptuously likened; and modern holders of the doctrine are occasionally made the subject of equally polite comparisons by its German, French, and English assailants.

When thus attacked, the Epicureans have always answered, that it is not they, but their accusers, who represent human nature in a degrading light; since the accusation supposes human beings to be capable of no pleasures except those of which swine are capable. If this supposition were true, the charge could not be gainsaid, but would then be no longer an imputation; for if the sources of pleasure were precisely the same to human beings and to swine, the rule of life which is good enough for the one would be good enough for the other. The comparison of the Epicurean life to that of beasts is felt as degrading, precisely because a beast's pleasures do not satisfy a human being's conceptions of happiness. Human beings have faculties more elevated than the animal appetites, and when once made conscious of them, do not regard anything as happiness which does not include their gratification. I do not, indeed, consider the Epicureans to have been by any means faultless in drawing out their scheme of consequences from the utilitarian principle. To do this in any sufficient manner, many Stoic, as well as Christian elements require to be included. But there is no known Epicurean theory of life which does not assign to the pleasures of the intellect, of the feelings and imagination, and of the moral sentiments, a much higher value as pleasures than to those of mere sensation. It must be admitted, however, that utilitarian writers in general have placed the superiority of mental over bodily pleasure chiefly in the greater permanency, safety, uncostliness, &c., of the former – that is, in their circumstantial advantages rather than in their intrinsic nature. And on all these points utilitarians have fully proved their case; but they might have taken the other, and, as it may be called, higher ground, with entire consistency. It is quite compatible with the principle of utility to recognise the fact, that some *kinds* of pleasure are more desirable and more valuable than others. It would be absurd that while, in estimating all other things, quality is considered as well as quantity, the estimation of pleasures should be supposed to depend on quantity alone.

If I am asked, what I mean by difference of quality in pleasures, or what makes one pleasure more valuable than another, merely as a pleasure, except its being greater in amount, there is but one possible answer. Of two pleasures, if there be one to which all or almost all who have experience of both give a decided preference, irrespective of any feeling of moral obligation to prefer it, that is the more desirable pleasure. If one of the two is, by those who are competently acquainted with both, placed so far above the other that they prefer it, even though knowing it to be attended with a greater amount of discontent, and would not resign it for any quantity of the other pleasure which their nature is capable of, we are justified in ascribing to the preferred enjoyment a superiority in quality, so far outweighing quantity as to render it, in comparison, of small account.

Now it is an unquestionable fact that those who are equally acquainted with, and equally capable of appreciating and enjoying, both, do give a most marked preference to the manner of existence which employs their higher faculties. Few human creatures would consent to be changed into any of the lower animals, for a promise of the fullest allowance of a beast's pleasures; no intelligent human being would consent to be a fool, no instructed person would be an ignoramus, no person of feeling and conscience would be selfish and base, even though they should be persuaded that the fool, the dunce, or the rascal is better satisfied with his lot than they are with theirs. They would not resign what they possess more than he, for the most complete satisfaction of all the desires which they have in common with him. If they ever fancy they would, it is only in cases of unhappiness so extreme, that to escape from it they would exchange their lot for almost any other, however undesirable in their own eyes. A being of higher faculties requires more to make him happy, is capable probably of more acute suffering, and certainly accessible to it at more points, than one of an inferior type; but in spite of these liabilities, he can never really wish to sink into what he feels to be a lower grade of existence. We may give what explanation we please of this unwillingness; we may attribute it to pride, a name which is given indiscriminately to some of the most and to some of the least estimable feelings of which mankind are capable; we may refer it to the love of liberty and personal independence, an appeal to which was with the Stoics one of the most effective means for the inculcation of it; to the love of power, or to the love of excitement, both of which do really enter into and contribute to it: but its most appropriate appellation is a sense of dignity, which all human beings possess in one form or other, and in some, though by no means in exact, proportion to their higher faculties, and which it is so essential a part of the happiness of those in whom it is strong, that nothing which conflicts with it could be, otherwise than momentarily, an object of desire to them. Whoever supposes that this preference takes place at a sacrifice of happiness – that the superior being, in anything like equal circumstances, is not happier than the inferior – confounds the two very different ideas, of happiness, and content. It is indisputable that the being whose capacities of enjoyment are low, has the greatest chance of having them fully satisfied; and a highly-endowed being will always feel that any happiness which he can look for, as the world is constituted, is imperfect. But he can learn to bear its imperfections, if they are at all bearable; and they will not make him envy the being who is indeed unconscious of the imperfections, but only because he feels not at all the good which those imperfections qualify. It is better to be a human being dissatisfied than a pig satisfied; better to be Socrates dissatisfied than a fool satisfied. And if the fool, or the pig, are of a different opinion, it is because they only know their own side of the question. The other party to the comparison knows both sides.

It may be objected, that many who are capable of the higher pleasures, occasionally, under the influence of temptation, postpone them to the lower. But this is quite compatible with a full appreciation of the intrinsic superiority of the higher. Men often, from infirmity of character, make their election for the nearer good, though they know it to be the less valuable; and this no less when the choice is between two bodily pleasures, than when it is between bodily and mental. They pursue sensual indulgences to the injury of health, though perfectly aware that health is the greater good. It may be further objected, that many who begin with youthful enthusiasm for everything noble, as they advance in years sink into indolence and selfishness. But I do not believe that those who undergo this very common change, voluntarily choose the lower description of pleasures in preference to the higher. I believe that before they devote themselves exclusively to the one, they have already become incapable of the other. Capacity for the nobler feelings is in most natures a very tender plant, easily killed, not only by hostile influences, but by mere want of sustenance; and in the majority of young persons it speedily dies away if the occupations to which their position in life has devoted them, and the society into which it has thrown them, are not favourable to keeping that higher capacity in exercise. Men lose their high aspirations as they lose their intellectual tastes, because they have not time or opportunity for indulging them; and they addict themselves to inferior pleasures, not because they deliberately prefer them, but because they are either the only ones to which they have access, or the only ones which they are any longer capable of enjoying. It may be questioned whether any one who has remained equally susceptible to both classes of pleasures, ever knowingly and calmly preferred the lower; though many, in all ages, have broken down in an ineffectual attempt to combine both.

From this verdict of the only competent judges, I apprehend there can be no appeal. On a question which is the best worth having of two pleasures, or which of two modes of existence is the most grateful to the feelings, apart from its moral attributes and from its consequences, the judgment of those who are qualified by knowledge of both, or, if they differ, that of the majority among them, must be admitted as final. And there needs be the less hesitation to accept this judgment respecting the quality of pleasures, since there is no other tribunal to be referred to even on the question of quantity. What means are there of determining which is the acutest of two pains, or the intensest of two pleasurable sensations, except the general suffrage of those who are familiar with both? Neither pains nor pleasures are homogeneous, and pain is always heterogeneous with pleasure. What is there to decide whether a particular pleasure is worth purchasing at the cost of a particular pain, except the feelings and judgment of the experienced? When, therefore, those feelings and judgment declare the pleasures derived from the higher faculties to be preferable *in kind,* apart from the question of intensity, to those of which the animal nature, disjoined from the higher faculties, is susceptible, they are entitled on this subject to the same regard.

I have dwelt on this point, as being a necessary part of a perfectly just conception of Utility or Happiness, considered as the directive rule of human conduct. But it is by no means an indispensable condition to the acceptance of the utilitarian standard; for that standard is not the agent's own greatest happiness, but the greatest amount of happiness altogether; and if it may possibly be doubted whether a noble character is always the happier for its nobleness, there can be no doubt that it makes other people happier, and that the world in general is immensely a gainer by it. Utilitarianism, therefore, could only attain its end by the general cultivation of nobleness of character, even if each individual were only benefited by the nobleness of others, and his own, so far as happiness is concerned, were a sheer deduction from the benefit. But the bare enunciation of such an absurdity as this last, renders refutation superfluous.

According to the Greatest Happiness Principle, as above explained, the ultimate end, with reference to and for the sake of which all other things are desirable (whether we are considering our own good or that of other people), is an existence exempt as far as possible from pain, and as rich as possible in enjoyments, both in point of quantity and quality; the test of quality, and the rule for measuring it against quantity, being the preference felt by those who, in their opportunities of experience, to which must be added their habits of self-consciousness and self-observation, are best furnished with the means of comparison. This, being, according to the utilitarian opinion, the end of human action, is necessarily also the standard of morality; which may accordingly be defined, the rules and precepts for human conduct, by the observance of which an existence such as has been described might be, to the greatest extent possible, secured to all mankind; and not to them only, but, so far as the nature of things admits, to the whole sentient creation.

Against this doctrine, however, arises another class of objectors, who say that happiness, in any form, cannot be the rational purpose of human life and action; because, in the first place, it is unattainable: and they contemptuously ask, What right hast thou to be happy? a question which Mr Carlyle clenches by the addition, What right, a short time ago, hadst thou even *to be*? Next, they say, that men can do *without* happiness; that all noble human beings have felt this, and could not have become noble but by learning the lesson of Entsagen, or renunciation; which lesson, thoroughly learnt and submitted to, they affirm to be the beginning and necessary condition of all virtue.

The first of these objections would go to the root of the matter were it well founded; for if no happiness is to be had at all by human beings, the attainment of it cannot be the end of morality, or of any rational conduct. Though, even in that case, something might still be said for the utilitarian theory; since utility includes not solely the pursuit of happiness, but the prevention or mitigation of unhappiness; and if the former aim be chimerical, there will be all the greater scope and more imperative need for the latter, so long at least as mankind think fit to live, and do not take refuge in the simultaneous act of suicide recommended under certain conditions by Novalis. When, however, it is thus positively asserted to be impossible that human life should be happy, the assertion, if not something like a verbal quibble, is at least an exaggeration. If by happiness be meant a continuity of highly pleasurable excitement, it is evident enough that this is impossible. A state of exalted pleasure lasts only moments, or in some cases, and with some intermissions, hours or days, and is the occasional brilliant flash of enjoyment, not its permanent and steady flame. Of this the philosophers who have taught that happiness is the end of life were as fully aware as those who taunt them. The happiness which they meant was not a life of rapture; but moments of such, in an existence made up of few and transitory pains, many and various pleasures, with a decided predominance of the active over the passive, and having as the foundation of the whole, not to expect more from life than it is capable of bestowing. A life thus composed, to those who have been fortunate enough to obtain it, has always appeared worthy of the name of happiness. And such an existence is even now the lot of many, during some considerable portion of their lives. The present wretched education, and wretched social arrangements, are the only real hindrance to its being attainable by almost all.

The objectors perhaps may doubt whether human beings, if taught to consider happiness as the end of life, would be satisfied with such a moderate share of it. But great numbers of mankind have been satisfied with much less. The main constituents of a satisfied life appear to be two, either of which by itself is often found sufficient for the purpose: tranquillity, and excitement. With much tranquillity, many find that they can be content with very little pleasure: with much excitement, many can reconcile themselves to a considerable quantity of pain. There is assuredly no inherent impossibility in enabling even the mass of mankind to unite both; since the two are so far from being incompatible that they are in natural alliance, the prolongation of either being a preparation for, and exciting a wish for, the other. It is only those in whom indolence amounts to a vice, that do not desire excitement after an interval of repose; it is only those in whom the need of excitement is a disease, that feel the tranquillity which follows excitement dull and insipid, instead of pleasurable in direct proportion to the excitement which preceded it. When people who are tolerably fortunate in their outward lot do not find in life sufficient enjoyment to make it valuable to them, the cause generally is, caring for nobody but themselves. To those who have neither public nor private affections, the excitements of life are much curtailed, and in any case dwindle in value as the time approaches when all selfish interests must be terminated by death: while those who leave after them objects of personal affection, and especially those who have also cultivated a fellow-feeling with the collective interests of mankind, retain as lively an interest in life on the eve of death as in the vigour of youth and health. Next to selfishness, the principal cause which makes life unsatisfactory, is want of mental cultivation. A cultivated mind – I do not mean that of a philosopher, but any mind to which the fountains of knowledge have been opened, and which has been taught, in any tolerable degree, to exercise its faculties – finds sources of inexhaustible interest in all that surrounds it; in the objects of nature, the achievements of art, the imaginations of poetry, the incidents of history, the ways of mankind past and present, and their prospects in the future. It is possible, indeed, to become indifferent to all this, and that too without having exhausted a thousandth part of it; but only when one has had from the beginning no moral or human interest in these things, and has sought in them only the gratification of curiosity.

Now there is absolutely no reason in the nature of things why an amount of mental culture sufficient to give an intelligent interest in these objects of contemplation, should not be the inheritance of every one born in a civilized country. As little is there an inherent necessity that any human being should be a selfish egotist, devoid of every feeling or care but those which centre in his own miserable individuality. Something far superior to this is sufficiently common even now, to give ample earnest of what the human species may be made. Genuine private affections, and a sincere interest in the public good, are possible, though in unequal degrees, to every rightly brought up human being. In a world in which there is so much to interest, so much to enjoy, and so much also to correct and improve, everyone who has this moderate amount of moral and intellectual requisites is capable of an existence which may be called enviable; and unless such a person, through bad laws, or subjection to the will of others, is denied the liberty to use the sources of happiness within his reach, he will not fail to find this enviable existence, if he escape the positive evils of life, the great source of physical and mental suffering – such as indigence, disease, and the unkindness, worthlessness, or premature loss of objects of affection. The main stress of the problem lies, therefore, in the contest with these calamities, from which it is a rare good fortune entirely to escape; which, as things now are, cannot be obviated, and often cannot be in any material degree mitigated. Yet no one whose opinion deserves a moment's consideration can doubt that most of the great positive evils of the world are in themselves removable, and will, if human affairs continue to improve, be in the end reduced within narrow limits. Poverty, in any sense implying suffering, may be completely extinguished by the wisdom of society, combined with the good sense and providence of individuals. Even that most intractable of enemies, disease, may be indefinitely reduced in dimensions by good physical and moral education, and proper control of noxious influences; while the progress of science holds out a promise for the future of still more direct conquests over this detestable foe. And every advance in that direction relieves us from some, not only of the chances which cut short our own lives, but, what concerns us still more, which deprive us of those in whom our happiness is wrapt up. As for vicissitudes of fortune, and other disappointments connected with worldly circumstances, these are principally the effect either of gross imprudence, of ill-regulated desires, or of bad or imperfect social institutions. All the grand sources, in short, of human suffering are in a great degree, many of them almost entirely, conquerable by human care and effort; and though their removal is grievously slow – though a long succession of generations will perish in the breach before the conquest is completed, and this world becomes all that, if will and knowledge were not wanting, it might easily be made – yet every mind sufficiently intelligent and generous to bear a part, however small and unconspicuous, in the endeavour, will draw a noble enjoyment from the contest itself, which he would not for any bribe in the form of selfish indulgence consent to be without.

And this leads to the true estimation of what is said by the objectors concerning the possibility, and the obligation, of learning to do without happiness. Unquestionably it is possible to do without happiness; it is done involuntarily by nineteen-twentieths of mankind, even in those parts of our present world which are least deep in barbarism; and it often has to be done voluntarily by the hero or the martyr, for the sake of something which he prizes more than his individual happiness. But this something, what is it, unless the happiness of others, or some of the requisites of happiness? It is noble to be capable of resigning entirely one's own portion of happiness, or chances of it: but, after all, this self-sacrifice must be for some end; it is not its own end; and if we are told that its end is not happiness, but virtue, which is better than happiness, I ask, would the sacrifice be made if the hero or martyr did not believe that it would earn for others immunity from similar sacrifices? Would it be made, if he thought that his renunciation of happiness for himself would produce no fruit for any of his fellow creatures, but to make their lot like his, and place them also in the condition of persons who have renounced happiness? All honour to those who can abnegate for themselves the personal enjoyment of life, when by such renunciation they contribute worthily to increase the amount of happiness in the world; but he who does it, or professes to do it, for any other purpose, is no more deserving of admiration than the ascetic mounted on his pillar. He may be an inspiring proof of what men *can* do, but assuredly not an example of what they *should*.

Though it is only in a very imperfect state of the world's arrangements that any one can best serve the happiness of others by the absolute sacrifice of his own, yet so long as the world is in that imperfect state, I fully acknowledge that the readiness to make such a sacrifice is the highest virtue which can be found in man. I will add, that in this condition of the world, paradoxical as the assertion may be, the conscious ability to do without happiness gives the best prospect of realizing such happiness as is attainable. For nothing except that consciousness can raise a person above the chances of life, by making him feel that, let fate and fortune do their worst, they have not power to subdue him: which, once felt, frees him from excess of anxiety concerning the evils of life, and enables him, like many a Stoic in the worst times of the Roman Empire, to cultivate in tranquillity the sources of satisfaction accessible to him, without concerning himself about the uncertainty of their duration, any more than about their inevitable end.

Meanwhile, let utilitarians never cease to claim the morality of self-devotion as a possession which belongs by as good a right to them, as either to the Stoic or to the Transcendentalist. The utilitarian morality does recognise in human beings the power of sacrificing their own greatest good for the good of others. It only refuses to admit that the sacrifice is itself a good. A sacrifice which does not increase, or tend to increase, the sum total of happiness, it considers as wasted. The only self-renunciation which it applauds, is devotion to the happiness, or to some of the means of happiness, of others; either of mankind collectively, or of individuals within the limits imposed by the collective interests of mankind.

I must again repeat, what the assailants of utilitarianism seldom have the justice to acknowledge, that the happiness which forms the utilitarian standard of what is right in conduct, is not the agent's own happiness, but that of all concerned. As between his own happiness and that of others, utilitarianism requires him to be as strictly impartial as a disinterested and benevolent spectator. In the golden rule of Jesus of Nazareth, we read the complete spirit of the ethics of utility. To do as you would be done by, and to love your neighbour as yourself, constitute the ideal of perfection of utilitarian morality. As the means of making the nearest approach to this ideal, utility would enjoin, first, that laws and social arrangements should place the happiness, or (as speaking practically it may be called) the interest, of every individual, as nearly as possible in harmony with the interest of the whole; and secondly, that education and opinion, which have so vast a power over human character, should so use that power as to establish in the mind of every individual an indissoluble association between his own happiness and the good of the whole; especially between his own happiness and the practice of such modes of conduct, negative and positive, as regard for the universal happiness prescribes: so that not only he may be unable to conceive the possibility of happiness to himself, consistently with conduct opposed to the general good, but also that a direct impulse to promote the general good may be in every individual one of the habitual motives of action, and the sentiments connected therewith may fill a large and prominent place in every human being's sentient existence. If the impugners of the utilitarian morality represented it to their own minds in this its true character, I know not what recommendation possessed by any other morality they could possibly affirm to be wanting to it: what more beautiful or more exalted developments of human nature any other ethical system can be supposed to foster, or what springs of action, not accessible to the utilitarian, such systems rely on for giving effect to their mandates.

The objectors to utilitarianism cannot always be charged with representing it in a discreditable light. On the contrary, those among them who entertain anything like a just idea of its disinterested character, sometimes find fault with its standard as being too high for humanity. They say it is exacting too much to require that people shall always act from the inducement of promoting the general interests of society. But this is to mistake the very meaning of a standard of morals, and confound the rule of action with the motive of it. It is the business of ethics to tell us what are our duties, or by what test we may know them; but no system of ethics requires that the sole motive of all we do shall be a feeling of duty; on the contrary, ninety-nine hundredths of all our actions are done from other motives, and rightly so done, if the rule of duty does not condemn them. It is the more unjust to utilitarianism that this particular misapprehension should be made a ground of objection to it, inasmuch as utilitarian moralists have gone beyond almost all others in affirming that the motive has nothing to do with the morality of the action, though much with the worth of the agent. He who saves a fellow creature from drowning does what is morally right, whether his motive be duty, or the hope of being paid for his trouble: he who betrays the friend that trusts him, is guilty of a crime, even if his object be to serve another friend to whom he is under greater obligations.* But to speak only of actions done from

* An opponent, whose intellectual and moral fairness it is a pleasure to acknowledge (the Rev. J. Llewellyn Davies), has objected to this passage, saying, 'Surely the rightness or wrongness of saving a man from drowning does depend very much upon

the motive of duty, and in direct obedience to principle: it is a misapprehension of the utilitarian mode of thought, to conceive it as implying that people should fix their minds upon so wide a generality as the world, or society at large. The great majority of good actions are intended, not for the benefit of the world, but for that of individuals, of which the good of the world is made up; and the thoughts of the most virtuous man need not on these occasions travel beyond the particular persons concerned, except so far as is necessary to assure himself that in benefiting them he is not violating the rights – that is, the legitimate and authorized

the motive with which it is done. Suppose that a tyrant, when his enemy jumped into the sea to escape from him, saved him from drowning simply in order that he might inflict upon him more exquisite tortures, would it tend to clearness to speak of that rescue as 'a morally right action?' Or suppose again, according to one of the stock illustrations of ethical inquiries, that a man betrayed a trust received from a friend, because the discharge of it would fatally injure that friend himself or some one belonging to him, would utilitarianism compel one to call the betrayal 'a crime' as much as if it had been done from the meanest motive?'

I submit, that he who saves another from drowning in order to kill him by torture afterwards, does not differ only in motive from him who does the same thing from duty or benevolence; the act itself is different. The rescue of the man is, in the case supposed, only the necessary first step of an act far more atrocious than leaving him to drown would have been. Had Mr Davies said, 'The rightness or wrongness of saving a man from drowning does depend very much'—not upon the motive, but—'upon the *intention*,' no utilitarian would have differed from him. Mr Davies, by an oversight too common not to be quite venial, has in this case confounded the very different ideas of Motive and Intention. There is no point which utilitarian thinkers (and Bentham pre-eminently) have taken more pains to illustrate than this. The morality of the action depends entirely upon the intention—that is, upon what the agent *wills to do*. But the motive, that is, the feeling which makes him will so to do, if it makes no difference in the act, makes none in the morality: though it makes a great difference in our moral estimation of the agent, especially if it indicates a good or a bad habitual *disposition*—a bent of character from which useful, or from which hurtful actions are likely to arise.[T] expectations – of any one else. The multiplication of happiness is, according to the utilitarian ethics, the object of virtue: the occasions on which any person (except one in a thousand) has it in his power to do this on an extended scale, in other words, to be a public benefactor, are but exceptional; and on these occasions alone is he called on to consider public utility; in every other case, private utility, the interest or happiness of some few persons, is all he has to attend to. Those alone, the influence of whose actions extends to society in general, need concern themselves habitually about so large an object. In the case of abstinences indeed – of things which people forbear to do, from moral considerations, though the consequences in the particular case might be beneficial – it would be unworthy of an intelligent agent not to be consciously aware that the action is of a class which, if practised generally, would be generally injurious, and that this is the ground of the obligation to abstain from it. The amount of regard for the public interest implied in this recognition, is no greater than is demanded by every system of morals; for they all enjoin to abstain from whatever is manifestly pernicious to society.

The same considerations dispose of another reproach against the doctrine of utility, founded on a still grosser misconception of the purpose of a standard of morality, and of the very meaning of the words right and wrong. It is often affirmed that utilitarianism renders men cold and unsympathizing; that it chills their moral feelings towards individuals; that it makes them regard only the dry and hard consideration of the consequences of actions, not taking into their moral estimate the qualities from which those actions emanate. If the assertion means that they do not allow their judgment respecting the rightness or wrongness of an action to be influenced by their opinion of the qualities of the person who does it, this is a complaint not against utilitarianism, but against having any standard of morality at all; for certainly no known ethical standard decides an action to be good or bad because it is done by a good or a bad man, still less because done by an amiable, a brave, or a benevolent man, or the contrary. These considerations are relevant, not to the estimation of actions, but of persons; and there is nothing in the utilitarian theory inconsistent with the fact that there are other things which interest us in persons besides the rightness and wrongness of their actions. The Stoics, indeed, with the paradoxical misuse of language which was part of their system, and by which they strove to raise themselves above all concern about anything but virtue, were fond of saying that he who has that has everything; that he, and only he, is rich, is beautiful, is a king. But no claim of this description is made for the virtuous man by the utilitarian doctrine. Utilitarians are quite aware that there are other desirable possessions and qualities besides virtue, and are perfectly willing to allow to all of them their full worth. They are also aware that a right action does not necessarily indicate a virtuous character, and that actions which are blameable often proceed from qualities entitled to praise. When this is apparent in any particular case, it modifies their estimation, not certainly of the act, but of the agent. I grant that they are, notwithstanding, of opinion, that in the long run the best proof of a good character is good actions; and resolutely refuse to consider any mental disposition as good, of which the predominant tendency is to produce bad conduct. This makes them unpopular with many people; but it is an unpopularity which they must share with every one who regards the distinction between right and wrong in a serious light; and the reproach is not one which a conscientious utilitarian need be anxious to repel.

If no more be meant by the objection than that many utilitarians look on the morality of actions, as measured by the utilitarian standard, with too exclusive a regard, and do not lay sufficient stress upon the other beauties of character which go towards making a human being loveable or admirable, this may be admitted. Utilitarians who have cultivated their moral feelings, but not their sympathies nor their artistic perceptions, do fall into this mistake; and so do all other moralists under the same conditions. What can be said in excuse for other moralists is equally available for them, namely, that if there is to be any error, it is better that it should be on that side. As a matter of fact, we may affirm that among utilitarians as among adherents of other systems, there is every imaginable degree of rigidity and of laxity in the application of their standard: some are even puritanically rigorous, while others are as indulgent as can possibly be desired by sinner or by sentimentalist. But on the whole, a doctrine which brings prominently forward the interest that mankind have in the repression and prevention of conduct which violates the moral law, is likely to be inferior to no other in turning the sanctions of opinion against such violations. It is true, the question, What does violate the moral law? is one on which those who recognise different standards of morality are likely now and then to differ. But difference of opinion on moral questions was not first introduced into the world by utilitarianism, while that doctrine does supply, if not always an easy, at all events a tangible and intelligible mode of deciding such differences.

It may not be superfluous to notice a few more of the common misapprehensions of utilitarian ethics, even those which are so obvious and gross that it might appear impossible for any person of candour and intelligence to fall into them: since persons, even of considerable mental endowments, often give themselves so little trouble to understand the bearings of any opinion against which they entertain a prejudice, and men are in general so little conscious of this voluntary ignorance as a defect, that the vulgarest misunderstandings of ethical doctrines are continually met with in the deliberate writings of persons of the greatest pretensions both to high principle and to philosophy. We not uncommonly hear the doctrine of utility inveighed against as a *godless* doctrine. If it be necessary to say anything at all against so mere an assumption, we may say that the question depends upon what idea we have formed of the moral character of the Deity. If it be a true belief that God desires, above all things, the happiness of his creatures, and that this was his purpose in their creation, utility is not only not a godless doctrine, but more profoundly religious than any other. If it be meant that utilitarianism does not recognise the revealed will of God as the supreme law of morals, I answer, that an utilitarian who believes in the perfect goodness and wisdom of God, necessarily believes that whatever God has thought fit to reveal on the subject of morals, must fulfil the requirements of utility in a supreme degree. But others besides utilitarians have been of opinion that the Christian revelation was intended, and is fitted, to inform the hearts and minds of mankind with a spirit which should enable them to find for themselves what is right, and incline them to do it when found, rather than to tell them, except in a very general way, what it is: and that we need a doctrine of ethics, carefully followed out, to *interpret* to us the will of God. Whether this opinion is correct or not, it is superfluous here to discuss; since whatever aid religion, either natural or revealed, can afford to ethical investigation, is as open to the utilitarian moralist as to any other. He can use it as the testimony of God to the usefulness or hurtfulness of any given course of action, by as good a right as others can use it for the indication of a transcendental law, having no connexion with usefulness or with happiness.

Again, Utility is often summarily stigmatized as an immoral doctrine by giving it the name of Expediency, and taking advantage of the popular use of that term to contrast it with Principle. But the Expedient, in the sense in which it is opposed to the Right, generally means that which is expedient for the particular interest of the agent himself; as when a minister sacrifices the interests of his country to keep himself in place. When it means anything better than this, it means that which is expedient for some immediate object, some temporary purpose, but which violates a rule whose observance is expedient in a much higher degree. The Expedient, in this sense, instead of being the same thing with the useful, is a branch of the hurtful. Thus, it would often be expedient, for the purpose of getting over some momentary embarrassment, or attaining some object immediately useful to ourselves or others, to tell a lie. But inasmuch as the cultivation in ourselves of a sensitive feeling on the subject of veracity, is one of the most useful, and the enfeeblement of that feeling one of the most hurtful, things to which our conduct can be instrumental; and inasmuch as any, even unintentional, deviation from truth, does that much towards weakening the trustworthiness of human assertion, which is not only the principal support of all present social well-being, but the insufficiency of which does more than any one thing that can be named to keep back civilization, virtue, everything on which human happiness on the largest scale depends; we feel that the violation, for a present advantage, of a rule of such transcendant expediency, is not expedient, and that he who, for the sake of a convenience to himself or to some other individual, does what depends on him to deprive mankind of the good, and inflict upon them the evil, involved in the greater or less reliance which they can place in each other's word, acts the part of one of their worst enemies. Yet that even this rule, sacred as it is, admits of possible exceptions, is acknowledged by all moralists; the chief of which is when the withholding of some fact (as of information from a malefactor, or of bad news from a person dangerously ill) would save an individual (especially an individual other than oneself) from great and unmerited evil, and when the withholding can only be effected by denial. But in order that the exception may not extend itself beyond the need, and may have the least possible effect in weakening reliance on veracity, it ought to be recognised, and, if possible, its limits defined; and if the principle of utility is good for anything, it must be good for weighing these conflicting utilities against one another, and marking out the region within which one or the other preponderates.

Again, defenders of utility often find themselves called upon to reply to such objections as this – that there is not time, previous to action, for calculating and weighing the effects of any line of conduct on the general happiness. This is exactly as if any one were to say that it is impossible to guide our conduct by Christianity, because there is not time, on every occasion on which anything has to be done, to read through the Old and New Testaments. The answer to the objection is, that there has been ample time, namely, the whole past duration of the human species. During all that time mankind have been learning by experience the tendencies of actions; on which experience all the prudence, as well as all the morality of life, are dependent. People talk as if the commencement of this course of experience had hitherto been put off, and as if, at the moment when some man feels tempted to meddle with the property or life of another, he had to begin considering for the first time whether murder and theft are injurious to human happiness. Even then I do not think that he would find the question very puzzling; but, at all events, the matter is now done to his hand. It is truly a whimsical supposition that if mankind were agreed in considering utility to be the test of morality, they would remain without any agreement as to what *is* useful, and would take no measures for having their notions on the subject taught to the young, and enforced by law and opinion. There is no difficulty in proving any ethical standard whatever to work ill, if we suppose universal idiocy to be conjoined with it; but on any hypothesis short of that, mankind must by this time have acquired positive beliefs as to the effects of some actions on their happiness; and the beliefs which have thus come down are the rules of morality for the multitude, and for the philosopher until he has succeeded in finding better. That philosophers might easily do this, even now, on many subjects; that the received code of ethics is by no means of divine right; and that mankind have still much to learn as to the effects of actions on the general happiness, I admit, or rather, earnestly maintain. The corollaries from the principle of utility, like the precepts of every practical art, admit of indefinite improvement, and, in a progressive state of the human mind, their improvement is perpetually going on. But to consider the rules of morality as improvable, is one thing; to pass over the intermediate generalizations entirely, and endeavour to test each individual action directly by the first principle, is another. It is a strange notion that the acknowledgment of a first principle is inconsistent with the admission of secondary ones. To inform a traveller respecting the place of his ultimate destination, is not to forbid the use of landmarks and direction-posts on the way. The proposition that happiness is the end and aim of morality, does not mean that no road ought to be laid down to that goal, or that persons going thither should not be advised to take one direction rather than another. Men really ought to leave off talking a kind of nonsense on this subject, which they would neither talk nor listen to on other matters of practical concernment. Nobody argues that the art of navigation is not founded on astronomy, because sailors cannot wait to calculate the Nautical Almanack. Being rational creatures, they go to sea with it ready calculated; and all rational creatures go out upon the sea of life with their minds made up on the common questions of right and wrong, as well as on many of the far more difficult questions of wise and foolish. And this, as long as foresight is a human quality, it is to be presumed they will continue to do. Whatever we adopt as the fundamental principle of morality, we require subordinate principles to apply it by: the impossibility of doing without them, being common to all systems, can afford no argument against any one in particular: but gravely to argue as if no such secondary principles could be had, and as if mankind had remained till now, and always must remain, without drawing any general conclusions from the experience of human life, is as high a pitch, I think, as absurdity has ever reached in philosophical controversy.

The remainder of the stock arguments against utilitarianism mostly consist in laying to its charge the common infirmities of human nature, and the general difficulties which embarrass conscientious persons in shaping their course through life. We are told that an utilitarian will be apt to make his own particular case an exception to moral rules, and, when under temptation, will see an utility in the breach of a rule, greater than he will see in its observance. But is utility the only creed which is able to furnish us with excuses for evil doing, and means of cheating our own conscience? They are afforded in abundance by all doctrines which recognise as a fact in morals the existence of conflicting considerations; which all doctrines do, that have been believed by sane persons. It is not the fault of any creed, but of the complicated nature of human affairs, that rules of conduct cannot be so framed as to require no exceptions, and that hardly any kind of action can safely be laid down as either always obligatory or always condemnable. There is no ethical creed which does not temper the rigidity of its laws, by giving a certain latitude, under the moral responsibility of the agent, for accommodation to peculiarities of circumstances; and under every creed, at the opening thus made, self-deception and dishonest casuistry get in. There exists no moral system under which there do not arise unequivocal cases of conflicting obligation. These are the real difficulties, the knotty points both in the theory of ethics, and in the conscientious guidance of personal conduct. They are overcome practically with greater or with less success according to the intellect and virtue of the individual; but it can hardly be pretended that any one will be the less qualified for dealing with them, from possessing an ultimate standard to which conflicting rights and duties can be referred. If utility is the ultimate source of moral obligations, utility may be invoked to decide between them when their demands are incompatible. Though the application of the standard may be difficult, it is better than none at all: while in other systems, the moral laws all claiming independent authority, there is no common umpire entitled to interfere between them; their claims to precedence one over another rest on little better than sophistry, and unless determined, as they generally are, by the unacknowledged influence of considerations of utility, afford a free scope for the action of personal desires and partialities. We must remember that only in these cases of conflict between secondary principles is it requisite that first principles should be appealed to. There is no case of moral obligation in which some secondary principle is not involved; and if only one, there can seldom be any real doubt which one it is, in the mind of any person by whom the principle itself is recognised.

PART III
DEMOCRACY AND FREEDOM

6 *Law of Libel and Liberty of the Press*

(*Westminster Review*, III, 1825.)

On the Law of Libel; with Strictures on the self-styled Constitutional Association. 8vo. pp. 73. London. John Hunt. 1823.

The Law of Libel. By Richard Mence, Esq. of the Middle Temple, Barrister. 8vo. 2 Vols. in one, pp. 595. London, 1824.

The two publications which we have chosen to head this article, possess considerable merit, and we do not hesitate to recommend them to our readers, as worthy of an attentive perusal.

The first, though no name appears in the title-page is the acknowledged production of a known and tried friend of the people. It consists of a series of essays, all of which, except the last, appeared nearly two years since in a weekly newspaper. It comprises a summary exposure of many of the abominations contained in what is called the Law of Libel, as well as in the administration of that Law; and a brief review of the acts of a body of men, now sunk into obscurity, who were at one time notorious under the name of the Constitutional Association. We will not say that the author has completely exhausted the subject; but we consider no small praise to be his due; for having said so much, to the purpose, in the narrow compass within which, by the original design, he was unavoidably confined.

Mr Mence's work attracted our attention, from being advertised as dedicated to the Constitutional Association. What might be expected from a work, appearing under such auspices, our readers have no occasion to be informed. We, however, had not proceeded far in the perusal, before we found Mr Mence to be, not a humble aspirant after ministerial patronage, content to lend himself to the purposes of those who would keep the human mind in perpetual bondage; but one who does not shrink from exposing, even at the risk of his professional success, the vices of existing institutions; one who dares give utterance to great and important truths, however little acceptable to the rich and powerful; and who would be, for that reason alone, deserving of high praise, had he executed his task with far less ability than he had displayed.

Without entering into a critical examination of the merits and defects of these two works, we embrace this opportunity of delivering our sentiments upon the highly important subject of which they refer: availing ourselves of the language of either or both of them, as often as it appears peculiarly adapted to our purpose.

We shall divide our remarks into two parts; in one of which we shall discuss the general question, to what extent restraints upon the freedom of the press can be considered as warranted by sound principles of political philosophy; and in the other, we shall take a brief review of the English Law, and of the doctrines of English Lawyers, on this subject: and we pledge ourselves to prove, that the Law of England is as unfavourable to the liberty of the press, as that of the most despotic government which ever existed; and, consequently, that whatever degree of that liberty is enjoyed in this country, exists, not in consequence of the law, but in spite of it.

The general question has usually been disposed of in a very summary way. It has, in fact, been regularly assumed, first, that to employ the press in any other than a certain manner, is inconceivably wicked; and secondly, that, for this reason, it is the duty of the magistrate to prevent it by fine and imprisonment, if not by means still more certainly and more promptly effectual.

The author of the article 'Liberty of the Press', in the Supplement to the Encyclopaedia Britannica, has, however, set the example of rather a different sort of reasoning; and (what was never completely or consistently done before) he has pointed out the considerations on which this question really turns. We have no higher ambition than that of treading in his steps; and, taking his principles as our guide, we shall endeavour to unravel the sophistry, and expose the mischievous designs of the enemies to free discussion.

That the press may be so employed as to require punishment, we are very far from denying: it may be made the instrument of almost every imaginable crime.

'There is scarcely a right,* for the violation of which, scarcely an operation of government, for the disturbance of which, the press may not be employed as an instrument. The offences capable of being committed by the press are indeed nearly coextensive with the whole field of delinquency.

'It is not, however, necessary to give a separate definition of every such violation or disturbance, when committed by the press, for that would be to write the penal code a second time; first describing each offence as it appears in ordinary cases; and then describing it anew for the case in which the press is the particular instrument.

'If, for the prevention of the violation of rights, it were necessary to give a separate definition, on account of every instrument which might be employed as a means of producing the several violations, the penal code would be endless. In general the instrument or means is an immaterial circumstance. The violation itself, and the degree of alarm which may attend it, are the principal objects of consideration. If a man is put in fear of his life, and robbed of his purse, it is of no consequence whether he is threatened with a pistol, or with a sword. In the deposition of a theft, of a

* Article 'Liberty of the Press' (in the Supplement to the Enc. Brit. near the beginning). This invaluable essay is from the pen of Mr Mill, the historian of British India.

fraud, or a murder, it is not necessary to include an account of all the sorts of means by which these injuries may be perpetrated. It is sufficient if the injury itself is accurately described. The object is, to prevent the injury, not merely when produced by one sort of means or another sort of means, but by any means.

'As far as persons and property are concerned, the general definition of the acts by which rights are liable to be violated, has always been held sufficient; and has been regarded as including not less the cases in which the instrumentality of the press has been employed, than those in which any other means have been employed to the same end. Nobody ever thought of a particular law for restraining the press on account of the cases in which it may have been rendered subservient to the perpetration of a murder or theft. It is enough that a law is made to punish him who has been guilty of the murder or theft, whether he has employed the press or any thing else as the means for accomplishing his end.'*

There are some species of acts, however, of which the press if not the sole, may, at any rate, be regarded as the most potent instrument: these are, the publication of facts, and the expression of opinions; and to one or other of these heads belong those uses of the press, against which the Law of Libel is principally directed.

* Montesquieu saw pretty clearly the only case in which the expression of opinions and sentiments could be a fit object of punishment: although he did not venture to extend the doctrine further than to the case of *words,* and even among words, only to these which are called treasonable.

'Les paroles qui sont jointes à une action, prennent la nature de cette action. Ainsi un homme qui va dans la place publique exhorter les sujets à la révolte, devient coupable de lèse-majesté, parceque les paroles sont jointes à l'action, et y participent. Ce ne sont point les paroles que l'on punit; mais une action commise dans laquelle on emploie les paroles. Elles ne deviennent des crimes, que lorsqu'elles préparant, qu'elles accompagnent, ou qu'elles suivent une action criminelle. On renverse tout, si l'on fait des paroles un crime capital, au lieu de les regarder comme le signe d'un crime capital.' *Esprit des Lois,* liv. xii, ch. 12.

It is not pretended that, in the language of English Law, the word Libel is strictly confined to one meaning. It includes, on the contrary, a number of acts, of a very heterogeneous nature, resembling one another scarcely at all, except in having penalties attached to them by the authorized interpreters of the law. A threatening letter, demanding money, is a libel. An indecent picture is a libel. For the present, however, we may confine our remarks to the question regarding the publication of facts and the expression of opinions.

To begin with the latter. If the magistrate is to be intrusted with power to suppress all opinions which he, in his wisdom, may pronounce to be michievous – to what control can this power be subjected? What security is it possible to take against its abuse? For without some security all power, and of course this power, is sure to be abused, just as often as its abuse can serve any purpose of the holder.

It is the boast of English lawyers that the offence of treason is defined; so strictly defined, that nothing is ambiguous, nothing arbitrary, nothing left to the discretion of the judge. This, they tell us, is one of the chief bulwarks of our liberty: implying, that if it *were* left to the judge to say what should and what should not be treason, every thing would be treason which the government did not like. Yet why should definition be required in the case of treason, not required in the case of libel? Is the government less interested in misdecision? Is the judge less dependent on the government? Is a packed special jury less subservient? Or are the judge and jury angels when they judge of libel, men only when they judge of treason?

It would be hardy to assert, that to give the right of pronouncing upon libels to the judge, is any thing more than another name for giving it to the government. But there are many subjects, and these the most important of all, on which it is the interest of the government, not that the people should think right, but, on the contrary, that they should think wrong: on these subjects, therefore, the government is quite sure, if it has the power to suppress, not the false and mischievous opinions, but the great and important truths. It is the interest of rulers that the people should hold slavish opinions in politics: it is equally so, that they should hold slavish opinions in religion: all opinions, therefore, whether in politics or religion, which are not slavish, the government, if it dares, will be sure to suppress. It is the interest of rulers that the people should believe all their proceedings to be the best possible: everything, therefore, which has a tendency to make them think otherwise, and among the rest, all strictures, however well deserved, government will use its most strenuous exertions to prevent. If these endeavours could succeed, if it could suppress all censure, its dominion, to whatever degree it might pillage and oppress the people, would be for ever secured.

This is so palpable, that a man must be either insincere or imbecile to deny it: and no one, we suppose, will openly affirm that rulers should have the power to suppress all opinions which they may call mischievous – all opinions which they may dislike. Where, then, is the line to be drawn? At what point is the magistrate's discretionary power of suppressing opinions to end? Can it be limited in such a manner as to leave him the power of suppressing really mischievous opinions, without giving him that of silencing every opinion hostile to the indefinite extension of his power?

It is manifest, even at first sight, that no such limit can be set. If the publication of opinions is to be restrained, merely because they are mischievous, there must be somebody to judge, what opinions are mischievous, and what the reverse. It is obvious, that there is no certain and universal rule for determining whether an opinion is useful or pernicious; and that if any person be authorized to decide, unfettered by such a rule, that person is a despot. To decide what opinions shall be permitted, and what prohibited, is to choose opinions for the people: since they cannot adopt opinions which are not suffered to be presented to their minds. Whoever chooses opinions for the people, possesses absolute control over their actions, and may wield them for his own purposes with perfect security.

It thus appears, by the closest ratiocination, that there is no medium between perfect freedom of expressing opinions, and absolute despotism. Whenever you invest the rulers of the country with any power to suppress opinions, you invest them with *all* power; and absolute power of suppressing opinions would amount, if it *could* be exercised, to a despotism far more perfect than any which has yet existed, because there is no country in which the power of suppressing opinions has ever, in practice, been altogether unrestrained.

How, then, it may be asked, if to have any power of silencing opinions is to have all power – since the government of Great Britain certainly has that power in a degree – how do we account for the practical freedom of discussion, which to a considerable extent undoubtedly prevails in this country? The government having the power to destroy it, why is it suffered to exist?

Why? For the same reason, for which we have a habeas corpus act, with a government possessing the power to suspend or repeal it: for the same reason for which a jury is sometimes allowed to acquit a prisoner, whom the aristocracy wish to destroy: for the same reason for which we are not taxed up to the highest amount which could be extorted from us, without impairing our power of being useful slaves. The aristocracy do not submit to these restraints because they like them, but because they do not venture to throw them off. This is conformable to the theory of the British constitution itself.

Even a Turkish Sultan is restrained by the fear of exciting insurrection. The power of shackling the press may, like all other power, be controlled in its exercise by public opinion, and to a very great, though far from a sufficient, extent, it has been and is so controlled in Great Britain. By law, however – notwithstanding the assertions of lawyers, which assertions, when it suits them, they never scruple to contradict – liberty of discussion, on any topic by which the interests of the aristocracy can be affected, does not exist at all in this country, as we have already shewn, upon general principles, and shall prove in the sequel from the actual words of the highest legal authorities.

The preliminary inquiry, however, would not be complete, unless, having discussed the consequences of restraining the press, we were also to inquire what would be the consequences of leaving it free.

It is evident, at first sight, that, whatever might be the evils of freedom, they could not be worse than the evils of restraint. The worst that could happen, if the people chose opinions for themselves, would be, that they would choose wrong opinions. But this evil, as we have seen, is not contingent, but unavoidable, if they allow any other person to choose opinions for them. Nor would it be possible that the opinions, however extravagant, which might become prevalent in a state of freedom, could exceed in mischievousness those which it would be the interest, and therefore the will, of rulers, to dictate: since there cannot be more mischievous opinions, than those which tend to perpetuate arbitrary power. There would, however, be one great difference. Under a free system, if error would be promulgated, so would truth: and truth never fails, in the long run, to prevail over error. Under a system of restraint, the errors which would be promulgated from authority would be the most mischievous possible, and would not be suffered to be refuted.

That truth, if it has fair play, always in the end triumphs over error, and becomes the opinion of the world, is a proposition which rests upon the broadest principles of human nature, and to which it would be easy to accumulate testimonials from almost every author, whatever may be his political leanings, who has distinguished himself in any branch of politics, morals, or theology. It is a proposition which the restrictors themselves do not venture to dispute. They continually protest, that their opinions have nothing to fear from discussion; the sole effect of which, according to them, is, to exhibit their irrefragable certainty in a still stronger light than before. And yet they do not scruple to punish men for doing that which, if their own assertions be correct, merits not punishment, but reward.

Although, however, the worst enemies of discussion, do not deny, as a general proposition, its tendency to unveil the truth, there is a certain number of subjects on which, if they are to be believed, discussion tends, not to enlighten, but to mislead. Among these are all the subjects on which it is the interest of rulers that the people *should* be misled; the political religion of the country, its political institutions, and the conduct and character of its rulers.

On the first of these topics, we have delivered our opinions so fully in our third number, that we shall in the present confine ourselves principally to the three latter: all of which substantially resolve themselves into one.

That there is no subject of greater importance, no one needs to be told: and to say this, is to say that there is no subject on which it is of greater importance that the people should be righly informed. As the stability of a good government wholly depends upon its being acknowledged by the people to be good, so, on the other hand, the reform of a bad one wholly depends upon its being believed by the people to be bad. In the correctness of the estimate which the people form of the goodness of their government, their whole happiness is involved; since misgovernment includes every misery which is capable of afflicting mankind: and misgovernment is alike the consequence, whether the people believe a good government to be a bad one, or a bad government to be a good one.

We have been thus particular in laying down first principles, because the language held on this subject by rulers implies, that it is indeed the greatest of calamities, for the people to believe a good government to be bad, but that their considering a bad government to be good, is no evil at all, or at most a very trifling one. The evil, however, as we have already observed, is in both cases the same; or rather, the one is an evil, chiefly because it leads to the other: that the people should think ill of a good government is principally to be lamented, because it may occasion their acquiescence in a worse.

If, therefore, there be any subject on which the people cannot, without the greatest danger, trust the power of choosing opinions for them out of their own hands, it is this. And if such power cannot safely be given to any one, least of all can it be given to the rulers of the country.

If the people were compelled to take their opinions implicitly from some one who might have an interest in persuading them that their government is worse than it is, the greatest evils, it is admitted, would be the consequence. To think ill of a good government, and well of a bad one, are evils of equal magnitude. If, therefore, the privilege of dictating opinions to the people, on the subject of their government, be intrusted to persons interested in persuading them that their government is better than it is, the mischief cannot consistently be affirmed to be less. That rulers are so interested, will not be denied. What inference, then, are we to draw? or rather, how can the inference be evaded, that, if rulers are suffered to choose what opinions the people shall hold concerning their government, all the evils of misrule are rendered perpetual?

Such a choice, however, is made by rulers, as often as they inflict punishment upon any person for criticizing institutions, or censuring the conduct of government: unless they are willing to prohibit, under equal penalties, the expression of praise.

To forbid the expression of one opinion, and give encouragement to that of another, is surely to make a choice. To punish censure of rulers, while praise is permitted, is to say, 'tis fit that the people should think well of their government, whether good or bad; and to take the most effectual mode of compelling them to do so.

Against this reasoning it is impossible that any rational objection can be urged. Cavils, indeed, may be brought against it: but there are few conclusions of equal importance, the proof of which affords so little hold even for cavil.

When it is asserted, that to restrain discussion is to choose opinions for the people, and that rulers, if permitted to dictate opinions to their subjects, having an interest in choosing the most mischievous of all opinions, will act as that interest directs; there is only one objection which can by possibility be raised. It cannot be said, that to fetter discussion is not to choose opinions, nor that rulers are not interested in making a bad choice. But, it may be said, that our rulers are men in whom the confidence of the people may be reposed; and that, although it be confessedly their interest to make a bad choice, they will disregard that interest, and make a good one.

To such a pinnacle of absurdity men may always be driven, when they attempt to argue in defence of mischievous power. They begin by boldly denying the possibility of abuse: when this can no longer be maintained, they fly for refuge to the characters of the individuals, and insist with equal pertinacity, that in their hands power may be trusted without fear of being abused. This is a compliment of which the rulers for the time being, be they who they may, always receive as much as they can pay for: dead rulers are not so fortunate. That all rulers in time past abused their power when they could, is allowed: but an exception is made in favour of the present. This is a species of reasoning, however, which will pass current with nobody in the present day: we cannot be forced back to the times when rulers were thought not to be made like human beings, but to be free from all the passions and appetites by which other men are misled. If uncontrolled power can exist, and not be abused, then away with the British, and all other constitutions, and let us return to the despotism of our wise and venerable ancestors. But if men will abuse all other powers, when unrestrained, so they will that of controlling the press: if rulers will avail themselves of all other means to render themselves despotic, they will not pass over an expedient so simple and effectual as that of suppressing, in as far as they dare, all opinions hostile to the extension of their authority. And perfect freedom of discussion is, as we have already proved, the only alternative.

The objections which have been urged against the principle of free discussion, though infinitely diversified in shape, are at bottom only one assertion: the incapacity of the people to form correct opinions. This assumption is indeed the stronghold of all the disguised or undisguised partisans of despotism. It has been the unremitting, and hitherto, unhappily, the successful endeavour of rulers, to make it be believed that the most dreadful calamities would be the effect of any attempt to obtain securities that their power should be employed for the benefit, not of themselves, but of the community. With this view, it has been their uniform practice to vilify those whom they are striving to enslave. If people were permitted to choose opinions for themselves, they would be sure, it is alleged, to choose the most mischievous and dangerous opinions. Being utterly incapable either of thinking or of acting for themselves, they are quite sure, unless kept in awe by priests and aristocracies, to become blind instruments in the hands of factious demagogues, who would employ them to subvert all establishments, and to throw every thing into the wildest anarchy and confusion. This language, by the way, is a practical illustration of the impartiality of the Law of Libel. It restrains all declaration, even of unfavourable truth with regard to the aristocracy: it gives full indulgence, and there is plenty of encouragement, to the propagation of all manner of unfavourable lies against the people. The conspiracy have thus all that is necessary for their purpose. Give a dog a bad name, and hang him: so they try with the people. Whether the object be to coerce them by standing armies, or to muzzle them by libel law, the motive always is pure loving-kindness, to save the unoffending, that is, the aristocratic part of mankind, from the jaws of ravenous wolves and tigers, the people.

Such a language is calculated to act upon men by their fears, not by their reason: otherwise a little reflection would show, that the incapacity of the people, were it admitted, proves nothing, or, at least, nothing to the purpose. The practical conclusion would be the same, even if the people were so destitute of reasoning power, as to be utterly incapable of distinguishing truth from falsehood: since there is no alternative, but to let them choose their own opinions, or to give the choice to persons interested in misleading them.

An ignorant man, even if he decide at hap-hazard, has at least a chance of being sometimes in the right. But he who adopts every opinion which rulers choose to dictate, is always in the wrong, when it is their interest that he should be so, that is, on the most momentous of all topics.

Another question, which it does not suit those who make the ignorance of the people a plea for enslaving them to put, is, why are they ignorant? because to this question there can be only one answer, namely, that if they are ignorant, it is precisely because that discussion, which alone can remove ignorance, has been withheld from them. And although their masters may find it convenient to speak of their ignorance as incurable, we take the liberty of demurring to this conclusion, until the proper remedy shall have been tried. This remedy is, instruction: and of instruction, discussion is the most potent instrument. Discussion, therefore, has a necessary tendency to remedy its own evils. For the evils which spring from an undue veneration for authority, there is no such cure: and the longer the disease continues, without the remedying influence of discussion, the more inveterate it becomes.

But, the assertion itself, by which so many terrors have been conjured up – the incapacity of the people to choose correct opinions – upon what evidence does it rest? Upon history? No; for history proves, that just in proportion as the people have been permitted to choose opinions for themselves, in that proportion have they been moral, intelligent, and happy: and it is precisely in those countries in which the greatest pains has been taken to shut out discussion, that the people, when once roused from their habitual apathy, have proved themselves to be most ignorant and ferocious. No people which had ever enjoyed a free press, could have been guilty of the excesses of the French Revolution. By what artifices, then, have governments contrived to spread a vague apprehension of danger from discussion so widely among the unthinking part of mankind? By availing themselves of that universal law of human nature, by which men are prone to dread whatever they do not understand, and they who foresee the least, uniformly fear the most. The evils which they endure, habit has rendered tolerable: but change, because they cannot foresee its consequences, is the object of their terror and aversion. And though history does not prove that discussion produces evil, but the contrary, there is abundant proof from history, that it produces change: change, not indeed in any thing good, but in every thing that is bad, bad laws, bad judicature, and bad government. That it leads to such changes is the very reason for which it is most to be desired, but it is also the reason why short-sighted persons hold it in terror.

Nor is there any difficulty in convincing the understanding of any one who will coolly apply his attention to the subject. The real difficulty is, to quiet fears. We cannot confide in persons whose fears appear to us to fall always in the wrong place. Nothing is more to be feared than a habit of fearing, whenever any thing is propsed for the good of mankind. The man who is always fearing evil to the many from the many, never from the few, appears to us an object of very rational fear.

The ignorance of the people is a mere pretext for a line of conduct which would have been equally pursued without any such pretext. This appears from the little regard paid to it in the practice of rulers themselves. The proper course in regard to ignorant persons, they say truly, is to guard them against deception: now, as rulers dare not openly lay claim to impeccability, they cannot deny that there may be deception on both sides: on the side of praise, as well as on the side of blame. To praise, however, both of rulers and of institutions, the most unlimited latitude has been given: censure alone has been restricted. Every one is free to represent the government and its functionaries as better than they are; and that to any extent: but woe to him who presumes, with whatever truth, to cast any blame upon either! Does this look as if it were believed that the people are ignorant? No! it looks as if it were feared that they would be too clear-sighted.

It seems not very consistent, in those whose case rests wholly upon the people's incapacity of judging to propose as a remedy for that incapacity, that nothing but an ex-parte statement should be presented to them. Is incapacity to judge cured by hearing only one side? Is ignorance remedied by placing it in a situation where the most perfect wisdom could scarcely escape being misled? To make the ignorance of the people a pretext for refusing them the means of judging, when it is precisely on account of their ignorance that they stand most in need of those means, would excite laughter, if it did not excite indignation. In other countries, it is maintained that the people ought not to judge of public affairs. To prevent them from hearing evidence, therefore, is, at any rate, consistent. In this country it is admitted that the people should judge; and it is, nevertheless, asserted, that they should hear only one side!

To support this monstrous absurdity, there is, in addition to the grand assumption of the incapacity of the people, another question which it has been customary to beg. This is, that the people hate their rulers, and are strongly disposed to judge unfavourably, both of them and of their actions. So utterly false is this assumption, that, on the contrary, there is no fact to which the testimony of experience is more unvarying, than to the strong disposition of the people, to think much better of their rulers and of their institutions than they deserve. The love of ease, perhaps the strongest principle of human nature, and beyond all comparison stronger, in the majority of mankind, than the hope of any remote and contingent advantage, is constantly urging them to avoid innovation, and rest satisfied with things as they are: with what success, every one has it in his power to observe. Who is there that has not seen a hundred instances of evil needlessly endured, for one of good wantonly abandoned and evil adopted? Is there, then, no inconsistency in supposing that in public matters the case is directly reversed?

Nor is the love of ease the only principle which is constantly in operation, to warp the judgments of the people in favour of their rulers. He must have looked at mankind with a resolution not to see the truth, who can be blind to the excessive veneration of the poor for title, rank, and riches, a veneration arising from the habitual propensity of mankind to over-estimate advantages which they do not possess; and which was enumerated by Adam Smith among the most fertile sources of false judgments in morality which could be named. With these two principles strongly on one side, and nothing but reason on the other, knowledge must be far advanced among the people before they learned to venerate rulers only as far as they deserve veneration. Accordingly, all history bears testimony to the constancy with which the most dreadful mis-government has been suffered to prevail in almost every country of the globe: but the advocates of restriction may safely be challenged to produce one instance from history, in which the people have risen against a good government and overthrown it.

So strong, and so durable, is the veneration of the people for their rulers: nor has it ever yet been eradicated by anything short of the most grinding oppression. What epithet, then, can be too severe for the conduct of those who would prevent this feeling from giving way, like all other mischievous feelings, with the progress of civilization; who would deny a hearing to opinions and arguments which tend to weaken the inordinate reverence of the people for every ruler, good or bad, and give free scope to those which tend to render that blind reverence, and all its consequent miseries, everlasting!

Although our sentiments on the subject of free discussion in religion have already been fully stated, we will quote one passage from an essay to which we have before referred: * merely to show that the same arguments apply to religion, which we have already stated with a more immediate reference to politics:

'Religion, in some of its shapes, has in most countries

* The Article 'Liberty of the Press,' near the end.

been placed on the footing of an institution of the state. Ought the freedom of the press to be as complete with regard to this, as we have seen that it ought to be in regard to all other institutions of the state? If any one says that it ought not, it is incumbent upon him to shew, wherein the principles which are applicable to the other institutions, fail in their application to this.

'We have seen, that, in regard to all other institutions, it is unsafe for the people to permit any but themselves to choose opinions for them. Nothing can be more certain, than that it is unsafe for them to permit any but themselves to choose for them in religion.

'If they part with the power of choosing their own religious opinions, they part with every power. It is well known with what ease religious opinions can be made to embrace every thing upon which the unlimited power of rulers and the utmost degradation of the people depend. The doctrine of *passive obedience* and non-resistance was a *religious doctrine*. Permit any man, or any set of men, to say what shall and what shall not be religious opinions, you make them despotic immediately.

'This is so obvious, that it requires neither illustration nor proof.

'But if the people here, too, must choose opinions for themselves, discussion must have its course; the same propositions which we have proved to be true in regard to other institutions, are true in regard to this; and no opinion ought to be impeded more than another, by any thing but the adduction of evidence on the opposite side.'

The argument drawn from the unsafeness of permitting governments to choose a religion for their subjects, cogent as it is, ranks only as one among a host of arguments, for leaving the people to follow their own reason, in matters of religion, as in every thing else.

In an age when the slightest difference of opinion on such a subject was deemed a perfectly sufficient reason for bringing the unhappy minority to the stake, it was not wonderful that Infidelity also should be considered a crime. But now, when a Churchman no more thinks of persecuting a Calvinist, or a Calvinist of persecuting a Churchman, than we think of punishing a man because he happens to be taller, or shorter, than ourselves; it is truly strange that there should be any one who can so blind himself as not to see, that the same reasons which make him a friend to toleration in other cases, bind him also to tolerate Infidelity.

The expression of opinions having been disposed of, it remains to be considered, whether in any case there is sufficient reason for placing restrictions upon the statement of facts. It must be admitted that the case of facts, and that of opinion, are not precisely similar. False opinions must be tolerated for the sake of the true: since it is impossible to draw any line by which true and false opinions can be separated from one another. There is no corresponding reason for permitting the publication of false statements of fact. The truth or falsehood of an alleged fact, is matter, not of opinion, but of evidence; and may be safely left to be decided by those, on whom the business of deciding upon evidence in other cases devolves.

It is maintained, however, by lawyers, that there ought to be other restrictions upon the statement of facts, besides the punishment of falsehood: there being some facts, as they allege, which, even if true, ought not to be made public. On this it is to be observed, that the same reasoning which proves that there should be perfect freedom of expressing opinions, proves also that there should be perfect freedom of expressing true facts. It is obviously upon facts, that all true opinions must be founded; if rulers, therefore, have, on any subject, on their own conduct, for example, the power of keeping from the knowledge of the people all facts which it does not suit them to disclose, they do, in fact, choose opinions for the people on that subject, just as completely as if they assumed the power of doing so, by a positive enactment.

There is one case, and only one, in which there might appear to be some doubt of the propriety of permitting the truth to be told without reserve. This is, when the truth, without being of any advantage to the public, is calculated to give annoyance to private individuals. That there are such cases must be allowed; and also that it would be desirable, in such cases, that the truth should be suppressed, if it could be done by any other means than law, or arbitrary power. It must, however, be borne in mind, that, if there are cases in which a truth unpleasant to individuals is of no advantage to the public, there are others in which it is of the greatest; and that the truths which it most imports to the public to know, are precisely those which give most annoyance to individuals, whose vices and follies they expose. Tory lawyers, indeed, for whom no doctrine is too extravagant which tends to uphold their power, or that of their employers, have asserted that one man has no right whatever to censure another: that to do so is an act of judicial authority which no individual is entitled to exercise: and that to expose vices and follies, instead of being one of the most important of all services to mankind, is a gross and unwarrantable usurpation of superiority.* We hope that none but Tory lawyers are hardly enough to profess concurrence in doctrines like these. Since, then, there is no one who can be trusted to decide which are useful, which the unimportant truths; and the consequences of suppressing both would, beyond comparison, exceed in mischievousness the consequences of allowing both to be heard; the practical conclusion needs not to be stated.

We have yet to notice a shift, to which recourse has frequently been had, since the spread of liberal opinions has rendered it scarcely safe to acknowledge the same degree of enmity to discussion, which was formerly avowed. We allude to the doctrine, that *calm* and *fair* discussion should be permitted, but that ridicule and invective ought to be chastised.

This is so much the doctrine which has been fashionable of late, that most of our readers probably believe it to be the law: and so, according to the *dicta* of judges, it is: but according to other *dicta* of the same judges, it is also the

* See Holt on the Law of Libel, *passim.*

law, that any discussion, unless it be all on one side, and even a bare statement of acknowledged facts, is a libel.

The doctrine, however, being as we have said, a fashionable one, it is necessary to say something on it; and we observe, in the first place, that if argument may be permitted with safety, there can be little hazard in tolerating ridicule and invective; since, on all questions of importance, it is, in the long run, the balance of argument which always determines the decision of the majority. First, from the very nature of the weapons themselves: the operation of invective and ridicule being in a great measure limited to those whose minds are already made up. They may stimulate partizans, but they are not calculated to make converts. If a man does not renounce his opinion from conviction, it is scarcely by hearing himself laughed at, or reviled for holding it, that he will be prevailed upon to give it up. Such means usually have no effect but to make him adhere to his opinion still more pertinaciously than before. And secondly, because ridicule and invective, if they may be used on one side, may be used also on the other; and against falsehood, for obvious reasons, with greater effect than against truth.

In the next place, if exclusion is to be put upon ridicule and invective, why is it not impartial? If any advantage can be derived from the employment of such weapons, why is it permitted to one set of opinions, withheld from another? Or is it that ridicule and invective then only tend to mislead, when they are employed on the side adverse to rulers? To deny any advantage to censure, which is extended to praise, is the same thing, though in a less aggravated degree, with the total prohibition of censure. Its effect, in as far as it has any, is to give an undue preponderance to praise: its tendency is, to make the people think better of their rulers than they deserve; and, to that extent rulers are enabled to oppress with impunity.

Suppose, for instance, that a writer is permitted to say, in as many words, that ministers or parliament have acted improperly, have engaged, for instance, in an unjust war; but, if he says this, and moreover expresses indignation that it should be so, he is punished. By expressing indignation, he gives it to be understood, that the evil, in his opinion, is great, and its authors deserving of punishment. If he refrains from expressing indignation, he virtually says, that the evil is not great, and its authors not deserving of punishment. Is it of no consequence, then, that the public should be informed, whether an evil is great or small? whether its authors are criminal, or the reverse? We fully subscribe to the manly and liberal sentiments of Mr Mence on this subject. 'It is not only no crime, but a positive duty, never to state crimes drily and coldly, and without the language of just and honest indignation. And our law, or supposed law of libel, by repressing the exercise of this duty, ministers to and encourages every kind of vice; and corrupts and undermines the manners and morals of the people.' i. 162.

Great as are these evils, they are not the greatest which the prohibition of ridicule and invective carries along with it: nor is it for the mere purpose of securing exclusively to themselves any advantage which such weapons can bestow, that rulers cling so closely to the privilege of putting them down. It is because they know well that, if they are permitted to suppress ridicule and invective, they have it in their power to suppress all unfavourable representation. Who is to judge, what is invective, and what is fair and temperate discussion? None but rulers themselves: for no line can be drawn. All censure is invective. To censure is to ascribe misconduct. Even error is misconduct, in those to whose management the great affairs of a community are intrusted. When to err is to put to hazard the welfare of a nation, it is a crime for those who cannot avoid error to remain at the helm. To impute even error, therefore, is equivalent to invective, and might be construed as employing it. The mere statement of a great crime is itself invective. It implies, and is meant to imply, moral guilt: if it fails of doing so, the statement is so far imperfect. It is impossible, therefore, to prohibit invective, without prohibiting all discussion, or leaving it to rulers to decide what sort of discussion shall be punished, and what left free.

'The question is,* whether *indecent* discussion should be prohibited? To answer this question, we must, of course, inquire what is meant by indecent.

'In English libel law, where this term holds so distinguished a place, is it not defined?

'English legislators have not hitherto been good at defining; and English lawyers have always vehemently condemned, and grossly abused it. The word "indecent," therefore, has always been a term under which it was not difficult, on each occasion, for the judge to include whatever he did not like. "Decent" and "what the judge likes," have been pretty nearly synonymous.' And while *indecent* discussion is prohibited by law, they always will be synonymous.

The doctrine which we have now exposed, is merely one of the shifts to which English rulers, from their peculiar situation, have been compelled to have recourse.

In other countries, where the system to be upheld is one of undisguised despotism, the utter incapacity of the people to judge rightly, and the unspeakable wickedness of their presuming to judge at all, on the subject of government, are the avowed doctrines of rulers. The people, it is there contended, have no business to form any opinion on the acts of government. They have nothing to do with their rulers except to obey them. The magistrate, as he ought to have absolute control over the actions of all under his dominion, ought likewise to have power equally unlimited over their opinions. And this doctrine, if it has no other merit, has at least the recommendation of consistency.

The language of English rulers, down to the Revolution in 1688, was precisely similar. At that period, however, a new government was established; and this government, having come in upon the popular ground of resistance to kings, could not avoid admitting, that the people ought to be permitted to judge both of rulers and of institutions; since to deny this, would have been to give up the principle upon which its own dominion was founded. At the same

* Article 'Liberty of the Press,' as before referred to.

time, having the same interests as any other government, it was desirous of suppressing, as far as possible, all censure upon its proceedings. Accordingly, the course which, since that time, it has pursued, has been one of perpetual compromise. It has admitted, in the fullest and most unequivocal terms, that discussion on all subjects of government and legislation ought to be free. It has even maintained, that the privilege of canvassing the acts of their government, is the birthright of Englishmen: that we owe to it all that we hold dear; that without it, there can be no security for good government. At the same time, in the teeth of these large professions, it has maintained, that censure of established governments ought not to be permitted; and it has assumed to itself, in practice, the privilege of visiting such censure, as often as it has thought fit, with some of the severest penalties of the law.

In this see-saw, English rulers have been followed by English lawyers. We shall select our first instances from Mr Holt's celebrated treatise on the Law of Libel: a work which, having been declared by the late lord Ellenborough from the bench to contain an accurate expression of his own sentiments, and being now generally received among lawyers as one of their standard works, may be considered unexceptionable authority, both for the law itself, and for the sentiments of rulers upon it. Observe what he says of the unspeakable importance of free discussion: –

'Our constitution, in fact, as it at present exists, in a church reformed from the errors of superstition, and in a system of liberty equally remote from feudal anarchy, and monarchical despotism, is almost entirely, under Providence, the fruit of a free press. It was this which awakened the minds of men from that apathy in which ignorance of their rights, and of the duties of their rulers, left them. It was by these means that moral and religious knowledge, the foundations of all liberty, was refracted, multiplied, and circulated; and instead of existing in masses, and in the single points of schools and universities, was rendered the common atmosphere in which we all live and breathe. It was from the press that originated, what is, in fact, the main distinction of the ancient and modern world, public opinion. A single question will be sufficient to put the importance of this subject in the strongest point of view. In the present state of knowledge and manners, is it possible that a Nero or Tiberius would be suffered to live or reign' – 1st ed. pp. 39, 40.

Judging from this passage, who would not conceive it to be the doctrine of English lawyers, that mankind are indebted for all that is of greatest value, to censure of existing institutions: such censure as tends to produce the most radical changes, both in church and state, and even the dethronement and destruction of a bad sovereign?

Now mark the language of the same writer, only a few pages afterwards.

'In *every society*, therefore, the liberty of the press may justly be restricted within those limits which are necessary to maintain the establishment, and are necessary to maintain its exercise.' – p. 45.

'Every society' admits of no exception. It includes the worst governed, as well as the best. According to Mr Holt, therefore, in this passage, all governments, no matter how bad, should be maintained. They are establishments, and that alone is a sufficient recommendation. It is to a free press, indeed, that we owe 'a church reformed from the errors of superstition, and a system of liberty equally remote from feudal anarchy and monarchical despotism;' but as these were obtained by overthrowing a former system, and as 'the limits necessary to maintain the establishment' are by no means to be passed, the writings which led to the Revolution ought to have been suppressed, and that great event, with all its glorious consequences, ought never to have been suffered to take place.

The difference, therefore, between the doctrine of rulers in England, and that of rulers elsewhere, exists only in name; and is not indicative of any difference in their real sentiments, but only in their power of giving expression to them without danger.

If there be any truth in the great principles of human nature, or any validity in the reasoning, upon which the British constitution is founded, there is no ruler who would not, if he could, suppress all censure of himself, of his measures, or of any of the arrangements which contribute to his authority. The British constitution supposes, that rulers always wish to abuse their power, and, of course, wish to remove every check which has a tendency to prevent them from abusing their power. But the great check to abuses of all sorts, is a free press. It is of the utmost importance, therefore, to observe, that all rulers have the strongest possible interest in destroying the freedom of the press: that they are under an absolute necessity of hating it; and that although they may not, at any one moment, have a fixed and regular plan for effecting its destruction, they are obstinately averse to any, even the most trifling, extension of it; and are eager to seize every opportunity for restraining it within the narrowest practicable limits.

The necessity for veiling this disposition by the tricks of language, has taught our rulers to devise a number of artful phrases, by the help of which they contrive, in the same breath, to give and take away the right of free discussion, and which, as often as they have occasion for the punishment of an obnoxious writer, serve them to beg the question in favour of their object. A trick of this kind, which has done them much good service, is the well-known profession, that they are friends to the *liberty* of the press, but enemies to its *licentiousness*.

Let us examine what this means. The liberty of the press, we are told, is good; that is, as we suppose, discussion, if not in all cases, at any rate in some cases, ought to be free. But the licentiousness of the press, it seems, is an evil; which we must presume to mean, that there are certain other cases in which discussion ought not to be free: but what cases? Of this we are not informed; for the word licentiousness, far from marking the distinction, is merely a vague epithet of blame. Their meaning, therefore, must be, that they are to judge what is the liberty of the press, and what is licentiousness. But this is to have the whole power of choosing opinions for the people. Allow them to decide what is, or is not licentiousness, and every thing will be licentiousness which implies censure of themselves, which involves any doctrine hostile to the indefinite increase and perpetual duration of their power. With them, indeed, to use the language of Mr Mence, 'the liberty of the press is a liberty of flattering, fawning, trifling, prosing, but not of writing freely, or fairly, or usefully, or in a way to engage attention, or have a chance of exciting interest, upon men or manners, or upon political, or legal, or religious, or moral subjects.'[8]

We regard it, then, as one of the most favourable signs of the times, that this indiscriminating reverence for all the instruments of judicature is giving way; that the proceedings of judges begin to obtain their due share of examination, and their misconduct of reprobation. And we take this opportunity of declaring our conviction, that this great and salutary change has been in a great degree owing to the indefatigable exertions of the Morning Chronicle; a journal in which we have now been long accustomed to look for excellence of all sorts, but which has displayed, more particularly, in its strictures on the language and conduct of judicial functionaries, a degree of true courage, of ability, and of morality in its highest and least common shape, which it has been but too rarely our lot to witness in the periodical press of this country.

The two following conclusions may now, we think, be regarded as fully established:

That the law of England, as delivered by its authorized interpreters, the judges, however earnestly the same judges may occasionally disavow this doctrine, prohibits all unfavourable representation with respect to institutions, and with respect to the government and its acts:

And, consequently, that if any freedom of discussion is permitted to exist, it is only because it cannot be repressed; the reason why it cannot be repressed, being, the dread of public opinion.

And now, having established these two propositions, we have only further to recommend them to the most serious consideration of our readers.

The importance of free discussion, though frequently dwelt upon by public writers, is seldom fully appreciated by those who, not being themselves exposed to the danger of becoming its martyrs, erroneously consider themselves little affected by its violations. It concerns in fact equally every member of the community. It is equal in value to good government, because without it good government cannot exist. Once remove it, and not only are all existing abuses perpetuated, but all which, in the course of successive ages, it has overthrown, revive in a moment, along with that ignorance and imbecility, against which it is the only safeguard. Conceive the horrors of an oriental despotism – from this and worse we are protected only by the press. Carry next the imagination, not to any living example of prosperity and good government, but to the furthest limit of happiness which is compatible with human nature; and behold that which may in time be attained, if the restrictions under which the press still groans, merely for the security of the holders of mischievous power, be removed. Such are the blessings of a free press: and again and again be it repeated, there cannot be a free press without freedom of censure.

7 *The Spirit of the Age*

(*Examiner*, 6 January-29 May 1831.[9])

The first of the leading peculiarities of the present age is, that it is an age of transition. Mankind have outgrown old institutions and old doctrines, and have not yet acquired new ones. When we say outgrown, we intend to prejudge nothing. A man may not be either better or happier at six-and-twenty, than he was at six years of age: but the same jacket which fitted him then, will not fit him now.

The prominent trait just indicated in the character of the present age, was obvious a few years ago only to the more discerning: at present it forces itself upon the most inobservant. Much might be said, and shall be said on a fitting occasion, of the mode in which the old order of things has become unsuited to the state of society and of the human mind. But when almost every nation on the continent of Europe has achieved, or is in the course of rapidly achieving, a change in its form of government; when our own country, at all former times the most attached in Europe to its old institutions, proclaims almost with one voice that they are vicious both in the outline and in the details, and that they *shall* be renovated, and purified, and made fit for civilized man, we may assume that a part of the effects of the cause just now pointed out, speak sufficiently loudly for themselves. To him who can reflect, even these are but indications which tell of a more vital and radical change. Not only, in the conviction of almost all men, things as they are, are wrong – but, according to that same conviction, it is not by remaining in the old ways that they can be set right. Society demands, and anticipates, not merely a new machine, but a machine constructed in another manner. Mankind will not be led by their old maxims, nor by their old guides; and they will not choose either their opinions or their guides as they have done heretofore. The ancient constitutional texts were formerly spells which would call forth or allay the spirit of the English people at pleasure: what has become of the charm? Who can hope to sway the minds of the public by the old maxims of law, or commerce, or foreign policy, or ecclesiastical policy? Whose feelings are now roused by the mottoes and watch-words of Whig and Tory? And what Whig or Tory could command ten followers in the warfare of politics by the weight of his own personal authority? Nay, what landlord could call forth his tenants, or what manufacturer his men? Do the poor respect the rich, or adopt their sentiments? Do the young respect the old, or adopt their sentiments? Of the feelings of our ancestors it may almost be said that we retain only such as are the natural and necessary growth of human society, however constituted; and I only adopt the energetic expression of a member of the House of Commons, less than two years ago, in saying of the young men, even of that rank in society, that they are ready to advertise for opinions.

Since the facts are so manifest, there is the more chance that a few reflections on their causes, and on their probable consequences, will receive whatever portion of the reader's attention they may happen to deserve.

With respect, then, to the discredit into which old institutions and old doctrines have fallen, I may premise, that this discredit is, in my opinion, perfectly deserved. Having said this, I may perhaps hope, that no perverse interpretation will be put upon the remainder of my observations, in case some of them should not be quite so comfortable to the sentiments of the day as my commencement might give reason to expect. The best guide is not he who, when people are in the right path, merely praises it, but he who shows them the pitfalls and the precipices by which it is endangered; and of which, as long as they were in the wrong road, it was not so necessary that they should be warned.

There is one very easy, and very pleasant way of accounting for this general departure from the modes of thinking of our ancestors: so easy, indeed, and so pleasant, especially to the hearer, as to be very convenient to such writers for hire or for applause, as address themselves not to the men of the age that is gone by, but to the men of the age which has commenced. This explanation is that which ascribes the altered state of opinion and feeling to the growth of the human understanding. According to this doctrine, we reject the sophisms and prejudices which misled the uncultivated minds of our ancestors, because we have learnt too much, and have become too wise, to be imposed upon by such sophisms and such prejudices. It is our knowledge and our sagacity which keep us free from these gross errors. We have now risen to the capacity of perceiving our true interests; and it is no longer in the power of imposters and charlatans to deceive us.

I am unable to adopt this theory. Though a firm believer in the improvement of the age, I do not believe that its improvement has been of this kind. The grand achievement of the present age is the *diffusion* of *superficial* knowledge; and that surely is no trifle, to have been accomplished by a single generation. The persons who are in possession of knowledge adequate to the formation of sound opinions by their own lights, form also a constantly increasing number, but hitherto at all times a small one. It would be carrying the notion of the march of intellect too far, to suppose that an average man of the present day is superior to the greatest men of the eighteenth century; yet they *held* many opinions which we are fast renouncing. The intellect of the age, therefore, is not the cause which we are in search of.

Not increase of wisdom, but a cause of the reality of which we are better assured, may serve to account for the decay of prejudices; and this is, increase of discussion. Men may not reason, better, concerning the great questions in which human nature is interested, but they reason more. Large subjects are discussed more, and longer, and by more minds. Discussion has penetrated deeper into society; and if no greater numbers than before have attained the higher degrees of intelligence, fewer grovel in that state of abject stupidity, which can only co-exist with utter apathy and sluggishness.

The progress which we have made, is precisely that sort of progress which increase of discussion suffices to produce, whether it be attended with increase of wisdom or no. To discuss, and to question established opinions, are merely two phrases for the same thing. When all opinions are questioned, it is in time found out what are those which will not bear a close examination. Ancient doctrines are then put upon their proofs; and those which were originally errors, or have become so by change of circumstances, are thrown aside. Discussion does this. It is by discussion, also, that true opinions are discovered and diffused. But this is not so certain a consequence of it as the weakening of error. To be rationally assured that a given doctrine is *true,* it is often necessary to examine and weigh an immense variety of facts. One single well-established fact, clearly irreconcilable with a doctrine, is sufficient to prove that it is *false*. Nay, opinions often upset themselves by their own incoherence; and the impossibility of their being well-founded may admit of being brought home to a mind not possessed of so much as one positive truth. All the inconsistencies of an opinion with itself, with obvious facts, or even with other prejudices, discussion evolves and makes manifest: and indeed this mode of refutation, requiring less study and less real knowledge than any other, is better suited to the inclination of most disputants. But the moment, and the mood of mind, in which men break loose from an error, is not, except in natures very happily constituted, the most favourable to those mental processes which are necessary to the investigation of truth. What led them wrong at first, was generally nothing else but the incapacity of seeing more than one thing at a time; and that incapacity is apt to stick to them when they have turned their eyes in an altered direction. They usually resolve that the new light which has broken in upon them shall be the sole light; and they wilfully and passionately blew out the ancient lamp, which, though it did not show them what they now see, served very well to enlighten the objects in its immediate neighbourhood. Whether men adhere to old opinions or adopt new ones, they have in general an invincible propensity to split the truth, and take half, or less than half of it; and a habit of erecting their quills and bristling up like a porcupine against any one who brings them the other half, as if he were attempting to deprive them of the portion which they have.

I am far from denying, that, besides getting rid of error, we are also continually enlarging the stock of positive truth. In physical science and art, this is too manifest to be called in question; and in the moral and social sciences I believe it to be as undeniably true. The wisest men in every age generally surpass in wisdom the wisest of any preceding age, because the wisest men can possess and profit by the constantly increasing accumulation of the ideas of all ages: but the multitude (by which I mean the majority of all ranks) have the ideas of their own age, and no others: and if the multitude of one age are nearer to the truth than the multitude of another, it is only in so far as they are guided and influenced by the authority of the wisest among them.

I have said that the present age is an age of transition: I shall now attempt to point out one of the most important consequences of this fact. In all other conditions of mankind, the uninstructed have faith in the instructed. In an age of transition, the divisions among the instructed nullify their authority, and the uninstructed lose their faith in them. The multitude are without a guide, and society is exposed to all the errors and dangers which are to be expected when persons who have never studied any branch of knowledge comprehensively and as a whole attempt to judge for themselves upon particular parts of it.

It is, therefore, one of the necessary conditions of humanity, that the majority must either have wrong opinions, or no fixed opinions, or must place the degree of reliance warranted by reason, in the authority of those who have made moral and social philosophy their peculiar study. It is right that every man should attempt to understand his reason as far as his reason will carry him, and cultivate the faculty as high as possible. But reason itself will teach most men that they must, in the last resort, fall back upon the authority of still more cultivated minds, as the ultimate sanction of the convictions of their reason itself.

But where is the authority which commands this confidence, or deserves it? Nowhere: and here we see the peculiar character, and at the same time the peculiar inconvenience, of a period of moral and social transition. At all other periods there exists a large body of received doctrine, covering nearly the whole field of the moral relations of man, and which no one thinks of questioning, backed as it is by the authority of all, or nearly all, persons, supposed to possess knowledge enough to qualify them for giving an opinion on the subject. This state of things does not now exist in the civilized world – except, indeed, to a certain limited extent in the United States of America. The progress of inquiry has brought to light the insufficiency of the ancient doctrines; but those who have made the investigation of social truths their occupation, have not yet sanctioned any new body of doctrine with their unanimous or nearly unanimous, consent. The true opinion is recommended to the public by no greater weight of authority than hundreds of false opinions; and, even at this day, to find any thing like a united body of grave and commanding authority, we must revert to the doctrines from which the progressiveness of the human mind, or, as it is more popularly called, the improvement of the age, has set us free.

In the mean time, as the old doctrines have gone out, and the new ones have not yet come in, every one must judge for himself as he best may. Learn, and think for yourself, is reasonable advice for the day: but let not the business of the day be so done as to prejudice the work of the morrow. 'Les supériorités morales,' to use the words of Fiévée, 'finiront par s'entendre'; the first men of the age will one day join hands and be agreed: and then there is no power in itself, on earth or in hell, capable of withstanding them.

But ere this can happen there must be a change in the whole framework of society, as at present constituted. Worldly power must pass from the hands of the stationary part of mankind into those of the progressive part. There must be a moral and social revolution, which shall, indeed, take away no men's lives or property, but which shall leave to no man one fraction of unearned distinction or unearned importance.

For mankind to change their institutions while their minds are unsettled, without fixed principles, and unable to trust either themselves or other people, is, indeed, a fearful thing. But a bad way is often the best, to get out of a bad position. Let us place our trust for the future, not in the wisdom of mankind, but on something far surer – the force of circumstances – which makes men see that, when it is near at hand, which they could not foresee when it was at a distance, and which so often and so unexpectedly makes the right course, in a moment of emergency, at once the easiest and the most obvious.

The affairs of mankind, or of any of those smaller political societies which we call nations, are always either in one or the other of two states, one of them in its nature durable, the other essentially transitory. The former of these we may term the *natural* state, the latter the *transitional*.

Society may be said to be in its *natural* state, when worldly power, and moral influence, are habitually and undisputedly exercised by the fittest persons whom the existing state of society affords. Or, to be more explicit; when on the one hand, the temporal, or, as the French would say, the *material* interests of the community, are managed by those of its members who possess the greatest capacity for such management; and on the other hand, those whose opinions the people follow, whose feelings they imbibe, and who practically and by common consent, perform, no matter under what original title, the office of thinking for the people, are persons better qualified than any others whom the civilization of the age and country affords to think and judge rightly and usefully.

In these circumstances the people, although they may at times be unhappy and consequently discontented, habitually acquiesce in the law and institutions which they live under, and seek for relief through those institutions and not in defiance of them. Individual ambition struggles to ascend by no other paths than those which the law recognizes and allows. The ruling powers have no immediate interest in counteracting the progress of civilization; society is either stationary, or moves onward solely in those directions in which its progress brings it into no collision with the established order of things.

Society may be said to be in its *transitional* state, when it contains other persons fitter for worldly power and moral influence than those who have hitherto enjoyed them: when worldly power, and the greatest existing capacity for world affairs, are no longer united but severed; and when the authority which sets the opinions and forms the feelings of those who are not accustomed to think for themselves, does not exist at all, or, existing, resides anywhere but in the most cultivated intellects, and the most exalted characters, of the age.

When this is the posture of affairs, society has either entered or is on the point of entering into a state in which there are no established doctrines; in which the world of opinions is a mere chaos; and in which, as to worldly affairs, whosoever is dissatisfied with one thing or for any reason, flies at once to an alteration in the conditions of worldly power, as a means for obtaining something which would remove what he deems the cause of his dissatisfaction.

And this continues until a moral and social revolution (or it may be, a series of such) has replaced worldly power and moral influence in the hands of the most competent: when society is once more in its natural state, and resumes its onward progress, at the point where it was stopped before by the social system which it has shivered.

8 *Democracy and Government*

(*London Review* I and II, 1835;
reprinted as Appendix in *Dissertations and Discussions*
Vol. 1, 1859.[10])

From the principle of the necessity of identifying the interest of the government with that of the people, most of the practical maxims of a representative government are corollaries. All popular institutions are means towards rendering the identity of interest more complete. We say *more* complete, because (and this it is important to remark) perfectly complete it can never be. An approximation is all that is, in the nature of things, possible. By pushing to its utmost extent the accountability of governments to the people, you indeed take away from them the power of prosecuting their own interests at the expense of the people by force, but you leave to them the whole range and compass of fraud. An attorney is accountable to his client, and removable at his client's pleasure; but we should scarcely say that his interest is identical with that of his client. When the accountability is perfect, the interest of rulers approximates more and more to identity with that of the people, in proportion as the people are more enlightened. The identity would be perfect, only if the people were so wise, that it should no longer be practicable to employ deceit as an instrument of government; a point of advancement only one stage below that at which they could do without government altogether; at least, without force, and penal sanctions, not (of course) without guidance and organized co-operation.

Identification of interest between the rulers and the ruled, being therefore, in a literal sense, impossible to be realized, ought not to be spoken of as a condition which a government must absolutely fulfil; but as an end to be incessantly aimed at, and approximated to as nearly as circumstances render possible, and as is compatible with the regard due to other ends. For this identity of interest, even if it were wholly attainable, not being the sole requisite of good government, expediency may require that we should sacrifice some portion of it, or (to speak more precisely) content ourselves with a somewhat less approximation to it than might possibly be attainable, for the sake of some other end.

The only end, liable occasionally to conflict with that which we have been insisting on, and at all comparable to it in importance – the only other condition essential to good government – is this: That it be government by a select body, not by the public collectively: That political questions be not decided by an appeal, either direct or indirect, to the judgment or will of an uninstructed mass, whether of gentlemen or of clowns; but by the deliberately formed opinions of a comparatively few, specially educated for the task. This is an element of good government which has existed, in a greater or less degree, in some aristocracies, though unhappily not in our own; and has been the cause of whatever reputation for prudent and skilful administration those governments have enjoyed. It has seldom been found in any aristocracies but those which were avowedly such. Aristocracies in the guise of monarchies (such as those of England and France) have very generally been aristocracies of idlers; while the others (such as Rome, Venice, and Holland) might partially be considered as aristocracies of experienced and laborious men. Of all modern governments, however, the one by which this excellence is possessed in the most eminent degree is the government of Prussia – a most powerfully and strongly organized aristocracy of the most highly-educated men in the kingdom. The British government in India partakes (with considerable modifications) of the same character.

When this principle has been combined with other fortunate circumstances, and particularly (as in Prussia) with circumstances rendering the popularity of the government almost a necessary condition of its security, a very considerable degree of good government has occasionally been produced, without any express accountability to the people. Such fortunate circumstances, however, are seldom to be reckoned upon. But though the principle of government by persons specially brought up to it will not suffice to produce good government, good government cannot be had without it; and the grand difficulty in politics will for a long time be, how best to conciliate the two great elements on which good government depends; to combine the greatest amount of the advantage derived from the independent judgment of a specially instructed few, with the greatest degree of the security for rectitude of purpose derived from rendering those few responsible to the many.

What is necessary, however, to make the two ends perfectly reconcilable, is a smaller matter than might at first sight be supposed. It is not necessary that the many should themselves be perfectly wise; it is sufficient if they be duly sensible of the value of superior wisdom. It is sufficient if they be aware, that the majority of political questions turn upon considerations of which they, and all persons not trained for the purpose, must necessarily be very imperfect judges; and that their judgment must in general be exercised rather upon the characters and talents of the persons whom they appoint to decide these questions for them, than upon the questions themselves. They would then select as their representatives those whom the general voice of the instructed pointed out as the *most* instructed; and would retain them, so long as no symptom was manifested in their conduct, of being under the influence of interests or of feelings at variance with the public welfare. This implies no greater wisdom in the people than the very ordinary wisdom of knowing what things they are and are not sufficient judges of. If the bulk of any nation possess a fair share of this wisdom, the argument for universal suffrage, so far as respects that people, is irresistible; for the experience of ages, and especially of all great national emergencies, bears out the assertion, that whenever the multitude are really alive to the necessity of superior intellect, they rarely fail to distinguish those who possess it.

The idea of a rational democracy is, not that the people themselves govern, but that they have security for good government. This security they cannot have by any other means than by retaining in their own hands the ultimate control. If they renounce this, they give themselves up to tyranny. A governing class not accountable to the people are sure, in the main, to sacrifice the people to the pursuit of separate interests and inclinations of their own. Even their feelings of morality, even their ideas of excellence, have reference, not to the good of the people, but to their own good: their very virtues are class virtues – their noblest acts of patriotism and self-devotion are but the sacrifice of their private interests to the interests of their class. The heroic public virtue of a Leonidas was quite compatible with the existence of Helots. In no government will the interests of the people be the object, except where the people are able to dismiss their rulers as soon as the devotion of those rulers to the interests of the people becomes questionable. But this is the only fit use to be made of popular power. Provided good intentions can be secured, the best government (need it be said?) must be the government of the wisest, and these must always be a few. The people ought to be the masters, but they are masters who must employ servants more skilful than themselves: like a ministry when they employ a military commander, or the military commander when he employs an army surgeon. When the minister ceases to confide in the commander, he dismisses him and appoints another; but he does not send him instructions when and where to fight. He holds him responsible only for intentions and for results. The people must do the same. This does not render the control of the people nugatory. The control of a government over the commander of an army is not nugatory. A man's control over his physician is not nugatory, though he does not direct his physician what medicine to administer.

But in government, as in everything else, the danger is, lest those who can do whatever they will, may will to do more than is for their ultimate interest. The interest of the people is, to choose for their rulers the most instructed and the ablest persons who can be found; and having done so, to allow them to exercise their knowledge and ability for the good of the people, under the check of the freest discussion and the most unreserved censure, but with the least possible direct interference of their constituents – as long as it *is* the good of the people, and not some private end, that they are aiming at. A democracy thus administered would unite all the good qualities ever possessed by any government. Not only would its ends be good, but its means would be as well chosen as the wisdom of the age would allow; and the omnipotence of the majority would be exercised through the agency and according to the judgment of an enlightened minority, accountable to the majority in the last resort.

But it is not possible that the constitution of the democracy itself should provide adequate security for its being understood and administered in this spirit. This rests with the good sense of the people themselves. If the people can remove their rulers for one thing, they can for another. That ultimate control, without which they cannot have security for good government, may, if they please, be made the means of themselves interfering in the government, and making their legislators mere delgates for carrying into execution the preconceived judgment of the majority. If the people do this, they mistake their interest; and such a government, though better than most aristocracies, is not the kind of democracy which wise men desire.

Some persons, and persons too whose desire for enlightened government cannot be questioned, do not take so serious a view of this perversion of the true idea of an enlightened democracy. They say, it is well that the many should evoke all political questions to their own tribunal, and decide them according to their own judgment, because then philosophers will be compelled to enlighten the multitude, and render them capable of appreciating their more profound views. No one can attach greater value than we do to this consequence of popular government, so far as we believe it capable of being realized; and the argument would be irresistible, if, in order to instruct the people, all that is requisite were to will it; if it were only the *discovery* of political truths which required study and wisdom, and the evidences of them when discovered could be made apparent at once to any person of common sense, as well educated as every individual in the community might and ought to be. But the fact is not so. Many of the truths of politics (in political economy, for instance) are the result of a concatenation of propositions, the very first steps of which no one who has not gone through a course of study is prepared to concede; there are others, to have a complete perception of which requires much meditation and experience of human nature. How will philosophers bring these home to the perceptions of the multitude? Can they enable common sense to judge of science, or inexperience of experience? Every one who has even crossed the threshold of political philosophy knows, that on many of its questions the false view is greatly the most plausible; and a large portion of its truths are, and must always remain, to all but those who have specially studied them, paradoxes; as contrary, in appearance, to common sense, as the proposition that the earth moves round the sun. The multitude will never believe those truths, until tendered to them from an authority in which they have as unlimited confidence as they have in the unanimous voice of astronomers on a question of astronomy. That they should have no such confidence at present is no discredit to them; for where are the persons who are entitled to it? But we are well satisfied that it will be given, as soon as knowledge shall have made sufficient progress among the instructed classes themselves, to produce something like a general agreement in their opinions on the leading points of moral and political doctrine. Even now, on those points on which the instructed classes are agreed, the uninstructed have generally adopted their opinions.

9 *M. de Tocqueville on Democracy in America*

(*Edinburgh Review* LXXII, 1840; reprinted in *Dissertations and Discussions* Vol. II, 1859.)

It has been the rare fortune of M. de Tocqueville's book to have achieved an easy triumph, both over the indifference of our at once busy and indolent public to profound speculation, and over the particular obstacles which oppose the reception of speculations from a foreign, and, above all, from a French source. There is some ground for the remark often made upon us by foreigners, that the character of our national intellect is insular. The general movement of the European mind sweeps past us without our being drawn into it, or even looking sufficiently at it to discover in what direction it is tending; and, if we had not a tolerably rapid original movement of our own, we should long since have been left in the distance. The French language is almost universally cultivated on this side of the Channel; a flood of human beings perpetually ebbs and flows between London and Paris; national prejudices and animosities are becoming numbered among the things that were; yet the revolution which has taken place in the tendencies of French thought, which has changed the character of the higher literature of France, and almost that of the French language, seems hitherto, as far as the English public are concerned, to have taken place in vain. At a time when the prevailing tone of French speculation is one of exaggerated reaction against the doctrines of the eighteenth century, French philosophy, with us, is still synonymous with Encyclopedism. The Englishmen may almost be numbered who are aware that France has produced any great names in prose literature since Voltaire and Rousseau; and while modern history has been receiving a new aspect from the labours of men who are not only among the profoundest thinkers, but the clearest and most popular writers of their age, even those of their works which are expressly dedicated to the history of our own country, remain mostly untranslated, and in almost all cases unread.

To this general neglect M. de Tocqueville's book forms, however, as we have already said, a brilliant exception. Its reputation was as sudden, and is as extensive, in this country as in France, and in that large part of Europe which receives its opinions from France. The progress of political dissatisfaction, and the comparisons made between the fruits of a popular constitution on one side of the Atlantic, and of a mixed government with a preponderating aristocratic element on the other, had made the working of American institutions a party question. For many years, every book of travels in America had been a party pamphlet, or had at least fallen among partisans, and been pressed into the service of one party or of the other. When, therefore, a new book, of a grave and imposing character, on Democracy in America, made its appearance even on the other side of the British Channel, it was not likely to be overlooked, or to escape an attempt to convert it to party purposes. If ever political writer had reason to believe that he had laboured successfully to render his book incapable of such a use, M. de Tocqueville was entitled to think so. But though his theories are of an impartiality without example, and his practical conclusions lean towards Radicalism, some of his phrases are susceptible of a Tory application. One of these is 'the tyranny of the majority.' This phrase was forthwith adopted into the Conservative dialect, and trumpeted by Sir Robert Peel in his Tamworth oration, when, as booksellers' advertisements have since frequently reminded us, he 'earnestly requested the perusal' of the book by all and each of his audience. And we believe it has since been the opinion of the country gentlemen that M. de Tocqueville is one of the pillars of Conservatism, and his book a definitive demolition of America and of Democracy. The error has done more good than the truth would perhaps have done; since the result is, that the English public now know and read the first philosophical book ever written on Democracy, as it manifests itself in modern society; a book, the essential doctrines of which it is not likely that any future speculations will subvert, to whatever degree they may modify them; while its spirit, and the general mode in which it treats its subject, constitute it the beginning of a new era in the scientific study of politics.

The importance of M. de Tocqueville's speculations is not to be estimated by the opinions which he had adopted, be these true or false. The value of his work is less in the conclusions, than in the mode of arriving at them. He has applied to the greatest question in the art and science of government, those principles and methods of philosophizing to which mankind are indebted for all the advances made by modern times in the other branches of the study of nature. It is not risking too much to affirm of these volumes, that they contain the first analytical inquiry into the influence of democracy. For the first time, that phenomenon is treated of as something which, being a reality in nature, and no mere mathematical or metaphysical abstraction, manifests itself by innumerable properties, not by some one only; and must be looked at in many aspects before it can be made the subject even of that modest and conjectural judgment, which is alone attainable respecting a fact at once so great and so new. Its consequences are by no means to be comprehended in one single description, nor in one summary verdict of approval or condemnation. So complicated and endless are their ramifications, that he who sees furthest into them will longest hesitate before finally pronouncing whether the good or the evil of its influence, on the whole, preponderates.

M. de Tocqueville has endeavoured to ascertain and discriminate the various properties and tendencies of Democracy; the separate relations in which it stands towards the different interests of society, and the different moral and social requisites of human nature. In the investigation he has left much undone, as who could possibly avoid? and much which will be better done by those who come after him, and build upon his foundations. But he has earned the double honour of being the first to make the attempt; and of having done more towards the success of it than probably will ever again be done by any one individual. His method is, as that of a philosopher on such a subject must be – a combination of deduction with induction: his evidences are laws of human nature, on the one hand; the example of America and France, and other modern nations, so far as applicable, on the other. His conclusions never rest on either species of evidence alone; whatever he classes as an effect of Democracy, he has both ascertained to exist in those countries in which the state of society is democratic, and has also succeeded in connecting with Democracy by deductions *a priori,* showing that such would naturally be its influences upon beings constituted as mankind are, and placed in a world such as we know ours to be. If this be not the true Baconian and Newtonian method applied to society and government; if any better, or even any other be possible, M. de Tocqueville would be the first to say, *candidus imperti*; if not, he is entitled to say to political theorists, whether calling themselves philosophers or practical men, *his utere mecum.*

That part of 'Democracy in America' which was first published, professes to treat of the political effects of Democracy; the second (published only this year) is devoted to its influence upon society in the widest sense; upon the relations of private life, upon intellect, morals, and the habits and modes of feeling which constitute national character. The last is both a newer and a more difficult subject of enquiry than the first; there are fewer who are competent, or who will even think themselves competent, to judge M. de Tocqueville's conclusions. But, we believe, no one, in the least entitled to an opinion, will refuse to him the praise of having probed the subject to a depth which had never before been sounded; of having carried forward the controversy into a wider and a loftier region of thought; and pointed out many questions essential to the subject which had not been before attended to; – questions which he may or may not have solved, but of which, in any case, he has greatly facilitated the solution.

The comprehensiveness of M. de Tocqueville's views, and the impartiality of his feelings, have not led him into the common infirmity of those who see too many sides to a question, that of thinking them all equally important. He is able to arrive at a decided opinion. Nor has the more extensive range of considerations embraced in his Second Part, affected practically the general conclusions which resulted from his First. They may be stated as follows: – That Democracy, in the modern world, is inevitable; and that it is, on the whole, desirable; but desirable only under certain conditions, and those conditions capable, by human care and foresight, of being realized, but capable also of being missed. The progress and ultimate ascendency of the democratic principle has, in his eyes, the character of a law of nature. He thinks it an inevitable result of the tendencies of a progressive civilisation; by which expressions he by no means intends to imply either praise or censure. No human effort, no accident even, unless one which should throw back civilisation itself, can avail, in his opinion, to defeat, or even very considerably to retard, this progress. But though the fact itself appears to him removed from human control, its salutary or baneful consequences do not. Like other great powers of nature, the tendency, though it cannot be counteracted, may be guided to good. Man cannot turn back the rivers to their source; but it rests with himself whether they shall fertilize or lay waste his fields. Left to its spontaneous course, with nothing done to prepare before it that set of circumstances under which it can exist with safety, and to fight against its worse, by an apt employment of its better peculiarities, the probable effects of Democracy upon human well-being, and upon whatever is best and noblest in human character, appear to M. de Tocqueville extremely formidable. But with as much of wise effort devoted to the purpose as it is not irrational to hope for, most of what is mischievous in its tendencies may, in his opinion, be corrected, and its natural capacities of good so far strengthened and made use of, as to leave no cause for regret in the old state of society, and enable the new one to be contemplated with calm contentment, if without exultation.

It is necessary to observe that, by Democracy, M. de Tocqueville does not, in general, mean any particular form of government. He can conceive a Democracy under an absolute monarch. Nay, he entertains no small dread, lest, in some countries, it should actually appear in that form. By Democracy M. de Tocqueville understands equality of conditions; the absence of all aristocracy, whether constituted by political privileges, or by superiority in individual importance and social power. It is towards Democracy in this sense, towards equality between man and man, that he conceives society to be irresistibly tending. Towards Democracy in the other, and more common sense, it may or may not be travelling. Equality of conditions tends naturally to produce a popular government, but not necessarily. Equality may be equal freedom or equal servitude. America is the type of the first; France, he thinks, is in danger of falling into the second. The latter country is in the condition which, of all that civilized societies are liable to, he regards with the greatest alarm – a democratic state of society without democratic institutions. For, in democratic institutions, M. de Tocqueville sees not an aggravation but a corrective of the most serious evils incident to a democratic state of society. No one is more opposed than he is to that species of democratic radicalism which would admit at once to the highest of political franchises, untaught masses who have not yet been experimentally proved fit even for the lowest. But the ever increasing intervention of the people, and of all classes of the people, in their own affairs, he regards as a cardinal maxim in the modern art of government; and he believes that the nations of civilized Europe, though not all equally advanced, are all advancing, towards a condition in which there will be no distinctions of political rights, no great or very permanent distinctions of hereditary wealth; when, as there will remain no classes nor individuals capable of making head against the government – unless all are, and are fit to be alike citizens – all will, erelong, be equally slaves.

The opinion, that there is this irresistible tendency to equality of conditions, is perhaps, of all the leading doctrines of the book, that which most stands in need of confirmation to English readers. M. de Tocqueville devotes but little space to the elucidation of it. To French readers the historical retrospect upon which it rests is familiar; and facts known to every one establish its truth so far as relates to that country. But to the English public, who have less faith in irresistible tendencies, and who, while they require for every political theory a historical basis, are far less accustomed to link together the events of history in a connected chain, the proposition will hardly seem to be sufficiently made out. Our author's historical argument is, however, deserving of their attention.

> 'Let us recollect the situation of France seven hundred years ago, when the territory was divided amongst a small number of families, who were the owners of the soil and the rulers of the inhabitants: the right of governing descended with the family inheritance from generation to generation; force was the only means by which man could act on man; and landed property was the sole source of power.
>
> 'Soon, however, the political power of the clergy was founded, and began to extend itself: the clergy opened its ranks to all classes, to the poor and the rich, the villein and the lord; equality penetrated into the government through the church, and the being who as a serf must have vegetated in perpetual bondage, took his place as a priest in the midst of nobles, and not infrequently above the heads of kings.
>
> 'The different relations of men became more complicated and more numerous as society gradually became more stable and more civilized. Thence the want of civil

laws was felt; and the order of legal functionaries soon rose from the obscurity of the tribunals and their dusty chambers, to appear at the court of the monarch, by the side of the feudal barons in their ermine and their mail.

'Whilst the kings were ruining themselves by their great enterprises, and the nobles exhausting their resources by private wars, the lower orders were enriching themselves by commerce. The influence of money began to be perceptible in state affairs. The transactions of business opened a new road to power, and the financier rose to a state of political influence in which he was at once flattered and despised.

'Gradually the spread of mental acquirements, and the increasing taste for literature and the arts, opened chances of success to talent; knowledge became a means of government, intelligence became a social power, and the man of letters took a part in the affairs of the state.

'The value attached to the privileges of birth decreased in the exact proportion in which new paths were struck out to advancement. In the eleventh century nobility was beyond all price; in the thirteenth it might be purchased; it was conferred for the first time in 1270; and equality was thus introduced into the government through aristocracy itself.

'In the course of these seven hundred years, it sometimes happened that, in order to resist the authority of the crown, or to diminish the power of their rivals, the nobles granted a certain share of political rights to the people. Or, more frequently, the king permitted the inferior orders to enjoy a degree of power, with the intention of lowering the aristocracy.

'As soon as land was held on any other than a feudal tenure, and personal property began in its turn to confer influence and power, every improvement which was introduced in commerce or manufactures was a fresh element of the equality of conditions. Henceforward every new discovery, every new want which it engendered, and every new desire which craved satisfaction, was a step towards the universal level. The taste for luxury, the love of war, the sway of fashion, the most superficial as well as the deepest passions of the human heart, co-operated to enrich the poor and to impoverish the rich.

'From the time when the exercise of the intellect became a source of strength and of wealth, it is impossible not to consider every addition to science, every fresh truth, every new idea, as a germ of power placed within the reach of the people. Poetry, eloquence, and memory, the grace of wit, the glow of imagination, the depth of thought, and all the gifts which are bestowed by Providence without respect of persons, turned to the advantage of the democracy and even when they were in the possession of its adversaries, they still served its cause by throwing into relief the natural greatness of man; its conquests spread, therefore, with those of civilisation and knowledge; and literature became an arsenal, where the poorest and the weakest could always find weapons to their hand

'In perusing the pages of our history, we shall scarcely meet with a single great event, in the lapse of seven hundred years, which has not turned to the advantage of equality.

'The Crusades and the wars with the English decimated the nobles and divided their possessions; the erection of corporate towns introduced an element of democratic liberty into the bosom of feudal monarchy; the invention of fire-arms equalized the villein and the noble on the field of battle; printing opened the same resources to the minds of all classes; the post was established so as to bring the same information to the door of the poor man's cottage and to the gate of the palace; and Protestantism proclaimed that all men are alike able to find the road to heaven. The discovery of America offered a thousand new paths to fortune, and placed riches and power within the reach of the adventurous and the obscure.

'It we examine what has happened in France at intervals of fifty years, beginning with the eleventh century, we shall invariably perceive that a twofold revolution has taken place in the state of society. The noble has gone down on the social ladder, and the *roturier* has gone up; the one descends as the other rises. Every half century brings them nearer to each other.

'Nor is this phenomenon at all peculiar to France. Whithersoever we turn our eyes, we witness the same continual revolution throughout the whole of Christendom.

'Every where the various occurrences of national existence have turned to the advantage of democracy; all men have aided it by their exertions: those who have intentionally laboured in its cause, and those who have served it unwittingly; those who have fought for it, and those who have declared themselves its opponents, have all been driven along in the same track, have all laboured to one end, some ignorantly and some unwillingly; all have been blind instruments in the hands of God.

'The gradual development of the equality of conditions is therefore a providential fact, and possesses all the characteristics of a Divine decree: it is universal, it is durable, it constantly eludes all human interference, and all events as well as all men contribute to its progress.

'Would it be wise to imagine that a social impulse which dates from so far back can be checked by the efforts of a generation? Is it credible that the democracy which has annihilated the feudal system, and vanquished kings, will respect the citizen and the capitalists? Will it stop now that it is grown so strong, and its adversaries so weak?

'It is not necessary that God himself should speak in order to disclose to us the unquestionable signs of his will. We can discern them in the habitual course of nature, and in the invariable tendency of events.

'The Christian nations of our age seem to me to present a most alarming spectacle. The impulse which is bearing them along is so strong that it cannot be stopped, but it is not yet so rapid that it cannot be guided. Their fate is in their hands; yet a little while and it may be so no longer.' – (*Introduction to the First Part.**)

That such has been the actual course of events in modern history, nobody can doubt, and as truly in England as in France. Of old, every proprietor of land was sovereign over its inhabitants, while the cultivators could not call even their bodily powers their own. It was by degrees only, and in a succession of ages, that their personal emancipation was effected, and their labour became theirs to sell for whatever they could obtain for it. They became the rich men's equals in the eye of the law; but the rich had still the making of the law, and the administering of it; and the equality was at first little more than nominal. The poor, however, could now acquire property; the path was open to them to quit their own class for a higher; their rise even to a considerable station, gradually became a common occurrence; and to those who acquired a large fortune, the other powers and privileges of aristocracy were successively opened, until hereditary honours have become less a power in themselves, than a symbol and ornament of great riches. While individuals thus continually rose from the mass, the mass itself multiplied and strengthened; the towns obtained a voice in public affairs; the many, in the aggregate, became even in property more and more a match for the few; and the nation became a power, distinct from the small number of individuals who once disposed even of the crown, and determined all public affairs at their pleasure. The Reformation was the dawn of the government of public opinion. Even at that early period, opinion was not formed by the higher classes exclusively; and while the publicity of all state transactions, the liberty of petition and public discussion, the press – and of late, above all, the periodical press – have rendered public opinion more and more the supreme power, the

* In this, and our other extracts, we have followed generally, though not implicitly, Mr Reeve's translation. Though not always unexceptionable, it is spirited, and sometimes felicitous.

same causes have rendered the formation of it less and less dependent upon the initiative of the higher ranks. Even the direct participation of the people at large in the government had, in various ways, been greatly extended, before the political events of the last few years, when democracy has given so signal a proof of its progress in society, by the inroads it has been able to make into the political constitution. And in spite of the alarm which has been taken by the possessors of large property, who are far more generally opposed than they had been within the present generation to any additional strengthening of the popular element in the House of Commons, there is at this moment a much stronger party for a further parliamentary reform, than many good observers thought there was, twelve years ago, for that which has already taken place.

But there is a surer mode of deciding the point than any historical retrospect. Let us look at the powers which are even now at work in society itself.

To a superficial glance at the condition of our own country, nothing can seem more unlike any tendency to equality of condition. The inequalities of property are apparently greater than in any former period of history. Nearly all the land is parcelled out in great estates, among comparatively few families; and it is not the large but the small properties which are in process of extinction. A hereditary and titled nobility, more potent by their vast possessions than by their social precedency, are constitutionally and really one of the great powers in the state. To form part of their order is what every ambitious man aspires to, as the crowning glory of a successful career. The passion for equality of which M. de Tocqueville speaks, almost as if it were the great moral lever of modern times, is hardly known in this country even by name. On the contrary, all ranks seem to have a passion for inequality. The hopes of every person are directed to rising in the world, not to pulling the world down to him. The greatest enemy of the political conduct of the House of Lords, submits to their superiority of rank as he would to the ordinances of nature; and often thinks any amount of toil and watching repaid by a nod of recognition from one of their number.

We have put the case as strongly as it could be put by an adversary, and have stated as facts some things which, if they have been facts, are giving visible signs that they will not always be so. If we look back even twenty years, we shall find that the popular respect for the higher classes is by no means the thing it was; and although all who are rising wish for the continuance of advantages which they themselves hope to share, there are among those who do not expect to rise, increasing indications that a levelling spirit is abroad, and political discontents, in whatever manner originating, show an increasing tendency to take that shape. But it is the less necessary to dwell upon these things, as we shall be satisfied with making out, in respect to the tendency to equality in England, much less that M. de Tocqueville contends for. We do not maintain that the time is drawing near when there will be no distinction of classes; but we do contend that the power of the higher classes, both in government and in society, is diminishing; while that of the middle and even the lower classes is increasing, and likely to increase.

The constituent elements of political importance are property, intelligence, and the power of combination. In every one of these elements, is it the higher classes, or the other portion of society, that have lately made and are continuing to make the most rapid advances?

Even with regard to the element of property, there cannot be room for more than a momentary doubt. The class who are rich by inheritance, are so far from augmenting their fortunes, that it is much if they can be said to keep them up. A territorial aristocracy always live up to their means—generally beyond them. Our own is no exception to the rule; and as their control over the taxes becomes every day more restricted, and the liberal professions more overcrowded, they are condemned more and more to bear the burden of their own large families, which is no easy burden; and at the same time to leave to the heir the means of keeping up, without becoming embarrassed, the old family establishments. It is matter of notoriety how severely the difficulty of providing for younger sons is felt even in the highest rank; and that, as a provision for daughters, alliances are now courted which would not have been endured a generation ago. The additions to the 'money-power' of the higher ranks, consist of the riches of the *novi homines* who are continually aggregated to that class from among the merchants and manufacturers, and occasionally from the professions. But many of these are merely successors to the impoverished owners of the land they buy; and the fortunes of others are taken, in the way of marriage, to pay off the mortgages of older families. Even with these allowances, no doubt the number of wealthy persons is steadily on the increase; but what is this to the accumulation of capitals and growth of incomes in the hands of the middle class? It is that class which furnishes all the accessions to the aristocracy of wealth; and for one who makes a large fortune, fifty acquire, without exceeding, a moderate competency, and leave their children to work, like themselves, at the labouring oar.

In point of intelligence, it can still less be affirmed that the higher classes maintain the same proportional ascendency as of old. They have shared with the rest of the world in the diffusion of information. They have improved, like all other classes, in the decorous virtues. Their humane feelings and refined tastes form in general a striking contrast to the coarse habits of the same class a few generations ago. But it would be difficult to point out what new idea in speculation, what invention or discovery in the practical arts, what useful institution, or what permanently valuable book, Great Britain has owed for the last hundred years to her hereditary aristocracy, titled or untitled; – what great public enterprise, what important national movement in religion or politics, those classes have originated, or in which they have so much as taken the principal share. Considered in respect to active energies and laborious habits, to the stirring qualities which fit men for playing a considerable part in the affairs of mankind, few will say that our aristocracy have not deteriorated. It is, on the other hand, one of the commonplaces of the age, that knowledge and intelligence are spreading, in a degree which was formerly thought impossible, to the lower, and down even to the lowest rank. And this is a fact, not accomplished, but in the mere dawn of its accomplishment and which has shown hitherto but a slight promise of its future fruits. It is easy to scoff at the kind of intelligence which is thus diffusing itself; but it is intelligence still. The knowledge which is power, is not the highest description of knowledge only: any knowledge which gives the habit of forming an opinion, and the capacity of expressing that opinion, constitutes a political power; and if combined with the capacity and habit of acting in concert, a formidable one.

It is in this last element, the power of combined action, that the progress of the Democracy has been the most gigantic. What combination can do, has been shown by an experiment of now many years' duration, among a people the most backward in civilisation (thanks to English misgovernment,) between the Vistula and the Pyrenees. Even on this side of the Irish Channel we have seen something of what could be done by Political Unions, Antislavery Societies, and the like; to say nothing of the less advanced, but already powerful organization of the working classes, the progress of which has been suspended only by the temporary failure arising from the manifest impracticability of its present objects. And these various associations are not the machinery of democratic combination, but the occasional weapons which that spirit forges as it needs them. The real Political Unions of England are the Newspapers. It is these which tell every person what all other persons are feeling, and in what manner they are ready to act: it is by these that the people learn, it may truly be said, their own wishes, and through these that they declare them. The Newspapers and the Railroads are solving the problem of bringing the democracy of England to vote, like that of Athens, simultaneously in one *agora*; and the same agencies are rapidly effacing those local distinctions which rendered one part of our population strangers to another; and are making us more than ever (what is the first condition of a powerful public opinion) a homogeneous people. If America has been said to prove that in an extensive country a popular government may exist, England seems destined to afford the proof, that after a certain stage in civilisation it must; for as soon as the numerically stronger have the same advantages, in means of combination and celerity of movement, as the smaller number, they are the masters; and, except by their permission, no government can any longer exist.

It may be said, doubtless, that though the aristocratic class may be no longer in the ascendant, the power by which it is succeeded is not that of the numerical majority; that the middle class in this country is as little in danger of being outstripped by the democracy below, as of being kept down by the aristocracy above; and that there can be no difficulty for that class, aided as it would be by the rich, in making head by its property, intelligence, and power of combination, against any possible growth of those elements of importance in the inferior classes; and in excluding the mass of mere manual labourers from any share in political rights, unless such a restricted and subordinate one as may be found compatible with the complete ascendency of property.

We are disposed partially to agree in this opinion. Universal suffrage is never likely to exist where the majority are *prolétaires*; and we are not unwilling to believe that a labouring class in abject poverty, like the greatest part of our rural population, or which expends its surplus earnings in gin or in waste, like so much of the better paid population of the towns, may be kept politically in subjection, and that the middle classes are safe from the permanent rule of such a body, though perhaps not from its Swing outrages, or Wat Tyler insurrections. But this admission leaves the fact of a tendency towards democracy practically untouched. There is a democracy short of pauper suffrage; the working classes themselves contain a middle, as well as a lowest class. Not to meddle with the *vexata quaestio*, whether the lowest class is or is not improving in condition, it is certain that a larger and larger body of manual labourers are rising above that class, and acquiring at once decent wages and decent habits of conduct. A rapidly increasing multitude of our working people are becoming, in point of condition and habits, what all the American working people are. And if our boasted improvements are of any worth, there must be a growing tendency in society and government to make this condition of the labouring classes the general one. The nation must be most slenderly supplied with wisdom and virtue, if it cannot do something to improve its own physical condition, to say nothing of its moral. It is something gained, that well-meaning persons of all parties now at length profess to have this end in view. But in proportion as it is approached to, in proportion as the working class becomes what all proclaim their desire that it should be – well paid, well taught, and well conducted; in the same proportion will the opinions of that class tell, according to its numbers, upon the affairs of the country. Whatever portion of the class succeeds in thus raising itself, becomes a part of the ruling body; and if the suffrage be necessary to make it so, it will not be long without the suffrage.

Meanwhile, we are satisfied if it be admitted, that the government of England is progressively changing from the government of a few, to the government, not indeed of *the* many, but of many; – from an aristocracy with a popular infusion, to the *régime* of the middle class. To most purposes, in the constitution of modern society, the government of a numerous middle class is democracy. Nay, it not merely *is* democracy, but the only democracy of which there is yet any example; what is called universal suffrage in America arising from the fact that America is *all* middle class; the whole people being in a condition, both as to education and pecuniary means, corresponding to the middle class here. The consequences which we would deduce from this fact will appear presently, when we examine M. de Tocqueville's view of the moral, social, and intellectual influences of democracy. This cannot be done until we have briefly stated his opinions on the purely political branch of the question.

To this part of our task we shall now proceed; with as much conciseness as is permitted by the number and importance of the ideas, which, holding an essential place among the grounds of his general conclusions, have a claim not to be omitted even from the most rapid summary.

We have already intimated that M. de Tocqueville recognises such a thing as a democratic state of society without a democratic government; a state in which the people are all equal, and subjected to one common master, who selects indiscriminately from all of them the instruments of his government. In this sense, as he remarks, the government of the Pasha of Egypt is a specimen of democracy; and to this type (with allowance for difference of civilisation and manners) he thinks that all nations are in danger of approximating, in which the equalization of conditions has made greater progress than the spirit of liberty. Now this he holds to be the condition of France. The kings of France have always been the greatest of levellers; Louis XI, Richelieu, Louis XIV, alike laboured to break the power of the noblesse, and reduce all intermediate classes and bodies to the general level. After them came the Revolution, bringing with it the abolition of hereditary privileges, the emigration and dispossession of half the great landed proprietors, and the subdivision of large fortunes by the revolutionary law of inheritance. While the equalization of conditions was thus rapidly reaching its extreme limits, no corresponding progress of public spirit was taking place in the people at large. No institutions capable of fostering an interest in the details of public affairs were created by the Revolution: it swept away even those which despotism had spared; and if it admitted a portion of the population to a voice in the government, gave it them only on the greatest but rarest occasion – the election of the great council of the state. A political act, to be done only once in a few years, and for which nothing in the daily habits of the citizen has prepared him, leaves his intellect and moral dispositions very much as it found them; and the citizens not being encouraged to take upon themselves collectively that portion of the business of society which had been performed by the privileged classes, the central government easily drew to itself not only the whole local administration, but much of what, in countries like ours, is performed by associations of individuals. Whether the government was revolutionary or counter-revolutionary made no difference; under the one and the other, every thing was done *for* the people, and nothing *by* the people. In France, consequently, the arbitrary power of the magistrate in detail, is almost without limit. And when of late some attempts have been made to associate a portion of the citizens in the management of local affairs, comparatively few have been found, even among those in good circumstances, (any where but in the large towns,) who could be induced willingly to take any part in that management; who, when they had no personal object to gain, felt the public interest sufficiently their own interest, not to grudge every moment which they withdrew from their occupations or pleasures to bestow upon it. With all the eagerness and violence of party contests in France, a nation more passive in the hands of any one who is uppermost does not exist. M. de Tocqueville has no faith in the virtues, nor even in the prolonged existence, of a superficial love of freedom, in the face of a practical habit of slavery; and the question whether the French are to be a free people, depends, in his opinion, upon the possibility of creating a spirit and a habit of local self-government.

M. de Tocqueville sees the principal source and security of American freedom, not so much in the election of President and Congress by popular suffrage, as in the administration of nearly all the business of society by the people themselves. This it is, which, according to him, keeps up the habit of attending to the public interest, not in the gross merely, or on a few momentous occasions, but in its dry and troublesome details. This, too, it is which enlightens the people, which teaches them, by experience, how public affairs must be carried on. The dissemination of public business as widely as possible among the people, is in his opinion, the only means by which they can be fitted for the exercise of any share of power over the legislature, and generally, also, the only means by which they can be led to desire it.

For the particulars of this education of the American people by means of political institutions, we must refer to the work itself; of which it is one of the minor recommendations, that it has never been equalled even as a mere statement and explanation of the institutions of the United States. The general principle to which M. de Tocqueville has given the sanction of his authority, merits more consideration than it has yet received from the professed labourers in the cause of national education. It has often been said, and requires to be repeated still oftener, that books and discourses alone are not education; that life is a problem, not a theorem; that action can only be learned in action. A child learns to write its name only by a succession of trials; and is a man to be taught to use his mind and guide his conduct by mere precept? What can be learned in schools is important, but not all-important. The main branch of the education of human beings is their habitual employment, which must be either their individual vocation, or some matter of general concern, in which they are called to take a part. The private money-getting occupation of almost every one, is more or less a mechanical routine; it brings but few of his faculties into action, while its exclusive pursuit tends to fasten his attention and interest exclusively upon himself, and upon his family as an appendage of himself; – making him indifferent to the public, to the more generous objects and the nobler interests, and, in his inordinate regard for his personal comforts, selfish and cowardly. Balance these tendencies by contrary ones; give him something to do for the public, whether as a vestryman, a juryman, or an elector; and in that degree, his ideas and feelings are taken out of this narrow circle. He becomes acquainted with more varied business, and a larger range of considerations. He is made to feel that besides the interests which separate him from his fellow-citizens, he has interests which connect him with them; that not only the common weal is his weal, but that it partly depends upon his exertions. Whatever might be the case in some other constitutions of society, the spirit of a commercial people will be, we are persuaded, essentially mean and slavish wherever public spirit is not cultivated by an extensive participation of the people in the business of government in detail: nor will the desideratum of a general diffusion of intelligence among either the middle or lower classes, be realized, but by a corresponding dissemination of public functions, and a voice in public affairs.

Nor is this inconsistent with obtaining a considerable share of the benefits (and they are great) of what is called centralization. The principle of local self-government has been undeservedly discredited, by being associated with the agitation against the new poor-law. The most active agency of a central authority in collecting and communicating information, giving advice to the local bodies, and even framing general rules for their observance, is no hinderance, but an aid, to making the local liberties an instrument of educating the people. The existence of such a central agency allows of intrusting to the people themselves, or to local bodies representative of them, many things of too great national importance to be committed unreservedly to the localities, and completes the efficacy of local self-government as a means of instruction, by accustoming the people not only to judge of particular facts, but to understand, and apply, and feel practically the value of, principles. The mode of administration provided for the English poor-laws by the late act, seems to us to be in its general conception almost theoretically perfect. And the extension of a similar mixture of central and local management to several other branches of administration, thereby combining the best fruits of popular intervention with much of the advantage of skilled supervision and traditional experience, would, we believe, be entitled to no mean rank in M. de Tocqueville's list of correctives to the inconveniences of democracy.

In estimating the effects of Democratic Government as distinguished from a Democratic State of Society, M. de Tocqueville assumes the state of circumstances which exists in America; – a popular government in the state, combined with popular local institutions. In such a government he sees great advantages, balanced by no inconsiderable evils.

Among the advantages, one which figures in the foremost rank is that of which we have just spoken, the diffusion of intelligence; the remarkable impulse given by democratic institutions to the active faculties of that portion of the community, who in other circumstances are the most ignorant, passive, and apathetic. These are characteristics of America which strike all travellers. Activity, enterprise, and a respectable amount of information, are not the qualities of a few among the American citizens, nor even of many, but of all. There is no class of persons who are the slaves of habit and routine. Every American will carry on his manufacture, or cultivate his farm, by the newest and best methods applicable to the circumstances of the case. The poorest American understands and can explain the most intricate parts of his country's institutions; can discuss her interests, internal and foreign. Much of this may justly be attributed to the universality of easy circumstances, and to the education and habits which the first settlers in America brought with them; but our author is certainly not wrong in ascribing a certain portion of it to the perpetual exercise of the faculties of every man among the people, through the universal practice of submitting all public questions to his judgment.

> 'It is incontestable that the people frequently conduct public business very ill; but it is impossible that the people should take a part in public business without extending the circle of their ideas, and without quitting the ordinary routine of their mental acquirements. The humblest individual who is called upon to co-operate in the government of society acquires a certain degree of self-respect; and, as he possesses power, minds more enlightened than his own offer him their services. He is canvassed by a multitude of claimants who need his support; and who, seeking to deceive him in a thousand different ways, instruct him in their deceit. He takes a part in political undertakings which did not originate in his own

conception, but which give him a taste for other undertakings. New ameliorations are daily suggested to him in the property which he holds in common with others, and this gives him the desire of improving that property which is peculiarly his own. He is, perhaps, neither happier nor better than those who came before him; but he is better informed and more active. I have no doubt that the democratic institutions of the United States, joined to the physical constitution of the country, are the cause (not the direct, as is so often asserted, but the indirect cause) of the prodigious commercial activity of the inhabitants. It is not engendered by the laws, but it proceeds from habits acquired through participation in making the laws.

'When the opponents of Democracy assert that a single individual performs the functions which he undertakes better than the government of the people at large, it appears to me that they are perfectly right. The government of an individual, supposing an equal degree of instruction on either side, has more constancy, more perseverance, than that of a multitude; more combination in its plans, and more perfection in its details; and is better qualified judiciously to discriminate the characters of the men it employs. If any deny this, they have never seen a democratic government, or have formed their opinion only upon a few instances. It must be conceded, that even when local circumstances and the disposition of the people allow democratic institutions to subsist, they never display a regular and methodical system of government. Democratic liberty is far from accomplishing all the projects it undertakes with the skill of an adroit despotism. It frequently abandons them before they have borne their fruits, or risks them when the consequences may prove dangerous; but in the end it produces greater results than any absolute government. It does fewer things well, but it does a greater number of things. Not what is done by a democratic government, but what is done under a democratic government by private agency, is really great. Democracy does not confer the most skilful kind of government upon the people, but it produces that which the most skilful governments are frequently unable to awaken, namely, an all-pervading and restless activity – a superabundant force – an energy which is never seen elsewhere, and which may, under favourable circumstances, beget the most amazing benefits. These are the true advantages of democracy.' – (Reeve, vol. ii. chap. 2.)

The other great political advantage which our author ascribes to Democracy requires less illustration, because it is more obvious, and has been oftener treated of; that the course of legislation and administration tends always in the direction of the interest of the greater number. Although M. de Tocqueville is far from considering this quality of Democracy as the *panacea* in politics which it has sometimes been supposed to be, he expresses his sense of its importance, if in measured, in no undecided terms. America does not exhibit to us what we see in the best mixed constitutions – the class interests of small minorities wielding the powers of legislation, in opposition both to the general interest and to the general opinion of the community; still less does she exhibit what has been characteristic of most representative governments, and is only gradually ceasing to characterise our own – a standing league of class interests – a tacit compact among the various knots of men who profit by abuses, to stand by one another in resisting reform. Nothing can subsist in America that is not recommended by arguments which, in appearance at least, address themselves to the interest of the many. However frequently, therefore, that interest may be mistaken, the direction of legislation towards it is maintained in the midst of the mistakes; and if a community is so situated or so ordered that it can 'support the transitory action of bad laws, and can await without destruction the result of the *general tendency* of the laws,' that country, in the opinion of M. de Tocqueville, will prosper more under a democratic government than under any other. But, in aristocratic governments, the interest, or at best the honour and glory, of the ruling class, is considered as the public interest; and all that is most valuable to the individuals composing the subordinate classes, is apt to be immolated to that public interest with all the rigour of antique patriotism.

'The men who are intrusted with the direction of public affairs in the United States are frequently inferior, both in point of capacity and of morality, to those whom aristocratic institutions would raise to power. But their interest is identified and confounded with that of the majority of those fellow-citizens. They may frequently be faithless and frequently mistaken, but they will never systematically adopt a line of conduct hostile to the majority; and it is impossible that they should give a dangerous or an exclusive character to the government.

The mal-administration of a democratic magistrate is, moreover, a mere isolated fact, the effects of which do not last beyond the short period for which he is elected. Corruption and incapacity do not act as common interests which may connect men permanently with one another. A corrupt or an incapable magistrate will not concert his measures with another magistrate simply because that individual is corrupt and incapable like himself; and these two men will never unite their endeavours to promote or screen the corruption or inaptitude of their remote posterity. The ambition and the manoeuvres of the one will serve, on the contrary, to unmask the other. The vices of the magistrate in democratic states are usually those of his individual character.

'But, under aristocratic governments, public men are swayed by the interest of their order, which, if it is sometimes blended with the interests of the majority, is frequently distinct from them. This interest is a common and lasting bond which unites them together. It induces them to coalesce, and combine their efforts towards attaining an end which is not always the happiness of the greatest number; and it not only connects the persons in authority with each other, but links them also to a considerable portion of the governed, since a numerous body of citizens belongs to the aristocracy without being invested with official functions. The aristocratic magistrate, therefore, finds himself supported in his own natural tendencies by a portion of society itself, as well as by the government of which he is a member.

'The common object which connects the interest of the magistrates in aristocracies with that of a portion of their contemporaries, identifies it also with future generations of their order. They labour for ages to come as well as for their own time. The aristocratic magistrate is thus urged towards the same point by the passions of those who surround him, by his own, and, I might almost say, by those of his posterity. Is it wonderful that he should not resist? And hence it is that the class spirit often hurries along with it those whom it does not corrupt, and makes them unintentionally fashion society to their own particular ends, and prepare it for their own descendants.' (Reeve, *ibid.*)

These, then, are the advantages ascribed by our author to a democratic government. We are now to speak of its disadvantages.

According to the opinion which is prevalent among the more cultivated advocates of democracy, one of its greatest recommendations is, that, by means of it, the wisest and worthiest are brought to the head of affairs. The people, it is said, have the strongest interest in selecting the right men. It is presumed that they will be sensible of that interest; and, subject to more or less liability of error, will, in the main, succeed in placing a high, if not the highest degree of worth and talent in the highest situations.

M. de Tocqueville is of another opinion. He was forcibly struck with the general want of merit in the members of the American legislatures, and other public functionaries. He accounts for this not solely by the people's incapacity to discriminate merit, but partly also by their indifference to it. He thinks there is little preference for men of superior intellect, little desire to obtain their services for the public; occasionally even a jealousy of them, especially if they be also rich. They, on their part, have still less inclination to seek any such employment. Public offices are little lucrative, confer little power, and offer no guarantee of permanency: almost any other career holds out better pecuniary prospects to a man of ability and enterprise; nor will instructed men stoop to those mean arts, and those compromises of their private opinions, to which their less distinguished competitors willingly resort. The depositaries of power, after being chosen with little regard to merit, are, partly perhaps for that very reason, frequently changed. The rapid return of elections, and even a taste for variety, M. de Tocqueville thinks, on the part of electors, (a taste not unnatural wherever little regard is paid to qualifications,) produces a rapid succession of new men in the legislatures, and in all public posts. Hence, on the one hand, great instability in the laws – every new comer desiring to do something in the short time which he has; while, on the other hand, there is no political *carrière* – statesmanship is not a profession. There is no body of persons educated for public business, pursuing it as their occupation, and who transmit from one to another the results of their experience. There are no traditions, no science or art of public affairs. A functionary knows little, and cares less, about the principles on which his predecessor has acted; and his successor thinks as little about his. Public transactions are therefore conducted with a reasonable share indeed of the common sense and common information which are general in a democratic community, but with little benefit from specific study and experience; without consistent system, long-sighted views, or persevering pursuit of distant objects.

This is likely enough to be a true picture of the American Government, but can scarcely be said to be peculiar to it: there are now few governments remaining, whether representative or absolute, of which something of the same sort might not be said. In no country where the real government resides in the minister, and where there are frequent changes of Ministry, are far-sighted views of policy likely to be acted upon; whether the country be England or France, in the eighteenth century or in the nineteenth.[11] In so far as it is true that there is a deficiency of remarkable merit in the American public men, (and our author allows that there is a large number of exceptions,) the fact may perhaps admit of a less discreditable explanation. America needs very little government. She has no wars, no neighbours, no complicated international relations; no old society with its thousand abuses to reform; no half-fed and untaught millions crying for food and guidance. Society in America requires little but to be let alone. The current affairs which her Government has to transact can seldom demand much more than average capacity; and it may be in the Americans a wise economy, not to pay the price of great talents when common ones will serve their purpose. We make these remarks by way of caution, not of controversy. Like many other parts of our author's doctrines, that of which we are now speaking affords work for a succession of thinkers and of accurate observers, and must in the main depend on future experience to confirm or refute it.

We now come to that one among the dangers of Democracy, respecting which so much has been said, and which our author designates as 'the despotism of the majority.'

It is perhaps the greatest defect of M. de Tocqueville's book, that from the scarcity of examples, his propositions, even when derived from observation, have the air of mere abstract speculations. He speaks of the tyranny of the majority in general phrases, but gives hardly any instances of it, nor much information as to the mode in which it is practically exemplified. The omission was in the present instance the more excusable, as the despotism complained of was, at that time, politically at least, an evil in apprehension more than in sufferance; and he was uneasy rather at the total absence of security against the tyranny of the majority, than at the frequency of its actual exertion.

Events, however, which have occurred since the publication of the First Part of M. de Tocqueville's work, give indication of the shape which tyranny is most likely to assume when exercised by a majority.

It is not easy to surmise any inducements of interest, by which in a country like America, the greater number could be led to oppress the smaller. When the majority and the minority are spoken of as conflicting interests, the rich and the poor are generally meant; but where the rich are content with being rich, and do not claim as such any political privileges, their interest and that of the poor are the same; – complete protection to property, and freedom in the disposal of it, are alike important to both. When, indeed, the poor are so poor that they can scarcely be worse off, respect on their part for rights of property which they cannot hope to share, is never safely to be calculated upon. But where all have property, either in enjoyment or in reasonable hope, and an appreciable chance of acquiring a large fortune; and where every man's way of life proceeds upon the confident assurance that, by superior exertion, he will obtain a superior reward; the importance of inviolability of property is not likely to be lost sight of. It is not affirmed of the Americans that they make laws against the rich, or unduly press upon them in the imposition of taxes. If a labouring class, less happily circumstanced, could prematurely force themselves into influence over our own legislature, there might then be danger – not so much of violations of property, as of undue interference with contracts; unenlightened legislation for the supposed interest of the many; laws founded on mistakes in political economy. A minimum of wages, or a tax on machinery, might be attempted: as silly and as inefficacious attempts might be made to keep up wages by law, as were so long made by the British legislature to keep them down by the same means. We have no wish to see the experiment tried, but we are fully convinced that experience would correct the one error as it has corrected the other, and in the same way; namely, by the completest practical failure. .

It is not from the separate interests, real or imaginary,

of the majority, that minorities are in danger; but from its antipathies of religion, political party, or race: and experience in America seems to confirm what theory rendered probable, that the tyranny of the majority would not take the shape of tyrannical laws, but that of a dispensing power over all laws. The people of Massachusetts passed no law prohibiting Roman Catholic schools, or exempting Protestants from the penalties of incendiarism; they contented themselves with burning the Ursuline convent to the ground, aware that no jury would be found to redress the injury. In the same reliance the people of New York and Philadelphia sacked and destroyed the houses of the Abolitionists, and the schools and churches of their black fellow-citizens, while numbers who took no share in the outrage amused themselves with the sight. The laws of Maryland still prohibit murder and burglary; but in 1812, a Baltimore mob, after destroying the printing office of a newspaper which had opposed the war with England, broke into the prison to which the editors had been conveyed for safety, murdered one of them, left the others for dead; and the criminals were tried and acquitted. In the same city, in 1835, a riot which lasted four days, and the foolish history of which is related in M. Chevalier's 'Letters,' was occasioned by the fraudulent bankruptcy of the Maryland Bank. It is not so much the riots, in such instances, that are deplorable; these might have occurred in any country: – it is the impossibility of obtaining aid from an executive dependent upon the mob, or justice from juries which formed part of it: it is the apathetic cowardly truckling of disapproving lookers-on; almost a parallel to the passive imbecility of the people of Paris, when a handful of hired assassins perpetrated the massacres of September. For where the majority is the sole power, and a power issuing its mandates in the form of riots, it inspires a terror which the most arbitrary monarch often fails to excite. The silent sympathy of the majority may support on the scaffold the martyr of one man's tyranny; but if we would imagine the situation of a victim of the majority itself, we must look to the annals of religious persecution for a parallel.

Yet, neither ought we to forget that even this lawless violence is not so great, because not so lasting, an evil, as tyranny through the medium of the law. A tyrannical law remains; because, so long as it is submitted to, its existence does not weaken the general authority of the laws. But in America, tyranny will seldom use the instrument of law, because among the white population there is no permanent class to be tyrannized over. The subjects of oppression are casual objects of popular resentment, who cannot be reached by law, but only by occasional acts of lawless power; and to tolerate these, if they ever became frequent, would be consenting to live without law. Already in the United States, the spirit of outrage has raised a spirit of resistance to outrage; of moral resistance first, as was to be wished and expected: if that fail, physical resistance will follow. The majority, like other despotic powers, will be taught by experience, that it cannot enjoy both the advantages of civilized society, and the barbarian liberty of taking men's lives and property at its discretion. Let it once be generally understood that minorities will fight, and majorities will be shy of provoking them. The bad government of which there is any permanent danger under modern civilisation, is in the form of bad laws and bad tribunals: government by the *sic volo* either of a king or a mob, belongs to past ages, and can no more exist out of the pale of Asiatic barbarism.

The despotism, therefore, of the majority within the limits of civil life, though a real evil, does not appear to us to be a formidable one. The tyranny which we fear, and which M. de Tocqueville principally dreads, is of another kind – a tyranny not over the body but over the mind.

It is the complaint of M. de Tocqueville, as well as of other travellers in America, that in no country does there exist less independence of thought. In religion, indeed, the varieties of opinion which fortunately prevailed among those by whom the colonies were settled, has produced a toleration in law and in fact extending to the limits of Christianity. If by ill fortune there had happened to be a religion of the majority, the case would probably have been different.

On every other subject, when the opinion of the majority is made up, hardly any one, it is affirmed, dares to be of any other opinion, or at least to profess it. The statements are not clear as to the nature or amount of the inconvenience that would be suffered by any one who presumed to question a received opinion. It seems certain, however, that scarcely any person has that courage; that when public opinion considers a question as settled, no further discussion of it takes place; and that not only nobody dares (what every body may venture upon in Europe) to say any thing disrespectful to the public, or derogatory to its opinions, but that its wisdom and virtue are perpetually celebrated with the most servile adulation and sycophancy.

These considerations, which were much dwelt upon in the author's First Part, are intimately connected with the views promulgated, in his Second, respecting the influence of Democracy on Intellect.

The Americans, according to M. de Tocqueville, not only profess, but carry into practice, on all subjects except the fundamental doctrines of Christianity and Christian ethics, the habit of mind which has been so often inculcated as the one sufficient security against mental slavery – the rejection of authority, and the assertion of the right of private judgment. They regard the traditions of the past merely in the light of materials, and as 'a useful study for doing otherwise and better.' They are not accustomed to look for guidance either to the wisdom of ancestors, or to eminent contemporary wisdom, but require that the grounds on which they act shall be made level to their own comprehension. And, as is natural to those who govern themselves by common sense rather than by science, their cast of mind is altogether unpedantic and practical; they go straight to the end without favour or prejudice towards any set of means, and aim at the substance of things with something like a contempt for form.

From such habits and ways of thinking, the consequence which would be apprehended by some, would be a most licentious abuse of individual independence of thought. The fact proves the reverse. It is impossible, as our author truly remarks, that mankind in general should form all their opinions for themselves: an authority from which they mostly derive them may be rejected in theory, but it always exists in fact. That law above them, which older societies have found in the traditions of antiquity, or in the dogmas of priests or philosophers, the Americans find in the opinions of one another. All being nearly equal in circumstances, and all nearly alike in intelligence and knowledge, the only authority which commands an involuntary deference is that of numbers. The more perfectly each knows himself the equal of every single individual, the more insignificant and helpless he feels against the aggregate mass; and the more incredible it appears to him that the opinion of all the world can possibly be erroneous. 'Faith in public opinion,' says M. de Tocqueville, 'becomes in such countries a species of religion, and the majority its prophet.' The idea that the things which the multitude believe are still disputable, is no longer kept alive by dissentient voices; the right of private judgment, by being extended to the incompetent, ceases to be exercised even by the competent; and speculation becomes possible only within the limits traced, not as of old by the infallibility of Aristotle, but by that of 'our free and enlightened citizens,' or 'our free and enlightened age.'

On the influence of Democracy upon the cultivation of Science and Art, the opinions of M. de Tocqueville are highly worthy of attention. There are many who, partly from theoretic considerations, and partly from the marked absence in America of original efforts in literature, philosophy, or the fine arts, incline to believe that modern Democracy is fatal to them, and that wherever its spirit spreads they will take flight. M. de Tocqueville is not of this opinion. The example of America, as he observes, is not to the purpose, because America is, intellectually speaking, a province of England; – a province in which the great occupation of the inhabitants is making money; because for that they have peculiar facilities, and are therefore, like the people of Manchester or Birmingham, for the most part contented to receive the higher branches of knowledge ready-made from the capital. In a democratic nation, which is also free and generally educated, our author is far from thinking that there will be no public to relish or remunerate the works of science and genius. Although there will be a great shifting of fortunes, and no hereditary body of wealthy persons sufficient to form a class, there will be, he thinks, from the general activity, and the absence of artificial barriers, combined with the inequality of human intelligence, a far greater number of rich individuals (*infiniment plus nombreux*) than in an aristocratic society. There will be, therefore, though not so complete a leisure, yet a leisure extending perhaps to more persons; while from the closer contact and greater mutual intercourse between classes, the love of intellectual pleasures and occupations will spread downward very widely, among those who have not the same advantages of leisure. Moreover, talent and knowledge being, in a democratic society, the only means of rapid improvement in fortune, they will be, in the abstract at least, by no means undervalued: whatever measure of them any person is capable of appreciating, he will also be desirous of possessing. Instead, therefore, of any neglect of science and literature, the eager ambition which is universal in such a state of society, takes that direction as well as others, and the number of those who cultivate these pursuits becomes 'immense.'

It is from this fact – from the more active competition in the products of intellect, and the more numerous public to which they are addressed – M. de Tocqueville deduces the defects with which the products themselves will be chargeable. In the multiplication of their quantity he sees the deterioration of their quality. Distracted by so great a multitude, the public can bestow but a moment's attention on each; they will be adapted, therefore, chiefly for striking at the moment. Deliberate approval, and a duration beyond the hour, become more and more difficult of attainment. What is written for the judgments of a highly instructed few, amidst the abundance of writings may very probably never reach them; and their suffrage, which never gave riches, does not now confer even glory. But the multitude of buyers affords the possibility of great pecuniary success and momentary notoriety for the work which is made up to please at once and to please the many. Literature thus becomes not only a trade, but is carried on by the maxims usually adopted by other trades which live by the number, rather than by the quality of their customers; that much pains need not be bestowed on commodities intended for the general market, and that what is saved in the workmanship may be more profitably expended in self-advertisement. There will thus be an immense mass of third- and fourth-rate productions, and very few first-rate. Even the turmoil and bustle of a society in which every one is striving to get on, is in itself, our author observes, not favourable to meditation. 'Il règne dans le sein de ces nations un petit mouvement incommode, une sorte de roulement incessant des hommes les uns sur les autres, qui trouble et distrait l'esprit sans l'animer et l'élever.' Not to mention that the universal tendency to action, and to rapid action, directs the taste to applications rather than principles, and hasty approximations to truth rather than scientific accuracy in it.

Passing now from the province of intellect to that of Sentiments and Morals, M. de Tocqueville is of opinion that the general softening of manners, and the remarkable growth, in modern times, of humanity and philanthropy, are in great part the effect of the gradual progress of social equality. Where the different classes of mankind are divided by impassable barriers, each may have intense sympathies with his own class, more intense than it is almost possible to have with mankind in general; but those who are far below him in condition are so unlike himself, that he hardly considers them as human beings; and if they are refractory and troublesome, will be unable to feel for them even that kindly interest which he experiences for his more unresisting domestic cattle. Our author cites a well-known passage of Madame de Sévigné's Letters in exemplification of the want of feeling exhibited even by good sort of persons towards those with whom they have no *fellow*-feeling. In America, except towards the slaves, (an exception which proves the rule,) he finds the sentiments of philanthropy and compassion almost universal, accompanied by a general kindness of manner and obligingness of disposition, without much of ceremony and punctilio. As all feel that they are not above the passable need of the good-will and good offices of others, every one is ready to afford his own. The general equality penetrates also into the family relations: there is more intimacy, he thinks, than in Europe, between parents and children, but less, except in the earliest years, of paternal authority, and the filial respect which is founded upon it. These, however, are among the topics which we must omit; as well as the connexion which our author attempts to trace between equality of conditions and strictness of domestic morals, and some other remarks on domestic society in America, which do not appear to us to be of any considerable value.

M. de Tocqueville is of opinion, that one of the tendencies of a democratic state of society is to make every one, in a manner, retire within himself, and concentrate his interests, wishes, and pursuits within his own business and household.

The members of a democratic community are like the sands of the sea-shore, each very minute, and no one adhering to any other. There are no permanent classes, and therefore no *esprit de corps;* few hereditary fortunes, and therefore few local attachments, or outward objects consecrated by family feeling. A man feels little connexion with his neighbours, little with his ancestors, little with his posterity. There are scarcely any ties to connect any two men together, except the common one of country. Now, the love of country is not, in large communities, a passion of spontaneous growth. When a man's country is his town, where his ancestors have lived for generations, of which he knows every inhabitant, and has recollections associated with every street and building – in which alone, of all places on the earth, he is not a stranger – which he is perpetually called upon to defend in the field, and in whose glory or shame he has an appreciable share, made sensible by the constant presence and rivalry of foreigners; in such a state of things patriotism is easy. It was easy in the ancient republics, or in modern Switzerland. But in great communities an intense interest in public affairs is scarcely natural, except to a member of an aristocracy, who alone has so conspicuous a position, and is so personally identified with the conduct of the government, that his credit and consequence are essentially connected with the glory and power of the nation he belongs to; its glory and power, (observe,) not the well-being of the bulk of its inhabitants. It is difficult for an obscure person like the citizen of a Democracy, who is in no way involved in the responsibility of public affairs, and cannot hope to exercise more than the minutest influence over them, to have the sentiment of patriotism as a living and earnest feeling. There being, then, no intermediate objects for his attachments to fix upon, they fasten themselves on his own private affairs; and, according to national character and circumstances, it becomes his ruling passion either to improve his condition in life, or to take his ease and pleasure by the means which it already affords him.

As, therefore, the state of society becomes more democratic, it is more and more necessary to nourish patriotism by artificial means; and of these none are so efficacious as free institutions – a large and frequent intervention of the citizens in the management of public business. Nor does the love of country alone require this encouragement, but every feeling which connects men either by interest or sympathy with their neighbours and fellow-citizens. Popular institutions are the great means of rendering general in a people, and especially among the richer classes, the desire of being useful in their generation; useful to the public or to their neighbours without distinction of rank; as well as courteous and unassuming in their habitual intercourse.

> 'When the public is supreme, there is no man who does not feel the value of public good-will, or who does not endeavour to court it by drawing to himself the esteem and affection of those amongst whom he is to live. Many of the passions which congeal and keep asunder human hearts, are then obliged to retire, and hide below the surface. Pride must be dissembled; disdain does not

break out; selfishness is afraid of itself. Under a free government, as most public offices are elective, the men whose elevated minds or aspiring hopes are too closely circumscribed in private life, constantly feel that they cannot do without the population which surrounds them. Men learn at such times to think of their fellow-men from ambitious motives, and they frequently find it, in a manner, their interest to be forgetful of self.

'I may here be met by an objection, derived from electioneering intrigues, the meannesses of candidates, and the calumnies of their opponents. These are opportunities of animosity which occur the oftener the more frequent elections become. Such evils are, doubtless, great, but they are transient; whereas the benefits which attend them remain. The desire of being elected may lead some men for a time to mutual hostility; but this same desire leads all men, in the long run, mutually to support each other; and if it happens that an election accidentally severs two friends, the electoral system brings a multitude of citizens permanently together who would always have remained unknown to each other. Freedom engenders private animosities, but despotism gives birth to general indifference . . .

'A brilliant achievement may win for you the favour of a people at one stroke; but to earn the love and respect of the population which surrounds you, requires a long succession of little services and obscure good offices, a constant habit of kindness, and an established reputation for disinterestedness. Local freedom, then, which leads a great number of citizens to value the affections of their neighbours, and of those with whom they are in contact, perpetually draws men back to one another, in spite of the propensities which sever them; and forces them to render each other mutual assistance.

'In the United States, the more opulent citizens take great care not to stand aloof from the people: on the contrary, they constantly keep on easy terms with them; they listen to them; they speak to them every day. They know that the rich, in democracies, always stand in need of the poor; and that in democratic times a poor man's attachment depends more on manner than on benefits conferred. The very magnitude of such benefits, by setting the differences of conditions in a strong light, causes a secret irritation to those who reap advantage from them; but the charm of simplicity of manners is almost irresistible . . . This truth does not penetrate at once into the minds of the rich. They generally resist it as long as the democratic revolution lasts, and they do not acknowledge it immediately after that revolution is accomplished. They are very ready to do good to the people, but they still choose to keep them at arm's length; they think that is sufficient, but they are mistaken. They might spend fortunes thus, without warming the hearts of the population around them; that population does not ask them for the sacrifice of their money, but of their pride.

'It would seem as if every imagination in the United States were on the stretch to invent means of increasing the wealth and satisfying the wants of the public. The best informed inhabitants of each district are incessantly using their information to discover new means of augmenting the general prosperity; and, when they have made any such discoveries, they eagerly surrender them to the mass of the people . . .

'I have often seen Americans make great and real sacrifices to the public welfare; and I have a hundred times remarked that, in case of need, they hardly ever fail to lend faithful support to each other. The free institutions which the inhabitants of the United States possess, and the political rights of which they make so much use, remind every citizen, and in a thousand ways, that he lives in society. They every instant impress upon his mind the notion that it is the duty as well as the interest of men to make themselves useful to their fellow-creatures; and as he sees no particular reason for disliking them, since he is never either their master or their slave, his heart readily leans to the side of kindness. Men attend to the interests of the public, first by necessity, afterwards by choice; what was calculation becomes an instinct; and, by dint of working for the good of one's fellow-citizens, the habit and the taste for serving them is at length acquired.

'Many people in France consider equality of conditions as one evil, and political freedom as a second. When they are obliged to yield to the former, they strive at least to escape from the latter. But I contend that, in order to combat the evils which equality may produce, there is only one effectual remedy – namely, political freedom.' – (Reeve, vol. iii. chap. 4.)

With regard to the tone of moral sentiment characteristic of democracy, M. de Tocqueville holds an opinion which we think deserves the attention of moralists. Among a class composed of persons who have been born into a distinguished position, the habitual springs of action will be very different from those of a democratic community. Speaking generally, (and making abstraction both of individual peculiarities, and of the influence of moral culture,) it may be said of the first, that their feelings and actions will be mainly under the influence of pride; of the latter, under that of interest. Now, as in an aristocratic society the elevated class, though small in number, sets the fashion in opinion and feeling, even virtue will, in that state of society, seem to be most strongly recommended by arguments addressing themselves to self-interest. In the one, we hear chiefly of the beauty and dignity of virtue, the grandeur of self-sacrifice; in the other, of honesty the best policy, the value of character, and the common interest of every individual in the good of the whole.

Neither the one nor the other of those modes of feeling, our author is well aware, constitutes moral excellence; which must have a deeper foundation than either the calculations of self-interest, or the emotions of self-flattery. But as an auxiliary to that higher principle, and as far as possible a substitute for it when it is absent, the latter of the two, in his opinion, though the least sentimental, will stand the most wear.

'The principle of enlightened self-interest is not a lofty one, but it is clear and sure. It does not aim at mighty objects, but it attains, without impracticable efforts, all those at which it aims. As it lies within the reach of all capacities, every one can without difficulty apprehend and retain it. By its adaptation to human weaknesses it easily obtains great dominion; nor is its dominion precarious, since it employs self-interest itself to correct self-interest, and uses, to direct the passions, the very instrument which excites them.

'The doctrine of enlightened self-interest produces no great acts of self-sacrifice, but it suggests daily small acts of self-denial. By itself it cannot suffice to make a virtuous man, but it disciplines a multitude of citizens in habits of regularity, temperance, moderation, foresight, self-command: and, if it does not at once lead men to virtue by their will, it draws them gradually in that direction by their habits. If the principle of "interest rightly understood," were to sway the whole moral world, extraordinary virtues would doubtless be more rare; but I think that gross depravity would then also be less common. That principle, perhaps, prevents some men from rising far above the level of mankind; but a great number of others who were falling below that level, are caught and upheld by it. Observe some few individuals, they are lowered by it; survey mankind, it is raised.

'I am not afraid to say, that the principle of enlightened self-interest appears to me the best suited of all philosophical theories to the wants of the men of our time; and that I regard it as their chief remaining security against themselves. Towards it, therefore, the minds of the moralists of our age should turn; even should they judge it incomplete, it must nevertheless be adopted as necessary.

'No power upon earth can prevent the increasing equality of conditions from impelling the human mind to seek out what is useful, or from inclining every member of the community to concentrate his affections on himself. It must therefore be expected that personal interest will become more than ever the principal, if not the sole spring of men's actions; but it remains to be seen how each man will understand his personal interest.

'I do not think that the doctrine of self-interest, as it is professed in America, is self-evident in all its parts, but it contains a great number of truths so evident, that men, if they are but instructed, cannot fail to see them. Instruct them, then, at all hazards; for the age of implicit self-sacrifice and instinctive virtues is already flying far away from us, and the time is fast approaching when freedom, public peace, and social order itself, will not be able to exist without instruction.' – (Reeve, vol. iii. chap. 8.)

M. de Tocqueville considers a democratic state of society as eminently tending to give the strongest impulse to the taste for physical well-being. He ascribes this, not so much to the equality of conditions as to their mobility. In a country like America every one may acquire riches; no one, at least, is artificially impeded in acquiring them, and hardly any one is born to them. Now, these are the conditions under which the passions which attach themselves to wealth, and to what wealth can purchase, are the strongest. Those who are born in the midst of affluence, are generally more or less *blasé* as to its enjoyments. They take the comfort or luxury to which they have always been accustomed, as they do the air they breathe; it is not *le but de la vie,* but *une manière de vivre*. An aristocracy, when put to the proof, has in general shown a wonderful facility in enduring the loss of riches and of physical comforts. The very pride, nourished by the elevation which they owed to wealth, supports them under the privation of it. But to those who have chased riches laboriously for half their lives, to lose it is the loss of all; *une vie manquée*;

a disappointment greater than can be endured. In a democracy, again, there is no contented poverty. No one being forced to remain poor; many who were poor daily becoming rich, and the comforts of life being apparently within the reach of all, the desire to appropriate them descends to the very lowest rank. Thus, –

'The desire of acquiring the comforts of the world haunts the imagination of the poor, and the dread of losing them that of the rich. Many scanty fortunes spring up; those who possess them have a sufficient share of physical gratifications to conceive a taste for those pleasures – not enough to satisfy it. They never procure them without exertion, and they never indulge in them without apprehension. They are therefore always straining to pursue or to retain gratifications so precious, so incomplete, and so fugitive.

'If I enquire what passion is most natural to men who are at once stimulated and circumscribed by the obscurity of their birth, or the mediocrity of their fortune, I can discover none more peculiarly appropriate to them than this love of physical prosperity. The passion for physical comforts is essentially a passion of the middle classes; with those classes it grows and spreads, and along with them it becomes preponderant. From them it mounts into the higher orders of society, and descends into the mass of the people.

'I never met in America with any citizen so poor as not to cast a glance of hope and longing towards the enjoyment of the rich, or whose imagination did not indulge itself by anticipation in those good things which fate still obstinately withheld from him.

'On the other hand, I never perceived, amongst the wealthier inhabitants of the United States, that proud contempt of the indulgences of riches, which is sometimes to be met with even in the most opulent and dissolute aristocracies. Most of these wealthy persons were once poor; they have felt the stimulus of privation, they have long struggled with adverse fortune; and now that the victory is won, the passions which accompanied the contest have survived it; their minds are, as it were, intoxicated by the petty enjoyments which they have pursued for forty years.

'Not but that in the United States, as elsewhere, there are a certain number of wealthy persons, who, having come into their property by inheritance, possess, without exertion, an opulence they have not earned. But even these are not less devotedly attached to the pleasures of material life. The love of physical comfort is become the predominant taste of the nation; the great current of man's passions runs in that channel, and sweeps every thing along in its course.' – (Reeve, vol. iii. book ii. chap. 10.)

A regulated sensuality thus establishes itself – the parent of effeminacy rather than of debauchery; paying respect to the social rights of other people and to the opinion of the world; not 'leading men away in search of forbidden enjoyments, but absorbing them in the pursuit of permitted ones. This spirit is frequently combined with a species of religious morality; men wish to be as well off as they can in this world, without foregoing their chance of another.'

From the preternatural stimulus given to the desire of acquiring and of enjoying wealth, by the intense competition which necessarily exists where an entire population are the competitors, arises the restlessness so characteristic of American life.

'It is strange to see with what feverish ardour the Americans pursue their own welfare; and to watch the vague dread that constantly torments them lest they should not have chosen the shortest path which may lead to it. A native of the United States clings to this world's goods as if he were certain never to die, and is so hasty in grasping at all within his reach, that one would suppose he was constantly afraid of not living long enough to enjoy them. He clutches every thing, he holds nothing fast, but soon loosens his grasp to pursue fresh gratifications . . .

'At first sight there is something surprising in this strange unrest of so many happy men, uneasy in the midst of abundance. The spectacle is, however, as old as the world; the novelty is to see a whole people furnish an example of it . . .

'When all the privileges of birth and fortune are abolished, when all professions are accessible to all, and a man's own energies may place him at the top of any one of them, an easy and unbounded career seems open to his ambition, and he will readily persuade himself that he is born to no vulgar destinies. But this is an erroneous notion, which is corrected by daily experience. The same equality which allows every citizen to conceive these lofty hopes, renders all the citizens individually feeble. It circumscribes their powers on every side while it gives freer scope to their desires. Not only are they restrained by their own weakness, but they are met at every step by immense obstacles which they did not at first perceive. They have swept away the privileges of some of their fellow-creatures which stood in their way; they have to encounter the competition of all. The barrier has changed its shape rather than its place. When men are nearly alike, and all follow the same track, it is very difficult for any one individual to get on fast, and cleave a way through the homogeneous throng which surrounds and presses upon him. This constant strife between the wishes springing from the equality of conditions and the means it supplies to satisfy them, harasses and wearies the mind.' – (Reeve, vol. ii. book ii. chap. 13.)

And hence, according to M. de Tocqueville, it is, that while every one is devoured by ambition, hardly any one is ambitious on a large scale. Among so many competitors for but a few great prizes, none of the candidates starting from the vantage ground of an elevated social position, very few can hope to gain those prizes, and they not until late in life. Men in general, therefore, do not look so high. A vast energy of passion in a whole community is developed and squandered in the petty pursuit of petty advancements in fortune, and the hurried snatching of petty pleasures.

To sum up our author's opinion of the dangers to which mankind are liable as they advance towards equality of condition; his fear, both in government and in intellect and morals, is not of too great liberty, but of too ready submission; not of anarchy, but of servility; not of too rapid change, but of Chinese stationariness. As democracy advances, the opinions of mankind on most subjects of general interest will become, he believes, as compared with any former period, more rooted and more difficult to change; and mankind are more and more in danger of losing the moral courage and pride of independence which make them deviate from the beaten path either in speculation or in conduct. Even in politics, it is to be apprehended that, feeling their personal insignificance, and conceiving a proportionally vast idea of the importance of society at large; being jealous, moreover, of one another, but not jealous of the central power which derives its origin from the majority, or which at least is the faithful representative of its desire to annihilate every intermediate power; they should allow that central government to assume more and more control, engross more and more of the business of society; and, on condition of making itself the organ of the general mode of feeling and thinking, should suffer it to relieve mankind from the care of their own interests, and keep them under a kind of tutelage; – trampling meanwhile with considerable recklessness, as often as convenient, upon the rights of individuals, in the name of society and the public good.

Against these political evils the corrective to which our author looks is popular education, and, above all, the spirit of liberty, fostered by the extension and dissemination of political rights. Democratic institutions, therefore, are his remedy for the worst mischiefs to which a democratic state of society is exposed. As for those to which democratic institutions are themselves liable, these, he holds, society must struggle with, and bear with so much of them as it cannot find the means of conquering. For M. de Tocqueville is no believer in the reality of mixed governments. There is, he says, always and every where, a strongest power: in every government either the king, the aristocracy, or the people, have an effective predominance, and can carry any point on which they set their heart. 'When a community really comes to have a mixed government, that is, to be equally divided between two adverse principles, it is either falling into a revolutionary state or into dissolution.' M. de Tocqueville believes that the preponderant power which must exist every where, is mostly rightly placed in the body of the people. But he thinks it most pernicious that this power, whether residing in the people or elsewhere, should be 'checked by no obstacles which may retard its course, and force it to moderate its own vehemence.' The difference, in his eyes, is great between one sort of democratic institutions and another. That form of democracy should be sought out and devised, and in every way endeavoured to be carried into practice, which, on the one hand, most exercises and cultivates the intelligence and mental activity of the majority; and, on the other, breaks the headlong impulses of popular opinion, by delay, rigour of forms, and adverse discussion. 'The organization and the establishment of democracy,' on these principles, 'is the great political problem of our time.'

And when this problem is solved, there remains an equally serious one; to make head against the tendency of democracy towards bearing down individuality, and circumscribing the exercise of the human faculties within narrow limits. To sustain the higher pursuits of philosophy and art; to vindicate and protect the unfettered exercise of reason, and the moral freedom of the individual – these are purposes to which, under a democracy, the superior spirits, and the government so far as it is permitted, should devote their utmost energies.

'I shall conclude by one general idea, which comprises not only all the particular ideas which have been expressed in the present chapter, but also most of those which it is the object of this book to treat of.

'In the ages of aristocracy which preceded our own, there were private persons of great power, and a social authority of extreme weakness. The principal efforts of the men of those times were required to strengthen, aggrandize, and secure the supreme power; and, on the other hand, to circumscribe individual independence within narrower limits, and to subject private interests to the public. Other perils and other cares await the men of our age. Amongst the greater part of modern nations, the government, whatever may be its origin, its constitution, or its name, has become almost omnipotent, and private persons are falling, more and more, into the lowest stage of weakness and dependence.

'The general character of olden society was diversity; unity and uniformity were nowhere to be met with. In modern society, all things threaten to become so much alike, that the peculiar characteristics of each individual will be entirely lost in the uniformity of the general aspect. Our forefathers were ever prone to make an improper use of the notion, that private rights ought to be respected; and we are naturally prone, on the other hand, to exaggerate the idea, that the interest of an individual ought to bend to the interest of the many.

'The political world is metamorphosed; new remedies must henceforth be sought for new disorders. To lay down extensive, but distinct and immovable limits to the action of the ruling power; to confer certain rights on private persons, and secure to them the undisputed enjoyment of their rights; to enable individual man to maintain whatever independence, strength, and originality he still possesses; to raise him by the side of society at large, and uphold him in that position; – these appear to me the main objects for the legislator in the age upon which we are now entering.

'It would seem as if the rulers of our time sought only to use men in order to effect great things: I wish that they would try a little more to make great men; that they would set less value on the work, and more upon the workman; that they would never forget that a nation cannot long remain strong when every man belonging to it is individually weak; and that no form or combination of social polity has yet been devised to make an energetic people out of a community of citizens personally feeble and pusillanimous.' – (Reeve, vol. iv. chap. 3.)

If we were here to close this article, and leave these noble speculations to produce their effect without further comment, the reader probably would not blame us. Our recommendation is not needed in their behalf. That nothing on the whole comparable in profundity to them had yet been written on democracy, will scarcely be disputed by any one who has read even our hasty abridgement of them. We must guard, at the same time, against attaching to these conclusions, or to any others that can result from such enquiries, a character of scientific certainty that can never belong to them. Democracy is too recent a phenomenon, and of too great magnitude, for any one who now lives to comprehend its consequences. A few of its more immediate tendencies may be perceived or surmised; what other tendencies, destined to overrule or to combine with these, lie behind, there are not grounds even to conjecture. If we revert to any similar fact in past history, any change in human affairs approaching in greatness to what is passing before our eyes, we shall find that no prediction which could have been made at the time, or for many generations afterwards, would have borne any resemblance to what has actually been the course of events. When the Greek commonwealths were crushed, and liberty in the civilized world apparently extinguished by the Macedonian invaders; when a rude unlettered people of Italy stretched their conquests and their dominion from one end to the other of the known world; when that people in turn lost its freedom and its old institutions, and fell under the military despotism of one of its own citizens; – what similarity is there between the effects we now know to have been produced by these causes, and any thing which the wisest person could then have anticipated from them? When the Roman Empire, containing all the art, science, literature, and industry of the world, was overrun, ravaged, and dismembered by hordes of barbarians, everybody lamented the destruction of civilization in an event which is now admitted to have been the necessary condition of its renovation. When the Christian religion had existed but for two centuries, when the Pope was only beginning to assert his ascendency, what philosopher or statesman could have foreseen the destinies of Christianity, or the part which has been acted in history by the Catholic Church? It is thus with all other really great historical facts – the invention of gunpowder for instance, or of the printing-press; even when their direct operation is as exactly measurable, because as strictly mechanical, as these were, the mere scale on which they operate gives birth to endless consequences, of a kind which would have appeared visionary to the most far-seeing contemporary wisdom.

It is not, therefore, without a deep sense of the uncertainty attaching to such predictions, that the wise would hazard an opinion as to the fate of mankind under the new democratic dispensation. But without pretending to judge confidently of remote tendencies, those immediate ones which are already developing themselves require to be dealt with as we treat any of the other circumstances in which we are placed; – by encouraging those which are salutary, and working out the means by which such as are hurtful may be counteracted. To exhort men to this, and to aid them in doing it, is the end for which M. de Tocqueville has written: and in the same spirit we will now venture to make one criticism upon him; – to point out one correction, of which we think his views stand in need; and for want of which they have occasionally an air of over-subtlety and false refinement, exciting the distrust of common readers, and making the opinions themselves appear less true, and less practically important, than, it seems to us, they really are.

M. de Tocqueville then has, at least apparently, confounded the effects of Democracy with the effects of Civilization. He has bound up in one abstract idea the whole of the tendencies of modern commercial society, and given them one name – Democracy; thereby letting it be supposed that he ascribes to equality of conditions, several of the effects naturally arising from the mere progress of national prosperity, in the form in which that progress manifests itself in modern times.

It is no doubt true, that among the tendencies of commercial civilization, a tendency to the equalization of conditions is one, and not the least conspicuous. When a nation is advancing in prosperity – when its industry is expanding, and its capital rapidly augmenting – the number also of those who possess capital increases in at least as great a proportion; and though the distance between the two extremes of society may not be much diminished, there is a rapid multiplication of those who occupy the intermediate positions. There may be princes at one end of the scale and paupers at the other; but between them there will be a respectable and well-paid class of artisans, and a middle class who combine property and industry. This may be called, and is, a tendency to equalization. But this growing equality is only one of the features of progressive civilization; one of the incidental effects of the progress of industry and wealth: a most important effect, and one which, as our author shows, re-acts in a hundred ways upon the other effects, but not, therefore, to be confounded with the cause.

So far is it, indeed, from being admissible, that *mere* equality of conditions is the mainspring of those moral and social phenomena which M. de Tocqueville has characterized, that when some unusual chance exhibits to us equality of conditions by itself, severed from that commercial state of society and that progress of industry of which it is the natural concomitant, it produces few or none of the moral effects ascribed to it. Consider, for instance, the French of Lower Canada. Equality of conditions is more universal there than in the United States; for the whole people, without exception, are in easy circumstances, and there are not even that considerable number of rich individuals who are to be found in all the great towns of the American Republic. Yet do we find in Canada that *go-ahead spirit* – that restless impatient eagerness for improvement in circumstances – that mobility, that shifting and fluctuating, now up now down, now here now there – that absence of classes and class-spirit – that jealousy of superior attainments – that want of deference for authority and leadership – that habit of bringing things to the rule and square of each man's own understanding – which M. de Tocqueville imputes to the same cause in the United States? In all these respects the very contrary qualities prevail. We by no means deny, that where the other circumstances which determine these effects exist, equality of conditions has a very perceptible effect in corroborating them. We think M. de Tocqueville has shown that it has. But that it is the exclusive or even the principal cause, we think the example of Canada goes far to disprove.

For the reverse of this experiment, we have only to look at home. Of all countries in a state of progressive commercial civilization, Great Britain is that in which the equalization of conditions has made least progress. The extremes of wealth and poverty are wider apart, and there is a more numerous body of persons at each extreme, than in any other commercial community. From the habits of the population in regard to marriage, the poor have remained poor; from the laws which tend to keep large masses of property together, the rich have remained rich; and often, when they have lost the substance of riches, have retained its social advantages and outward trappings. Great fortunes are continually accumulated, and seldom redistributed. In this respect, therefore, England is the most complete contrast to the United States. But in commercial prosperity, in the rapid growth of industry and wealth, she is the next after America, and not very much inferior to her. Accordingly we appeal to all competent observers, whether, in nearly all the moral and intellectual features of American society, as represented by M. de Tocqueville, this country does not stand next to America? whether, with the single difference of our remaining respect for aristocracy, the American people, both in their good qualities and in their defects, resemble any thing so much as an exaggeration of our own middle class? whether the spirit which is gaining more and more the ascendant with us, is not, in a very great degree, American? and whether all the moral elements of an American state of society are not most rapidly growing up?

For example, that entire unfixedness in the social position of individuals – that treading upon the heels of one another – that habitual dissatisfaction of each with the position he occupies, and eager desire to push himself into the next above it – has not this become, and is it not becoming more and more, an English characteristic? In England, as well as in America, it appears to foreigners, and even to Englishmen recently returned from a foreign country, as if every body had but one wish – to improve his condition, never to enjoy it; as if no Englishman cared to cultivate either the pleasures or the virtues corresponding to his station in society, but solely to get out of it as quickly as possible; or if that cannot be done, and until it is done, to *seem* to have got out of it. 'The hypocrisy of luxury,' as M. de Tocqueville calls the maintaining an appearance beyond one's real expenditure, he considers as a democratic peculiarity. It is surely an English one. The highest class of all, indeed, is, as might be expected, comparatively exempt from these bad peculiarities. But the very existence of such a class, whose immunities and political privileges are attainable by wealth, tends to aggravate the struggle of the other classes for the possession of that passport to all other importance; and it perhaps required the example of America to prove, that the 'sabbathless pursuit of wealth' could be as intensely prevalent, where there were no aristocratic distinctions to tempt to it.

Again, the mobility and fluctuating nature of individual relations – the absence of permanent ties, local or personal; how often has this been commented on as one of the organic changes by which the ancient structure of English society is becoming dissolved? Without reverting to the days of clanship, or to those in which the gentry led a patriarchal life among their tenantry and neighbours, the memory of man extends to a time when the same tenants remained attached to the same landlords, the same servants to the same household; but this, with other old customs, after progressively retiring to the remote corners of our island, has nearly taken flight altogether; and it may now be said, that in all the relations of life, except those to which law and religion have given perpetuity, change has become the general rule, and constancy the exception.

The remainder of the tendencies which M. de Tocqueville has delineated, may mostly be brought under one general agency as their immediate cause, the growing insignificance of individuals in comparison with the mass. Now, it would be difficult to show any country in which this insignificance is more marked and conspicuous than in England, or any incompatibility between that tendency and aristocratic institutions. It is not because the individuals composing the mass are all equal, but because the mass itself has grown to so immense a size, that individuals are powerless in the face of it; and because the mass having, by mechanical improvements, become capable of acting simultaneously, can compel not merely any individual, but any number of individuals, to bend before it. The House of Lords is the richest and most powerful collection of persons in Europe, yet they not only could not prevent, but were themselves compelled to pass, the Reform Bill. The daily actions of every peer and peeress are falling more and more under the yoke of *bourgeois* opinion, they feel every day a stronger necessity of showing an immaculate front to the world. When they do venture to disregard common opinion, it is in a body, and when supported by one another; whereas formerly every nobleman acted on his own notions, and dared be as eccentric as he pleased. No rank in society is now exempt from the fear of being peculiar, the unwillingness to be, or to be thought, in any respect original. Hardly any thing now depends upon individuals, but all upon classes, and among classes mainly upon the middle class. That class is now the power in society, the arbiter of fortune and success. Ten times more money is made by supplying the wants, even the superfluous wants, of the middle, nay of the lower classes, than those of the higher. It is the middle class that now rewards even literature and art; the books by which most money is made are the cheap books; the greatest part of the profit of a picture is the profit of the engraving from it. Accordingly, all the intellectual effects which M. de Tocqueville ascribes to Democracy, are taking place under the Democracy of the middle class. There is a greatly augmented number of moderate successes, fewer great literary and scientific reputations. Elementary and popular treatises are immensely multiplied, superficial information far more widely diffused; but there are fewer who devote themselves to thought for its own sake, and pursue in retirement those profounder researches, the result of which can only be appreciated by a few. Literary productions are seldom highly finished – they are got up to be read by many, and to be read but once. If the work sells for a day, the author's time and pains will be better laid out in writing a second than in improving the first. And this is not because books are no longer written for the aristocracy: they never were so. The aristocracy (saving individual exceptions) never were a reading class. It is because books are now written for a numerous, and therefore an unlearned public; no longer principally for scholars and men of science, who have knowledge of their own, and are not imposed upon by half-knowledge – who have studied the great works of genius, and can make comparisons.*

As for the decay of authority, and diminution of respect for traditional opinions, this could not well be so far advanced among an ancient people – all whose political notions rest on an historical basis, and whose institutions themselves are built upon prescription, and not upon ideas of expediency – as in America, where the whole edifice of government was

* On this account, among others, we think M. de Tocqueville right in the great importance he attaches to the study of Greek and Roman literature; not as being without faults, but as having the contrary faults to those of our own day. Not only do those

constructed within the memory of man upon abstract principles. But surely this change also is taking place as fast as could be expected under the circumstances. And even this effect, though it has a more direct connexion with Democracy, has not an exclusive one. Respect for old opinions must diminish wherever science and knowledge are rapidly progressive. As the people in general become aware of the recent date of the most important physical discoveries, they are liable to form a rather contemptuous opinion of their ancestors. The mere visible fruits of scientific progress in a wealthy society, the mechanical improvements, the steam-engines, the railroads, carry the feeling of admiration for modern and disrespect for ancient times, down even to the wholly uneducated classes. For that other mental characteristic which M. de Tocqueville finds in America – a positive, matter-of-fact spirit – a demand that all things shall be made clear to each man's understanding, an indifference to the subtler proofs which address themselves to more cultivated and systematically exercised intellects; for what may be called, in short, the dogmatism of common sense, we need not look beyond our own country. There needs no Democracy to account for this – there needs only the habit of energetic action, without a proportional development of the taste for speculation. Bonaparte was one of the most remarkable

literatures furnish models of high finish and perfection in workmanship, to correct the slovenly habits of modern hasty writing, but they exhibit, in the military and agricultural commonwealths of antiquity, precisely that order of virtues in which a commercial society is apt to be deficient; and they altogether show human nature on a grander scale: with less benevolence but more patriotism, less sentiment but more self-control; if a lower average of virtue, more striking individual examples of it; fewer small goodnesses, but more of greatness, and appreciation of greatness; more which tends to exalt the imagination, and inspire high conceptions of the capabilities of human nature. If, as every one may see, the want of affinity of these studies to the modern mind is gradually lowering them in popular estimation, this is but a confirmation of the need of them, and renders it more incumbent upon those who have the power, to do their utmost towards preventing their decline.

examples of it; and the diffusion of half-instruction, without any sufficient provision made by society for sustaining the higher cultivation, tends greatly to encourage its excess.

Nearly all those moral and social influences, therefore, which are the subject of M. de Tocqueville's second part, are shown to be in full operation in aristocratic England. What connexion they have with equality is with the growth of the middle class, not with the annihilation of the extremes. They are quite compatible with the existence of peers and *prolétaires*; nay, with the most abundant provision of both those varieties of human nature. If we were sure of preserving for ever our aristocratic institutions, society would no less have to struggle against all these tendencies; and perhaps even the loss of those institutions would not have so much effect as is supposed in accelerating their triumph.

The evil is not in the preponderance of a democratic class, but of any class. The defects which M. de Tocqueville points out in the American, and which we see in the modern English mind, are the ordinary ones of a commercial class. The portion of society which is predominant in America, and that which is attaining predominance here, the American Many, and our middle class, agree in being commercial classes. The one country is affording a complete, and the other a progressive exemplification, that whenever any variety of human nature becomes preponderant in a community, it imposes upon all the rest of society its own type; forcing all either to submit to it or to imitate it.

It is not in China only that a homogeneous community is naturally a stationary community. The unlikeness of one man to another is not only a principle of improvement, but would seem almost to be the only principle. It is profoundly remarked by M. Guizot, that the short duration or stunted growth of the earlier civilizations arose from this, that in each of them some one element of human improvement existed exclusively, or so preponderatingly as to overpower all the others; whereby the community, after accomplishing rapidly all which that one element could do, either perished for want of what it could not do, or came to a halt, and became immoveable. It would be an error to suppose that such could not possibly be our fate. In the generalisation which pronounces the 'law of progress' to be an inherent attribute of human nature, it is forgotten that, among the inhabitants of our earth, the European family of nations is the only one which has ever shown any capability of spontaneous improvement, beyond a certain low level. Let us beware of supposing that we owe this peculiarity to any necessity of nature, and not rather to combinations of circumstances, which have existed nowhere else, and may not exist for ever among ourselves. The spirit of commerce and industry is one of the greatest instruments not only of civilization in the narrowest, but of improvement and culture in the widest sense: to it, or to its consequences, we owe nearly all that advantageously distinguishes the present period from the middle ages. So long as other co-ordinate elements of improvement existed beside it, doing what it left undone, and keeping its exclusive tendencies in equipoise by an opposite order of sentiments, principles of action, and modes of thought – so long the benefits which it conferred on humanity were unqualified. But example and theory alike justify the expectation, that with its complete preponderance would commence an era either of stationariness or of decline.

If to avert this consummation it were necessary that the class which wields the strongest power in society should be prevented from exercising its strength, or, that those who are powerful enough to overthrow the government, should not claim a paramount control over it, the case of civilized nations would be almost hopeless. But human affairs are not entirely governed by mechanical laws, nor men's characters wholly and irrevocably formed by their situation in life. Economical and social changes, though among the greatest, are not the only forces which shape the course of our species; ideas are not always the mere signs and effects of social circumstances, they are themselves a power in history. Let the idea take hold of the more generous and cultivated minds, that the most serious danger to the future prospects of mankind is in the unbalanced influence of the commercial spirit – let the wiser and better-hearted politicians and public teachers look upon it as their most pressing duty, to protect and strengthen whatever, in the heart of man or in his outward life, can form a salutary check in the exclusive tendencies of that spirit – and we should not only have individual testimonies against it, in all the forms of genius, from those who have the privilege of speaking not to their own age merely, but to all time; there would also gradually shape itself forth a national education, which, without overlooking any other of the requisites of human wellbeing, would be adapted to this purpose in particular.

What is requisite in politics for the same end, is not that public opinion should not be, what it is and must be, the ruling power; but that, in order to the formation of the best public opinion, there should exist somewhere a great social support for opinions and sentiments different from those of the mass. The shape which that support may best assume in a question of time, place, and circumstance; but (in a commercial country, and an age when, happily for mankind, the military spirit is gone by) there can be no doubt about the elements which must compose it: they are, an agricultural class, a leisured class, and a learned class.

The natural tendencies of an agricultural class are in many respects the reverse of those of a manufacturing and commercial. In the first place, from their more scattered position, and less exercised activity of mind, they have usually a greater willingness to look up to, and accept of, guidance. In the next place, they are the class who have local attachments; and it is astonishing how much of character depends upon this one circumstance. If the agricultural spirit is not felt in America as a counterpoise to the commercial, it is because American agriculturists have no local attachments; they range from place to place, and are to all intents and purposes a commercial class. But in an old country, where the same family has long occupied the same land, the case will naturally be different. From attachment to places follows attachment to persons who are associated with those places.

Though no longer the permanent tie which it once was, the connexion between tenants and landlords is one not lightly broken off; – one which both parties, when they enter into it, desire and hope to be permanent. Again, with attachment to the place comes generally attachment to the occupation; – a farmer seldom becomes anything but a farmer. The rage of money-getting can scarcely, in agricultural occupations, reach any dangerous height: except where bad laws have aggravated the natural fluctuations of price, there is little room for gambling; the rewards of industry and skill are here but moderate; an agriculturist can rarely make a large fortune. A manufacturer or merchant, unless he can outstrip others, knows that others will outstrip him, and ruin him; while, in the irksome drudgery to which he subjects himself as a means, there is nothing agreeable to dwell upon except the ultimate end. But agriculture is in itself an interesting occupation, which few wish to retire from, and which men of property and education often pursue merely for their amusement. Men so occupied are satisfied with less gain, and are less impatient to realize it. Our town population, it has long been remarked, is becoming almost as mobile and almost as uneasy as the American. It ought not to be so with our agriculturists; they ought to be the counterbalancing element in our national character; they should represent the type opposite to the commercial, – that of moderate wishes, tranquil tastes, cultivation of the excitements and enjoyments near at hand, and compatible with their existing position.

To attain this object, how much alteration may be requisite in the system of rack-renting and tenancy at will, we cannot undertake to show in this place. It is sufficiently obvious also that the Corn-Laws must disappear; there must be no feud raging between the commercial class and that by whose influence and example its excesses are to be tempered: men are not prone to adopt the characteristics of their enemies. Nor is this all. In order that the agricultural population should count for any thing in politics, or contribute its part to the formation of the national character, it is absolutely necessary that it should be educated. And let it be remembered that, in an agricultural people, the diffusion of information and intelligence must necessarily be artificial; – the work of government, or of the superior classes. In populous towns, the mere collision of man with man, the keenness of competition, the habits of society and discussion, the easy access to reading – even the dullness of the ordinary occupations, which drives men to other excitements – produce of themselves a certain development of intelligence. The least favoured class of a town population are seldom actually stupid, and have often in some directions a morbid keenness and acuteness. It is otherwise with the peasantry. Whatever it is desired that they should know, they must be taught; whatever intelligence is expected to grow up among them, must first be implanted, and sedulously nursed.

It is not needful to go into a similar analysis of the tendencies of the other two classes – a leisured, and a learned class. The capabilities which they possess for controlling the excess of the commercial spirit by a contrary spirit, are at once apparent. We regard it as one of the greatest advantages of this country over America, that it possesses both these classes; and we believe that the interests of the time to come are greatly dependent upon preserving them; and upon their being rendered, as they much require to be, better and better qualified for their important functions.

If we believed that the national character of England, instead of reacting upon the American character and raising it, was gradually assimilating itself to those points of it which the best and wisest Americans see with most uneasiness, it would be no consolation to us to think that we might possibly avoid American institutions; for we should have all the effects of her institutions, except those which are beneficial. The American Many are not essentially a different class from our ten-pound householders; and if the middle class are left to the mere habits and instincts of a commercial community, we shall have a 'tyranny of the majority,' not the less irksome because most of the tyrants may not be manual labourers. For it is a chimerical hope to overbear or outnumber the middle class; whatever modes of voting, whatever redistribution of the constituencies, are really necessary for placing the government in their hands – those, whether we like it or not, they will assuredly obtain.

The ascendency of the commercial class in modern society and politics is inevitable, and, under due limitations, ought not to be regarded as an evil. That class is the most powerful; but it needs not therefore be all-powerful. Now, as ever, the great problem in government is to prevent the strongest from becoming the only power; and repress the natural tendency of the instincts and passions of the ruling body to sweep away all barriers which are capable of resisting, even for a moment, their own tendencies. Any counterbalancing power can henceforth exist only by the sufferance of the commercial class; but that it should tolerate some such limitation, we deem as important as that it should not itself be held in vassalage.[12]

10 *Of Individuality, as One of the Elements of Well-Being*

(Chapter III of *On Liberty*, London, 1859.)

Such being the reasons which make it imperative that human beings should be free to form opinions, and to express their opinions without reserve; and such the baneful consequences to the intellectual, and through that to the moral nature of man, unless this liberty is either conceded, or asserted in spite of prohibition; let us next examine whether the same reasons do not require that men should be free to act upon their opinions – to carry these out in their lives, without hindrance, either physical or moral, from their fellow-men, so long as it is at their own risk and peril. This last proviso is of course indispensable. No one pretends that actions should be as free as opinions. On the contrary, even opinions lose their immunity when the circumstances in which they are expressed are such as to constitute their expression a positive instigation to some mischievous act. An opinion that corn-dealers are starvers of the poor, or that private property is robbery, ought to be unmolested when simply circulated through the press, but may justly incur punishment when delivered orally to an excited mob assembled before the house of a corn-dealer, or when handed about among the same mob in the form of a placard. Acts, of whatever kind, which, without justifiable cause, do harm to others, may be, and in the more important cases absolutely require to be, controlled by the unfavourable sentiments, and, when needful, by the active interference of mankind. The liberty of the individual must be thus far limited; he must not make himself a nuisance to other people. But if he refrains from molesting others in what concerns them, and merely acts according to his own inclination and judgment in things which concern himself, the same reasons which show that opinion should be free, prove also that he should be allowed, without molestation, to carry his opinions into practice at his own cost. That mankind are not infallible; that their truths, for the most part, are only half-truths; that unity of opinion, unless resulting from the fullest and freest comparison of opposite opinions, is not desirable, and diversity not an evil, but a good, until mankind are much more capable than at present of recognising all sides of the truth, are principles applicable to men's modes of action, not less than to their opinions. As it is useful that while mankind are imperfect there should be different opinions, so it is that there should be different experiments of living; that free scope should be given to varieties of character, short of injury to others; and that the worth of different modes of life should be proved practically, when any one thinks fit to try them. It is desirable, in short, that in things which do not primarily concern others, individuality should assert itself. Where, not the person's own character, but the traditions or customs of other people are the rule of conduct, there is wanting one of the principal ingredients of human happiness, and quite the chief ingredient of individual and social progress.

In maintaining this principle, the greatest difficulty to be encountered does not lie in the appreciation of means towards an acknowledged end, but in the indifference of persons in general to the end itself. If it were felt that the free development of individuality is one of the leading essentials of well-being; that it is not only a co-ordinate element with all that is designated by the terms civilisation, instruction, education, culture, but is itself a necessary part and condition of all those things; there would be no danger that liberty should be undervalued, and the adjustment of the boundaries between it and social control would present no extraordinary difficulty. But the evil is, that individual spontaneity is hardly recognised by the common modes of thinking as having any intrinsic worth, or deserving any regard on its own account. The majority, being satisfied with the ways of mankind as they now are (for it is they who make them what they are), cannot comprehend why those ways should not be good enough for everybody; and what is more, spontaneity forms no part of the ideal of the majority of moral and social reformers, but is rather looked on with jealousy, as a troublesome and perhaps rebellious obstruction to the general acceptance of what these reformers, in their own judgment, think would be best for mankind. Few persons, out of Germany, even comprehend the meaning of the doctrine which Wilhelm von Humboldt, so eminent both as a *savant* and as a politician, made the text of a treatise – that 'the end of man, or that which is prescribed by the eternal or immutable dictates of reason, and not suggested by vague and transient desires, is the highest and most harmonious development of his powers to a complete and consistent whole;' that, therefore, the object 'towards which every human being must ceaselessly direct his efforts, and on which especially those who design to influence their fellow-men must ever keep their eyes, is the individuality of power and development;' that for this there are two requisites, 'freedom, and variety of situations;' and that from the union of these arise 'individual vigour and manifold diversity,' which combine themselves in 'originality.'*

Little, however, as people are accustomed to a doctrine like that of von Humboldt, and surprising as it may be to them to find so high a value attached to individuality, the question, one must nevertheless think, can only be one of degree. No one's idea of excellence in conduct is that people should do absolutely nothing but copy one another. No one would assert that people ought not to put into their mode of life, and into the conduct of their concerns, any impress whatever of their own judgment, or of their own individual character. On the other hand, it would be absurd to pretend that people ought to live as if nothing whatever

* *The Sphere and Duties of Government,* from the German of Baron Wilhelm von Humboldt, pp. 11-13.

had been known in the world before they came into it; as if experience had as yet done nothing towards showing that one mode of existence, or of conduct, is preferable to another. Nobody denies that people should be so taught and trained in youth as to know and benefit by the ascertained results of human experience. But it is the privilege and proper condition of a human being, arrived at the maturity of his faculties, to use and interpret experience in his own way. It is for him to find out what part of recorded experience is properly applicable to his own circumstances and character. The traditions and customs of other people are, to a certain extent, evidence of what their experience has taught *them*; presumptive evidence, and as such, have a claim to his deference: but, in the first place, their experience may be too narrow; or they may not have interpreted it rightly. Secondly, their interpretation of experience may be correct, but unsuitable to him. Customs are made for customary circumstances and customary characters; and his circumstances or his character may be uncustomary. Thirdly, though the customs be both good as customs, and suitable to him, yet to conform to custom, merely *as* custom, does not educate or develop in him any of the qualities which are the distinctive endowment of a human being. The human faculties of perception, judgment, discriminative feeling, mental activity, and even moral preference, are exercised only in making a choice. He who does anything because it is the custom makes no choice. He gains no practice either in discerning or in desiring what is best. The mental and moral, like the muscular powers, are improved only by being used. The faculties are called into no exercise by doing a thing merely because others do it, no more than by believing a thing only because others believe it. If the grounds of an opinion are not conclusive to the person's own reason, his reason cannot be strengthened, but is likely to be weakened, by his adopting it: and if the inducements to an act are not such as are consentaneous to his own feelings and character (where affection, or the rights of others, are not concerned) it is so much done towards rendering his feelings and character inert and torpid, instead of active and energetic.

He who lets the world, or his own portion of it, choose his plan of life for him, has no need of any other faculty than the ape-like one of imitation. He who chooses his plan for himself, employs all his faculties. He must use observation to see, reasoning and judgment to foresee, activity to gather materials for decision, discrimination to decide, and when he has decided, firmness and self-control to hold to his deliberate decision. And these qualities he requires and exercises exactly in proportion as the part of his conduct which he determines according to his own judgment and feelings is a large one. It is possible that he might be guided in some good path, and kept out of harm's way, without any of these things. But what will be his comparative worth as a human being? It really is of importance, not only what men do, but also what manner of men they are that do it. Among the works of man, which human life is rightly employed in perfecting and beautifying, the first in importance surely is man himself. Supposing it were possible to get houses built, corn grown, battles fought, causes tried, and even churches erected and prayers said, by machinery – by automatons in human form – it would be a considerable loss to exchange for these automatons even the men and women who at present inhabit the more civilized parts of the world, and who assuredly are but starved specimens of what nature can and will produce. Human nature is not a machine to be built after a model, and set to do exactly the work prescribed for it, but a tree, which requires to grow and develop itself on all sides, according to the tendency of the inward forces which make it a living thing.

It will probably be conceded that it is desirable people should exercise their understandings, and that an intelligent following of custom, or even occasionally an intelligent deviation from custom, is better than a blind and simply mechanical adhesion to it. To a certain extent it is admitted that our understanding should be our own: but there is not the same willingness to admit that our desires and impulses should be our own likewise; or that to possess impulses of our own, and of any strength, is anything but a peril and a snare. Yet desires and impulses are as much a part of a perfect human being as beliefs and restraints: and strong impulses are only perilous when not properly balanced; when one set of aims and inclinations is developed into strength, while others, which ought to co-exist with them, remain weak and inactive. It is not because men's desires are strong that they act ill; it is because their consciences are weak. There is no natural connexion between strong impulses and a weak conscience. The natural connexion is the other way. To say that one person's desires and feelings are stronger and more various than those of another, is merely to say that he has more of the raw material of human nature, and is therefore capable, perhaps of more evil, but certainly of more good. Strong impulses are but another name for energy. Energy may be turned to bad uses; but more good may always be made of an energetic nature, than of an indolent and impassive one. Those who have most natural feeling are always those whose cultivated feelings may be made the strongest. The same strong susceptibilities which make the personal impulses vivid and powerful, are also the source from whence are generated the most passionate love of virtue, and the sternest self-control. It is through the cultivation of these that society both does its duty and protects its interests: not by rejecting the stuff of which heroes are made, because it knows not how to make them. A person whose desires and impulses are his own – are the expression of his own nature, as it has been developed and modified by his own culture – is said to have a character. One whose desires and impulses are not his own, has no character, no more than a steam-engine has a character. If, in addition to being his own, his impulses are strong, and are under the government of a strong will, he has an energetic character. Whoever thinks that individuality of desires and impulses should not be encouraged to unfold itself, must maintain that society has no need of strong natures – is not the better for containing many persons who have much character – and that a high general average of energy is not desirable.

In some early states of society, these forces might be, and were, too much ahead of the power which society then possessed of disciplining and controlling them. There has been a time when the element of spontaneity and individuality was in excess, and the social principle had a hard struggle with it. The difficulty then was to induce men of strong bodies or minds to pay obedience to any rules which required them to control their impulses. To overcome this difficulty, law and discipline, like the Popes struggling against the Emperors, asserted a power over the whole man, claiming to control all his life in order to control his character – which society had not found any other sufficient means of binding. But society has now fairly got the better of individuality; and the danger which threatens human nature is not the excess, but the deficiency, of personal impulses and preferences. Things are vastly changed since the passions of those who were strong by station or by personal endowment were in a state of habitual rebellion against laws and ordinances, and required to be rigorously chained up to enable the persons within their reach to enjoy any particle of security. In our times, from the highest class of society down to the lowest, every one lives as under the eye of a hostile and dreaded censorship. Not only in what concerns others, but in what concerns only themselves, the individual or the family do not ask themselves – what do I prefer? or, what would suit my character and disposition? or, what would allow the best and highest in me to have fair play, and enable it to grow and thrive? They ask themselves, what is suitable to my position? what is usually done by persons of my station and pecuniary circumstances? or (worse still) what is usually done by persons of a station and circumstances superior to mine? I do not mean that they choose what is customary in preference to what suits their own inclination. It does not occur to them to have any inclination, except for what is customary. Thus the mind itself is bowed to the yoke: even in what people do for pleasure, conformity is the first thing thought of; they like in crowds; they exercise choice only among things commonly done: peculiarity of taste, eccentricity of conduct, are shunned equally with crimes: until by dint of not following their own nature they have no nature to follow: their human capacities are withered and starved: they become incapable of any strong wishes or native pleasures, and are generally without either opinions or feelings of home growth, or properly their own. Now is this, or is it not, the desirable condition of human nature?

It is so, on the Calvinistic theory. According to that, the one great offence of man is self-will. All the good of which humanity is capable is comprised in obedience. You have no choice; thus you must do, and no otherwise: 'whatever is not a duty, is a sin.' Human nature being radically corrupt, there is no redemption for any one until human nature is killed within him. To one holding this theory of life, crushing out any of the human faculties, capacities, and susceptibilities, is no evil: man needs no capacity, but that of surrendering himself to the will of God: and if he uses any of his faculties for any other purpose but to do that supposed will more effectually, he is better without them. This is the theory of Calvinism; and it is held, in a mitigated form, by many who do not consider themselves Calvinists; the mitigation consisting in giving a less ascetic interpretation to the alleged will of God; asserting it to be his will that mankind should gratify some of their inclinations; of course not in the manner they themselves prefer, but in the way of obedience, that is, in a way prescribed to them by authority; and, therefore, by the necessary condition of the case, the same for all.

In some such insidious form there is at present a strong tendency to this narrow theory of life, and to the pinched and hidebound type of human character which it patronises. Many persons, no doubt, sincerely think that human beings thus cramped and dwarfed are as their Maker designed them to be; just as many have thought that trees are a much finer thing when clipped into pollards, or cut out into figures of animals, than as nature made them. But if it be any part of religion to believe that man was made by a good Being, it is more consistent with that faith to believe that this Being gave all human faculties that they might be cultivated and unfolded, not rooted out and consumed, and that he takes delight in every nearer approach made by his creatures to the ideal conception embodied in them, every increase in any of their capabilities of comprehension, of action, or of enjoyment. There is a different type of human excellence from the Calvinistic: a conception of humanity as having its nature bestowed on it for other purposes than merely to be abnegated. 'Pagan self-assertion' is one of the elements of human worth, as well as 'Christian self-denial.'* There is a Greek ideal of self-development, which the Platonic and Christian ideal of self-government blends with, but does not supersede. It may be better to be a John Knox than an Alcibiades, but it is better to be a Pericles than either; nor would a Pericles, if we had one in these days, be without anything good which belonged to John Knox.

It is not by wearing down into uniformity all that is individual in themselves, but by cultivating it, and calling it forth, within the limits imposed by the rights and interests of others, that human beings become a noble and beautiful object of contemplation; and as the works partake the character of those who do them, by the same process human life also becomes rich, diversified, and animating, furnishing more abundant aliment to high thoughts and elevating feelings, and strengthening the tie which binds every individual to the race, by making the race infinitely better worth belonging to. In proportion to the development of his individuality, each person becomes more valuable to himself, and is therefore capable of being more valuable to others. There is a greater fulness of life about his own existence, and when there is more life in the units there is more in the mass which is composed of them. As much compression as is necessary to prevent the stronger specimens of human nature from encroaching on the rights of others cannot be dispensed with; but for this there is ample compensation even in the point of view of human development. The means of development which the individual loses by being prevented from gratify-

* Sterling's *Essays.*

ing his inclinations to the injury of others, are chiefly obtained at the expense of the development of other people. And even to himself there is a full equivalent in the better development of the social part of his nature, rendered possible by the restraint put upon the selfish part. To be held to rigid rules of justice for the sake of others, develops the feelings and capacities which have the good of others for their object. But to be restrained in things not affecting their good, by their mere displeasure, develops nothing valuable, except such force of character as may unfold itself in resisting the restraint. If acquiesced in, it dulls and blunts the whole nature. To give any fair play to the nature of each, it is essential that different persons should be allowed to lead different lives. In proportion as this latitude has been exercised in any age, has that age been noteworthy to posterity. Even despotism does not produce its worst effects, so long as individuality exists under it; and whatever crushes individuality is despotism, by whatever name it may be called, and whether it professes to be enforcing the will of God or the injunctions of men.

Having said that the individuality is the same thing with development, and that it is only the cultivation of individuality which produces, or can produce, well-developed human beings, I might here close the argument: for what more or better can be said of any condition of human affairs than that it brings human beings themselves nearer to the best thing they can be? or what worse can be said of any obstruction to good than that it prevents this? Doubtless, however, these considerations will not suffice to convince those who most need convincing; and it is necessary further to show, that these developed human beings are of some use to the undeveloped – to point out to those who do not desire liberty, and would not avail themselves of it, that they may be in some intelligible manner rewarded for allowing other people to make use of it without hindrance.

In the first place, then, I would suggest that they might possibly learn something from them. It will not be denied by anybody, that originality is a valuable element in human affairs. There is always need of persons not only to discover new truths, and point out when what were once truths are true no longer, but also to commence new practices, and set the example of more enlightened conduct, and better taste and sense in human life. This cannot well be gainsaid by anybody who does not believe that the world has already attained perfection in all its ways and practices. It is true that this benefit is not capable of being rendered by everybody alike: there are but few persons, in comparison with the whole of mankind, whose experiments, if adopted by others, would be likely to be any improvement on established practice. But these few are the salt of the earth; without them, human life would become a stagnant pool. Not only is it they who introduce good things which did not before exist; it is they who keep the life in those which already exist. If there were nothing to be done, would human intellect cease to be necessary? Would it be a reason why those who do the old things should forget why they are done, and do them like cattle, not like human beings? There is only too great a tendency in the best beliefs and practices to degenerate into the mechanical; and unless there were a succession of persons whose ever-recurring originality prevents the grounds of those beliefs and practices from becoming merely traditional, such dead matter would not resist the smallest shock from anything really alive, and there would be no reason why civilisation should not die out, as in the Byzantine Empire. Persons of genius, it is true, are, and are always likely to be, a small minority; but in order to have them, it is necessary to preserve the soil in which they grow. Genius can only breathe freely in an *atmosphere* of freedom. Persons of genius are, *ex vi termini,* more individual than any other people – less capable, consequently, of fitting themselves, without hurtful compression, into any of the small number of moulds which society provides in order to save its members the trouble of forming their own character. If from timidity they consent to be forced into one of these moulds, and to let all that part of themselves which cannot expand under the pressure remain unexpanded, society will be little the better for their genius. If they are of a strong character, and break their fetters, they become a mark for the society which has not succeeded in reducing them to commonplace, to point out with solemn warning as 'wild,' 'erratic,' and the like; much as if one should complain of the Niagara river for not flowing smoothly between its banks like a Dutch canal.

I insist thus emphatically on the importance of genius, and the necessity of allowing it to unfold itself freely both in thought and in practice, being well aware that no one will deny the position in theory, but knowing also that almost every one, in reality, is totally indifferent to it. People think genius a fine thing if it enables a man to write an exciting poem, or paint a picture. But in its true sense, that of originality in thought and action, though no one says that it is not a thing to be admired, nearly all, at heart, think that they can do very well without it. Unhappily this is too natural to be wondered at. Originality is the one thing which unoriginal minds cannot feel the use of. They cannot see what it is to do for them: how should they? If they could see what it would do for them, it would not be originality. The first service which originality has to render them, is that of opening their eyes: which being once fully done, they would have a chance of being themselves original. Meanwhile, recollecting that nothing was ever yet done which some one was not the first to do, and that all good things which exist are the fruits of originality, let them be modest enough to believe that there is something still left for it to accomplish, and assure themselves that they are more in need of originality, the less they are conscious of the want.

In sober truth, whatever homage may be professed, or even paid, to real or supposed mental superiority, the general tendency of things throughout the world is to render mediocrity the ascendant power among mankind. In ancient history, in the Middle Ages, and in a diminishing degree through the long transition from feudality to the present time, the individual was a power in himself; and if he had either great talents or a high social position, he was a considerable power. At present individuals are lost in the crowd. In politics it is almost a triviality to say that public opinion now rules the world. The only power deserving the name is that of masses, and of governments while they make themselves the organ of the tendencies and instincts of masses. This is as true in the moral and social relations of private life as in public transactions. Those whose opinions go by the name of public opinion are not always the same sort of public: in America they are the whole white population; in England, chiefly the middle class. But they are always a mass, that is to say, collective mediocrity. And what is a still greater novelty, the mass do not now take their opinions from dignitaries in Church or State, from ostensible leaders, or from books. Their thinking is done for them by men much like themselves, addressing them or speaking in their name, on the spur of the moment, through the newspapers. I am not complaining of all this. I do not assert that anything better is compatible, as a general rule, with the present low state of the human mind. But that does not hinder the government of mediocrity from being mediocre government. No government by a democracy or a numerous aristocracy, either in its political acts or in the opinions, qualities, and tone of mind which it fosters, ever did or could rise above mediocrity, except in so far as the sovereign many have let themselves be guided (which in their best times they always have done) by the counsels and influence of a more highly gifted and instructed One or Few. The initiation of all wise or noble things comes and must come from the individuals; generally at first from some one individual. The honour and glory of the average man is that he is capable of following that initiative; that he can respond internally to wise and noble things, and be led to them with his eyes open. I am not countenancing the sort of 'hero-worship' which applauds the strong man of genius for forcibly seizing on the government of the world and making it do his bidding in spite of itself. All he can claim is, freedom to point out the way. The power of compelling others into it is not only inconsistent with the freedom and development of all the rest, but corrupting to the strong man himself. It does seem, however, that when the opinions of masses of merely average men are everywhere become or becoming the dominant power, the counterpoise and corrective to that tendency would be the more and more pronounced individuality of those who stand on the higher eminences of thought. It is in these circumstances most especially, that exceptional individuals, instead of being deterred, should be encouraged in acting differently from the mass. In other times there was no advantage in their doing so, unless they acted not only differently but better. In this age, the mere example of non-conformity, the mere refusal to bend the knee to custom, is itself a service. Precisely because the tyranny of opinion is such as to make eccentricity a reproach, it is desirable, in order to break through that tyranny, that people should be eccentric. Eccentricity has always abounded when and where strength of character has abounded; and the amount of eccentricity in a society has generally been proportional to the amount of genius, mental vigour, and moral courage it contained. That so few now dare to be eccentric marks the chief danger of the time.

I have said that it is important to give the freest scope possible to uncustomary things, in order that it may in time appear which of these are fit to be converted into customs. But independence of action, and disregard of custom, are not solely deserving of encouragement for the chance they afford that better modes of action, and customs more worthy of general adoption, may be struck out; nor is it only persons of decided mental superiority who have a just claim to carry on their lives in their own way. There is no reason that all human existence should be constructed on some one or some small number of patterns. If a person possesses any tolerable amount of common sense and experience, his own mode of laying out his existence is the best, not because it is the best in itself, but because it is his own mode. Human beings are not like sheep; and even sheep are not undistinguishably alike. A man cannot get a coat or a pair of boots to fit him unless they are either made to his measure, or he has a whole warehouseful to choose from: and is it easier to fit him with a life than with a coat, or are human beings more like one another in their whole physical and spiritual conformation than in the shape of their feet? If it were only that people have diversities of taste, that is reason enough for not attempting to shape them all after one model. But different persons also require different conditions for their spiritual development; and can no more exist healthily in the same moral, than all the variety of plants can in the same physical, atmosphere and climate. The same things which are helps to one person towards the cultivation of his higher nature are hindrances to another. The same mode of life is a healthy excitement to one, keeping all his faculties of action and enjoyment in their best order, while to another it is a distracting burthen, which suspends or crushes all internal life. Such are the differences among human beings in their sources of pleasure, their susceptibilities of pain, and the operation on them of different physical and moral agencies, that unless there is a corresponding diversity in their modes of life, they neither obtain their fair share of happiness, nor grow up to the mental, moral, and æsthetic stature of which their nature is capable. Why then should tolerance, as far as the public sentiment is concerned, extend only to tastes and modes of life which extort acquiescence by the multitude of their adherents? Nowhere (except in some monastic institutions) is diversity of taste entirely unrecognised; a person may, without blame, either like or dislike rowing, or smoking, or music, or athletic exercises, or chess, or cards, or study, because both those who like each of these things, and those who dislike them, are too numerous to be put down. But the man, and still more the woman, who can be accused either of doing 'what nobody does,' or of not doing 'what everybody does,' is the subject of as much depreciatory remark as if he or she had committed some grave moral delinquency. Persons require to possess a title, or some other badge of rank, or of the consideration of people of rank, to be able to indulge somewhat in the luxury of doing as they like without detriment to their estimation. To indulge somewhat, I repeat: for whoever allow themselves much of that indulgence, incur the risk of something worse than disparaging speeches—they are in peril of a commission *de lunatico,* and of having their property taken from them and given to their relations.*

There is one characteristic of the present direction of public opinion peculiarly calculated to make it intolerant of any marked demonstration of individuality. The general average of mankind are not only moderate in intellect, but also moderate in inclinations: they have no tastes or wishes strong enough to incline them to do anything unusual, and they consequently do not understand those who have, and class all such with the wild and intemperate whom they are accustomed to look down upon. Now, in addition to this fact which is general, we have only to suppose that a strong movement has set in towards the improvement of morals, and it is evident what we have to expect. In these days

* There is something both contemptible and frightful in the sort of evidence on which, of late years, any person can be judicially declared unfit for the management of his affairs; and after his death, his disposal of his property can be set aside, if there is enough of it to pay the expenses of litigation—which are charged on the property itself. All the minute details of his daily life are pried into, and whatever is found which, seen through the medium of the perceiving and describing faculties of the lowest of the low, bears an appearance unlike absolute commonplace, is laid before the jury as evidence of insanity, and often with success; the jurors being little, if at all, less vulgar and ignorant than the witnesses; while the judges, with that extraordinary want of knowledge of human nature and life which continually astonishes us in English lawyers, often help to mislead them. These trials speak volumes as to the state of feeling and opinion among the vulgar with regard to human liberty. So far from setting any value on individuality—so far from respecting the right of each individual to act, in things indifferent, as seems good to his own judgment and inclinations, judges and juries cannot even conceive that a person in a state of sanity can desire such freedom. In former days, when it was proposed to burn atheists, charitable people used to suggest putting them in a madhouse instead: it would be nothing surprising now-a-days were we to see this done, and the doers applauding themselves, because, instead of persecuting for religion, they had adopted so humane and Christian a mode of treating these unfortunates, not without a silent satisfaction at their having thereby obtained their deserts.

such a movement has set in; much has actually been effected in the way of increased regularity of conduct and discouragement of excesses; and there is a philanthropic spirit abroad, for the exercise of which there is no more inviting field than the moral and prudential improvement of our fellow-creatures. These tendencies of the times cause the public to be more disposed than at most former periods to prescribe general rules of conduct, and endeavour to make every one conform to the approved standard. And that standard, express or tacit, is to desire nothing strongly. Its ideal of character is to be without any marked character; to maim by compression, like a Chinese lady's foot, every part of human nature which stands out prominently, and tends to make the person markedly dissimilar in outline to commonplace humanity.

As is usually the case with ideals which exclude one-half of what is desirable, the present standard of approbation produces only an inferior imitation of the other half. Instead of great energies guided by vigorous reason, and strong feelings strongly controlled by a conscientious will, its result is weak feelings and weak energies, which therefore can be kept in outward conformity to rule without any strength either of will or of reason. Already energetic characters on any large scale are becoming merely traditional. There is now scarcely any outlet for energy in this country except business. The energy expended in this may still be regarded as considerable. What little is left from that employment is expended on some hobby; which may be a useful, even a philanthropic hobby, but is always some one thing, and generally a thing of small dimensions. The greatness of England is now all collective; individually small, we only appear capable of anything great by our habit of combining; and with this our moral and religious philanthropists are perfectly contented. But it was men of another stamp than this that made England what it has been; and men of another stamp will be needed to prevent its decline.

The despotism of custom is everywhere the standing hindrance to human advancement, being in unceasing antagonism to that disposition to aim at something better than customary, which is called, according to circumstances, the spirit of liberty, or that of progress or improvement. The spirit of improvement is not always a spirit of liberty, for it may aim at forcing improvements on an unwilling people; and the spirit of liberty, in so far as it resists such attempts, may ally itself locally and temporarily with the opponents of improvement; but the only unfailing and permanent source of improvement is liberty, since by it there are as many possible independent centres of improvement as there are individuals. The progressive principle, however, in either shape, whether as the love of liberty or of improvement, is antagonistic to the sway of Custom, involving at least emancipation from that yoke; and the contest between the two constitutes the chief interest of the history of mankind. The greater part of the world has, properly speaking, no history, because the despotism of Custom is complete. This is the case over the whole East. Custom is there, in all things, the final appeal; justice and right mean conformity to custom; the argument of custom no one, unless some tyrant intoxicated with power, thinks of resisting. And we see the result. Those nations must once have had originality; they did not start out of the ground populous, lettered, and versed in many of the arts of life; they made themselves all this, and were then the greatest and most powerful nations of the world. What are they now? The subjects or dependents of tribes whose forefathers wandered in the forests when theirs had magnificent palaces and gorgeous temples, but over whom custom exercised only a divided rule with liberty and progress. A people, it appears, may be progressive for a certain length of time, and then stop: when does it stop? When it ceases to possess individuality. If a similar change should befall the nations of Europe, it will not be in exactly the same shape: the despotism of custom with which these nations are threatened is not precisely stationariness. It proscribes singularity, but it does not preclude change, provided all change together. We have discarded the fixed costumes of our forefathers; every one must still dress like other people, but the fashion may change once or twice a year. We thus take care that when there is a change, it shall be for change's sake, and not from any idea of beauty or convenience; for the same idea of beauty or convenience would not strike all the world at the same moment, and be simultaneously thrown aside by all at another moment. But we are progressive as well as changeable: we continually make new inventions in mechanical things, and keep them until they are again superseded by better; we are eager for improvement in politics, in education, even in morals, though in this last our idea of improvement chiefly consists in persuading or forcing other people to be as good as ourselves. It is not progress that we object to; on the contrary, we flatter ourselves that we are the most progressive people who ever lived. It is individuality that we war against: we should think we had done wonders if we had made ourselves all alike; forgetting that the unlikeness of one person to another is generally the first thing which draws the attention of either to the imperfection of his own type, and the superioriy of another, or the possibility, by combining the advantages of both, of producing something better than either. We have a warning example in China – a nation of much talent, and, in some respects, even wisdom, owing to the rare good fortune of having been provided at an early period with a particularly good set of customs, the work, in some measure, of men to whom even the most enlightened European must accord, under certain limitations, the title of sages and philosophers. They are remarkable, too in the excellence of their apparatus for impressing as far as possible the best wisdom they possess upon every mind in the community, and securing that those who have appropriated most of it shall occupy the posts of honour and power. Surely the people who did this have discovered the secret of human progressiveness, and must have kept themselves steadily at the head of the movement of the world. On the contrary they have become stationary – have remained so for thousands of years; and if they are ever to be further improved, it must be by foreigners. They have succeeded beyond all hope in what English philanthropists are so industriously working at – in making a people all alike, all governing their thoughts and conduct by the same maxims and rules; and these are the fruits. The modern *régime* of public opinion is, in an unorganised form, what the Chinese educational and political systems are in an organised; and unless individuality shall be able successfully to assert itself against this yoke, Europe, notwithstanding its noble antecedents and its professed Christianity, will tend to become another China.

What is it that has hitherto preserved Europe from this lot? What has made the European family of nations an improving, instead of a stationary portion of mankind? Not any superior excellence in them, which, when it exists, exists as the effect not as the cause; but their remarkable diversity of character and culture. Individuals, classes, nations, have been extremely unlike one another: they have struck out a great variety of paths, each leading to something valuable, and although at every period those who travelled in different paths have been intolerant of one another, and each would have thought it an excellent thing if all the rest could have been compelled to travel his road, their attempts to thwart each other's development have rarely had any permanent success, and each has in time endured to receive the good which the others have offered. Europe is, in my judgment, wholly indebted to this plurality of paths for its progressive and many-sided development. But it already begins to possess this benefit in a considerably less degree. It is decidedly advancing towards the Chinese ideal of making all people alike. M. de Tocqueville, in his last important work, remarks how much more the Frenchmen of the present day resemble one another than did those even of the last generation. The same remark might be made of Englishmen in a far greater degree. In a passage already quoted from Wilhelm von Humboldt, he points out two things as necessary conditions of human development, because necessary to render people unlike one another; namely, freedom, and variety of situations. The second of these two conditions is in this country every day diminishing. The circumstances which surround different classes and individuals, and shape their characters, are daily becoming more assimilated. Formerly, different ranks, different neighbourhoods, different trades and professions, lived in what might be called different worlds; at present to a great degree in the same. Comparatively speaking, they now read the same things, listen to the same things, see the same things, go to the same places, have their hopes and fears directed to the same objects, have the same rights and liberties, and the same means of asserting them. Great as are the differences of position which remain, they are nothing to those which have ceased. And the assimilation is still proceeding. All the political changes of the age promote it, since they all tend to raise the low and to lower the high. Every extension of education promotes it, because education brings people under common influences, and gives them access to the general stock of facts and sentiments. Improvements in the means of communication promotes it, by bringing the inhabitants of distant places into personal contact, and keeping up a rapid flow of changes of residence between one place and another. The increase of commerce and manufactures promotes it, by diffusing more widely the advantages of easy circumstances, and opening all objects of ambition, even the highest, to general competition, whereby the desire of rising becomes no longer the character of a particular class, but of all classes. A more powerful agency than all these, in bringing about a general similarity among mankind, is the complete establishment, in this and other free countries, of the ascendancy of public opinion in the State. As the various social eminences which enabled persons entrenched on them to disregard the opinion of the multitude gradually become levelled; as the very idea of resisting the will of the public, when it is positively known that they have a will, disappears more and more from the minds of practical politicians; there ceases to be any social support for nonconformity – any substantive power in society which, itself opposed to the ascendancy of numbers, is interested in taking under its protection opinions and tendencies at variance with those of the public.

The combination of all these causes forms so great a mass of influence hostile to Individuality, that it is not easy to see how it can stand its ground. It will do so with increasing difficulty, unless the intelligent part of the public can be made to feel its value – to see that it is good there should be differences, even though not for the better, even though, as it may appear to them, some should be for the worse. If the claims of Individuality are ever to be asserted, the time is now, while much is still wanting to complete the enforced assimiliation. It is only in the earlier stages that any stand can be successfully made against the encroachment. The demand that all other people shall resemble ourselves grows by what it feeds on. If resistance waits till life is reduced nearly to one uniform type, all deviations from that type will come to be considered impious, immoral, even monstrous and contrary to nature. Mankind speedily become unable to conceive diversity, when they have been for some time unaccustomed to see it.

PART IV THE WORKING CLASS

11 *Claims of Labour*

(*Edinburgh Review* LXXXI, 1845;
reprinted in *Dissertations and Discussions*,
Vol. II, 1859.)

'Persons of a thoughtful mind,' says the introduction to this little volume, 'seeing closely the falsehood, the folly, and the arrogance of the age in which they live, are apt, occasionally, to have a great contempt for it; and I doubt not, that many a man looks upon the present time as one of feebleness and degeneracy. There are, however, signs of an increased solicitude for the *Claims of Labour,* which of itself is a thing of the highest promise, and more to be rejoiced over than all the mechanical triumphs which both those who would magnify, and those who would depreciate, the present age, would be apt to point to as containing its especial significance and merit.'

It is true that many are now inquiring, more earnestly that heretofore, 'how the great mass of the people are fed, clothed, and taught – and whether the improvement in their condition corresponds at all with the improvement of the condition of the middle and upper classes.' [P. 3.] And many are of opinion, with the writer from whom we quote, that the answer which can be given to these questions is an unsatisfactory one. Nor is the newly-awakened interest in the condition of the labouring people confined to persons, like this author, of feeling and reflection. To its claims upon the conscience and philanthropy of the more favoured classes, to its ever-strengthening demands upon their sense of self-interest, this cause now adds the more ephemeral attractions of the last new fashion. The *Claims of Labour* have become the question of the day: the current of public meetings, subscriptions, and associations, has for some time set strongly in that direction; and many minor topics which previously occupied the public mind, have either merged into that question, or been superseded by it. Even the Legislature, which seldom concerns itself much with new tendencies of opinion until they have grown too powerful to be safely overlooked, is invited, in each Session with increasing urgency, to provide that the labouring classes shall earn more, work less, or have their lot in some other manner alleviated; and in each Session yields more or less cheerfully, but still yields, though slowly yet increasingly, to the requisition.

That this impulse is salutary and promising, few will deny; but it would be idle to suppose that it has not its peculiar dangers, or that the business of doing good can be the only one for which *zeal* suffices, without *knowledge* or circumspection. A change from wrong to right, even in little things, is not so easy to make, as to wish for, and to talk about. Society cannot with safety, in one of its gravest concerns, pass at once from selfish supineness to restless activity. It has a long and difficult apprenticeship yet to serve; during which we shall be often reminded of the *dictum* of Fontenelle, that mankind only settle into the right course after passing through and exhausting all the varieties of error. But however this may be, the movement is not therefore to be damped or discouraged. If, in the attempt to benefit the labouring classes, we are destined to see great mistakes committed in practice, as so many errors are already advocated in theory, let us not lay the blame upon excess of zeal. The danger is, that men in general will care enough for the object, to be willing to sacrifice other people's interest to it, but not their own; and that the few who lead will make the sacrifice of their money, their times, even their bodily ease, in the cause; but will not do for its sake what to most men is so much more difficult – undergo the formidable labour of thought.

For several reasons, it will be useful to trace back this philanthropic movement to its small and unobvious beginnings – to note its fountain-head, and show what mingled streams have from time to time swelled its course.

We are inclined to date its origin from an event which would in vulgar apprehension seem to have a less title to that than to any other honourable distinction – the appearance of Mr Malthus's Essay on Population. Though the assertion may be looked upon as a paradox, it is historically true, that only from that time has the economical condition of the labouring classes been regarded by thoughtful men as susceptible of permanent improvement. We know that this was not the inference originally drawn from the truth propounded by Mr Malthus. Even by himself, that truth was at first announced as an inexorable law, which, by perpetuating the poverty and degradation of the mass of mankind, gave a *quietus* to the visions of indefinite social improvement which had agitated so fiercely a neighbouring nation. To these supposed corollaries from Mr Malthus's principle, it was, we believe, indebted for its early success with the more opulent classes, and for much of its lasting unpopularity with the poorer. But this view of its tendencies only continued to prevail while the theory itself was but imperfectly understood; and now lingers nowhere but in those dark corners into which no subsequent lights have penetrated. The first promulgator of a truth is not always the best judge of its tendencies and consequences; but Mr Malthus early abandoned the mistaken inferences he had at first drawn from his celebrated principle, and adopted the very different views now almost unanimously professed by those who recognise his doctrine.

So long as the necessary relation between the numbers of the labouring population and their wages had escaped attention, the poverty, bordering on destitution, of the great mass of mankind, being an universal fact, was (by one of those natural illusions from which human reason is still so incompletely emancipated) conceived to be inevitable; – a provision of nature, and as some said, an ordinance of God; a part of human destiny, susceptible merely of partial alleviation in individual cases, from public or private charity. The only persons by whom any other opinion seemed to be entertained, were those who prophesied advancements in physical knowledge and mechanical art, sufficient to alter the fundamental conditions of man's existence on earth; or who professed the doctrine, that poverty is a factitious thing, produced by the tyranny and rapacity of governments and of the rich. Even so recent a thinker, and one so much in advance of his predecessors, as Adam Smith, went no further than to say, that the labourers might be well off in a rapidly progressive state of the public wealth; – a state which has never yet comprehended more than a small portion of the earth's surface at once, and can nowhere last indefinitely; while they must be pinched and in a condition of hardship in the stationary state, which in a finite world, composed of matter not changeable in its properties, is the state towards which things must be at all times tending. The ideas, therefore, of the most enlightened men, anterior to Mr Malthus, led really to the discouraging anticipations for which his doctrine has been made accountable. But these anticipations vanished, so soon as the truths brought to light by Mr Malthus were correctly understood. It was then seen that the capabilities of increase of the human species, as of animal nature in general (being far greater than those of subsistence under any except very unusual circumstances), must be, and are, controlled, everywhere else, by one or two limiting principles – starvation, or prudence and conscience: That, under the operation of this conflict, the reward of ordinary unskilled labour is always and everywhere (saving temporary variations, and rare conjunctions of circumstances) at the lowest point to which the labours will consent to be reduced – the point below which they will not choose to propagate their species: That this *minimum*, though everywhere much too low for human happiness and dignity, is different in different places, and in different ages of the world; and, in an improving country, has on the whole a tendency to rise. These considerations furnished a sufficient solution of the state of extreme poverty in which the majority of mankind had almost everywhere been found existing, without supposing any inherent necessity in the case – any universal cause, other than the causes which have made human progress altogether so imperfect and slow as it is. And the explanation afforded a sure hope, that whatever accelerates that progress would tell with full effect upon the physical condition of the labouring classes. Whatever raises the civilization of the people at large – whatever accustoms them to require a higher standard of subsistence, comfort, taste, and enjoyment, affords of itself, according to this encouraging view of human prospects, the means of satisfying the wants which it engenders. In every moral or intellectual benefit conferred upon the mass of the people, this doctrine teaches us to see an assurance also of their physical advantage; a means of enabling them to improve their worldly circumstances – not in the vulgar way of 'rising in the world,' so often recommended to them – not by endeavouring to escape out of their class, as if to live by manual labour were a fate only endurable as a step to something else; but by raising the class itself, in physical well-being and in self-estimation. These are the prospects which the vilified population principle has opened to mankind. True, indeed the doctrine teaches this further lesson, that any attempt to produce the same result by other means – any scheme of beneficence which trusts for its moving power to anything but to the influence over the minds and habits of the people, which it either directly aims at, or may happen indirectly to promote – might, for any *general* effect of a beneficial kind which it can produce, as well be let alone. And, the doctrine being brought thus into conflict with those plans of easy beneficence which accord so well with the inclinations of man, but so ill with the arrangements of nature, we need not wonder that the epithets of 'Malthusians' and 'Political Economists' are so often considered equivalent to hard-hearted, unfeeling, and enemies of the poor; – accusations so far from being true, that no thinkers, of any pretensions to sobriety, cherish such hopeful views of the future social position of labour, or have so long made the permanent increase of its remuneration the turning-point of their political speculations, as those who most broadly acknowledge the doctrine of Malthus.

But if the permanent place now occupied in the minds of thinking men by the question of improving the condition of the labouring classes, may be dated from the new light cast by Malthus's speculations upon the determining laws of that condition, other causes are needful to account for the popularity of the subject as one of the topics of the day; and we believe they will be found in the stir and commotion of the national mind, consequent upon the passing of the Reform Bill.

It was foretold during the Reform crisis, that when the consequences of the Bill should have had time to manifest themselves, the direct effects with which all mouths were filled, would prove unimportant compared with those indirect effects which were never mentioned in discussion, and which hardly any one seemed to think of. The prophecy has been signally verified. Considered as a great constitutional change, both friends and enemies now seem rather surprised that they should have ascribed so much efficacy to the Bill, for good or for evil. But its indirect consequences have surpassed every calculation. The series of events, commencing with Catholic Emancipation, and consummated by the Reform Act, brought home for the first time to the existing generation a practical consciousness of living in a world of change. It gave the first great shock to old habits. It was to politics what the Reformation was to religion – it made reason the recognised standard, instead of authority. By making it evident to the public that they were on a new sea, it destroyed the force of the instinctive objection to new courses. Reforms have still to encounter opposition from those whose interests they affect, or seem to affect; but innovation is no longer under a ban, merely as innovation. The existing system has lost its *prestige*; it has ceased to be the system which Tories had been taught to venerate, and has not become that which Liberals were accustomed to desire. When any wide-spread social evil was brought before minds thus prepared, there was such a chance as there had not been for the last two hundred years, of its being examined with a real desire to find a remedy, or at least without a predetermination to leave things alone. That the evils of the condition of the working classes should be brought before the mind of the nation in the most emphatic manner, was the care of those classes themselves. Their 'petition of grievances' was embodied in the People's Charter.

The democratic movement among the operative classes, commonly known as Chartism, was the first open separation of interest, feeling, and opinion, between the labouring portion of the commonwealth and all above them. It was the revolt of nearly all the active talent, and a great part of the physical force, of the working classes, against their whole relation to society. Conscientious and sympathizing minds among the ruling classes, could not but be strongly impressed by such a protest. They could not but ask themselves, with misgiving, what there was to say in reply to it; how the existing social arrangements could best be justified to those who deemed themselves aggrieved by them. It seemed highly desirable that the benefits derived from those arrangements by the poor should be made less questionable – should be such as could not easily be overlooked. If the poor had reason for their complaints, the higher classes had not fulfilled their duties as governors; if they had no reason, neither had those classes fulfilled their duties in allowing them to grow up so ignorant and uncultivated as to be open to these mischievous delusions. While one sort of minds among the more fortunate classes were thus influenced by the political claims put forth by the operatives, there was another description upon whom that phenomenon acted in a different manner, leading, however, to the same result. While some, by the physical and moral circumstances which they saw around them, were made to feel that the condition of the labouring classes *ought* to be attended to, others were made to see that it *would* be attended to, whether they wished to be blind to it or not. The victory of 1832, due to the manifestation, though without the actual employment, of physical force, had taught a lesson to those who, from the nature of the case, have always the physical force on their side; and who only wanted the organization, which they were rapidly acquiring, to convert their physical power into a moral and social one. It was no longer disputable that something must be done to render the multitude more content with the existing state of things.

Ideas, unless outward circumstances conspire with them, have in general no very rapid or immediate efficacy in human affairs; and the most favourable outward circumstances may pass by, or remain inoperative, for want of ideas suitable to the conjuncture. But when the right circumstances and the right ideas meet, the effect is seldom slow in manifesting itself. In the posture of things which has been described, we attribute considerable effect to certain writers, by whom what many were either thinking or prepared to think, was for the first time expressly proclaimed. Among these must be reckoned Mr Carlyle, whose 'Chartism' and 'Past and Present' were openly, what much of his previous writings had been incidentally, an indignant remonstrance with the higher classes on their sins of omission against the lower; contrasted with what he deemed the superior efficiency, in that relation, of the rulers in older times. On both these points, he has met with auxiliaries from a direct opposite point of the political horizon; from those whom a spirit of reaction against the democratic tendencies of the age, had flung off with the greatest violence in the direction of feudal and sacerdotal ascendancy. As, in the Stuart times, there were said to be Church Puritans and State Puritans, so there are now Church Puseyites, and what may be called State Puseyites; of whom the so-called 'Young England' party aspires to be the parliamentary organ, and the *Times* newspaper makes itself to some extent the representative in the press: [13] men who look back with fondness to times when the poor had no notion of any other social state than to give obedience to the nearest great landholder, and receive protection; and who assert, in the meantime, the right of the poor to protection, in hopes that the obedience will follow.

To complete the explanation of this increase of sympathy for the poor, it ought to be noticed that, until lately, few were adequately aware of their real condition. The agitation against the Poor-Law, bad as it was and is, both in its objects and in its effects, had in it this good, that it incessantly invited attention to the details of distress. The inquiries emanating from the Poor-Law Commission, and the official investigations of the last few years, brought to light many facts which made a great impression upon the public; and the poverty and wretchedness of great masses of people were incidentally unveiled by the struggles of parties respecting the Corn-Laws. The Agriculturists attempted to turn the tables upon their opponents, by highly coloured pictures of the sufferings and degradation of the Factory people; and the League repaid the attack with interest, by sending emissaries into the rural districts, and publishing the deplorable poverty of the agricultural labourers.

From these multifarious causes a feeling has been awakened, which would soon be as influential in elections as the anti-slavery movement some years ago, and dispose of funds equal to those of the missionary societies, had it but as definite an object. The stream at present flows in a multitude of small channels. Societies for the protection of needlewomen, of governesses – associations to improve the buildings of the labouring classes, to provide them with baths, with parks and promenades, have started into existence. Legislative interference to abridge the hours of labour in factories has obtained large minorities, and once a passing majority, in the House of Commons; and attempts are multiplying to obtain, by the consent of employers, a similar abridgement in many departments of retail trade. In the rural districts, every expedient, practicable or not, for giving work to the unemployed, finds advocates; public meetings for the discussion and comparison of projects have lately been frequent; and the movement towards the 'allotment system' is becoming general.

If these, and other modes of relieving distress, were looked upon simply in the light of ordinary charity, they would not fill the large space they do in public discussion, and would not demand any special comment. To give money in alms has never been, either in this country or in most others, a rare virtue. Charitable institutions, and subscriptions for relief of the destitute, already abounded: and if new forms were brought into notice, nothing was more natural than to do for them what had already been done for others. People usually give alms to gratify their feelings of compassion, or to discharge what they think their duty by giving of their superfluity to alleviate the wants of individual sufferers; and beyond this they do not, nor are they, in general, qualified to look. But it is not in this spirit that the new schemes of benevolence are conceived. They are propounded as instalments of a great social reform. They are celebrated as the beginning of a new moral order, or an old order revived, in which the possessors of property are to resume their place as the paternal guardians of those less fortunate; and which, when established, is to cause peace and union throughout society, and to extinguish, not indeed poverty – that hardly seems to be thought desirable – but the more abject forms of vice, destitution, and physical wretchedness. What has hitherto been *done* in this brilliant career of improvement, is of very little importance compared with what is *said;* with the objects held up to pursuit, and the theories avowed. These are not now confined to speculative men and professed philanthropists. They are made familiar to every reader of newspapers, by sedulous inculcation from day to day.

It is therefore not superfluous to consider whether these theories, and the expectations built upon them, are rational or chimerical; whether the attempt to carry them out would in the end be found to accord or conflict with the nature of man, and of the world in which he is cast. It would be unfair to the theorists to try them by anything which has been commenced, or even projected. Were they asked if they expect any good to the general interest of the labouring people, from a Labourers' Friend Society, or a Society for Distressed Needlewomen, they would of course answer that they do not; that these are but the first leaf-buds of what they hope to nourish into a stately and spreading tree;

that they do not limit their intentions to mitigating the evils of a low remuneration of labour, but must have a high remuneration; in the words of the operatives in the late disturbances – 'a fair day's wages for a fair day's work,' – that they hope to secure this, and will be contented with nothing short of it. Here, then, is a ground on which we can fairly meet them. That object is ours also. The question is of means, not ends. Let us look a little into the means they propose.

Their theory appears to be, in few words, this – that it is the proper function of the possessors of wealth, and especially of the employers of labour and the owners of land, to take care that the labouring people are well off: – that they ought always to pay good wages; – that they ought to withdraw their custom, their patronage, and any other desirable thing at their disposal, from all employers who will not do the like; – that, at these good wages, they ought to give employment to as great a number of persons as they can afford; and to make them work for no greater number of hours in the twenty-four, than is compatible with comfort, and with leisure for recreation and improvement. That if they have land or houses to be let to tenants, they should require and accept no higher rents than can be paid with comfort; and should be ready to build, at such rents as can be conveniently paid, warm, airy, healthy, and spacious cottages, for any number of young couples who may ask for them.

All this is not said in direct terms; but something very little short of it is. These principles form the standard by which we daily see the conduct, both of classes and of individuals, measured and condemned; and if these principles are not true, the new doctrines are without a meaning. It is allowable to take this picture as a true likeness of the 'new moral world' which the present philanthropic movement aims at calling into existence.

Mankind are often cautioned by divines and moralists against unreasonableness in their expectations. We attach greater value to the more limited warning against inconsistency in them. The state of society which this picture represents, is a conceivable one. We shall not at present inquire if it is of all others the most eligible one, even as an Utopia. We only ask if its promoters are willing to accept this state of society, together with all its inevitable accompaniments.

It is quite possible to impose, as a moral or a legal obligation, upon the higher classes, that they shall be answerable for the well-doing and well-being of the lower. There have been times and places in which this has in some measure been done. States of society exist, in which it is the recognised duty of every owner of land, not only to see that all who dwell and work thereon are fed, clothed, and housed, in a sufficient manner; but to be, in so full a sense, responsible for their good conduct, as to indemnify all other persons for any damage they do, or offence they may commit. This must surely be the ideal state of society which the new philanthropists are contending for. Who are the happy labouring classes who enjoy the blessings of these wise ordinances? The Russian boors. There are other labourers, not merely tillers of the soil, but workers in great establishments partaking of the nature of Factories, for whom the laws of our own country, even in our own time, compelled their employers to find wholesome food, and sufficient lodging and clothing. Who were these? The slaves on a West India estate. The relation sought to be established between the landed and manufacturing classes and the labourers, is therefore by no means unexampled. The former have before now been forced to maintain the latter, and to provide work for them, or support them in idleness. But this obligation never has existed, and never will nor can exist, without, as a counteravailing element, absolute power, or something approaching to it, in those who are bound to afford this support, over those entitled to receive it. Such a relation has never existed between human beings, without ultimate[14] degradation to the character of the dependent class. Shall we take another example, in which things are not carried quite so far as this? There are governments in Europe who look upon it as part of their duty to take care of the physical well-being and comfort of the people. The Austrian government, in its German dominions, does so. Several of the minor German governments do so. But with paternal care is connected paternal authority. In these states we find severe restrictions on marriage. No one is permitted to marry, unless he satisfies the authorities that he has a rational prospect of being able to support a family.

Thus much, at least, it might have been expected that the apostles of the new theory would have been prepared for. They cannot mean that the working classes should combine the liberty of action of independent citizens, with the immunities of slaves. There are but two modes of social existence for human beings: they must be left to the natural consequences of their mistakes in life; or society must guard against the mistakes, by prevention or punishment. Which will the new philanthropists have? If it is really to be incumbent on whoever have more than a mere subsistence, to give, so far as their means enable them, good wages and comfortable homes to all who present themselves, it is not surely intended that these should be permitted to follow the instinct of multiplication at the expense of others, until all are reduced to the same level as themselves. We should therefore have expected that the philanthropists would have accepted the condition, and contended for such a measure of restriction as might prevent the good they meditate from producing an overbalance of evil. To our surprise, we find them the great sticklers for the domestic liberty of the poor. The outcry against the Poor-Law finds among them its principal organs. Far from being willing that a man should be subject, when out of the poorhouse, to any restraints other than his own prudence may dictate, they will not submit to its being imposed upon him while actually supported at the expense of others. It is they who talk of Union Bastiles. They cannot bear that even a workhouse should be a place of regulation and discipline; that any extrinsic restraint should be applied even there. Their bitterest quarrel with the present system of relief is, that it enforces the separation of the sexes.

The higher and middle classes might or ought to be willing to submit to a very considerable sacrifice of their own means, for improving the condition of the existing generation of labourers, if by this they could hope to provide similar advantages for the generation to come. But why should they be called upon to make these sacrifices, merely that the country may contain a greater number of people, in as great poverty and as great liability to destitution as now? If whoever has too little, is to come to them to make it more, there is no alternative but restrictions on marriage, combined with such severe penalties on illegitimate births, as it would hardly be possible to enforce under a social system in which all grown persons are, nominally at least, their own masters. Without these provisions, the millennium promised would, in little more than a generation, sink the people of any country in Europe to one level of poverty. If, then, it is intended that the law, or the people of property, should assume a control over the multiplication of the people, tell us so plainly, and inform us how you propose to do it. But it will doubtless be said, that nothing of this sort would be endurable; that such things are not to be dreamt of in the state of English society and opinion; that the spirit of equality, and the love of individual independence, have so pervaded even the poorest class, that they would not take plenty to eat and drink, at the price of having their most personal concerns regulated for them by others. If this be so, all schemes for withdrawing wages from the control of supply and demand, or raising the people by other means than by such changes in their minds and habits as shall make them fit guardians of their own physical condition, are schemes for combining incompatibilities. They ought to be shielded, we hope they already are so, by public or private charity, from actual want of mere necessaries, and from any other extreme of bodily suffering. But if the whole income of the country were divided among them in wages or poor-rates, still, until there is a change in themselves, there can be no lasting improvement in their outward condition.

And how is this change to be effected, while we continue

inculcating upon them that their wages are to be regulated for them, and that to keep wages high is other people's business and not theirs? All classes are ready enough, without prompting, to believe that whatever ails them is not their fault, but the crime of somebody else; and that they are granting an indemnity to the crime if they attempt to get rid of the evil by any effort or sacrifice of their own. The National Assembly of France has been much blamed for talking in a rhetorical style about the rights of man, and neglecting to say anything about the duties. The same error is now in the course of being repeated with respect to the rights of poverty. It would surely be no derogation from any one's philanthropy to consider, that it is one thing to tell the poor that the rich ought to take care of them; and that it is rather idle in these days to suppose that a thing will not be overheard by the poor, because it is not designed for their ears. It is most true that the rich have much to answer for in their conduct to the poor. But in the matter of their poverty, there is no way in which the rich *could* have helped them, but by inducing them to help themselves; and if, while we stimulate the rich to repair this omission, we do all that depends on us to inculcate upon the poor that they need not attend to the lesson, we must be little aware of the sort of feelings and doctrines with which the minds of the poor are already filled. If we go on in this course, we may succeed in bursting society asunder by a Socialist revolution; but the poor, and their poverty, we shall leave worse than we found them.

The first remedy, then, is to abstain from directly counteracting our own end. The second, and most obvious, is Education. And this indeed is not the principal, but the sole remedy, if understood in its widest sense. Whatever acts upon the minds of the labouring classes, is properly their education. But their minds, like those of other people, are acted upon by the whole of their social circumstances; and often the part of their education which is least efficacious as such, is that which goes by the name.

Yet even in that comparatively narrow sense, too much

stress can hardly be laid upon its importance. We have scarcely seen more than the small beginnings of what might be effected for the country even by mere schooling. The religious rivalries, which are the unhappy price the course of our history has compelled us to pay for such religious liberty as we possess, have as yet thwarted every attempt to make this benefit universal. But if the children of different religious bodies cannot be instructed together, each can be instructed apart. And if we may judge from the zeal manifested, and the sums raised, both by the Church and by Dissenters, since the abandonment of the Government measure two years ago, there is no deficiency of pecuniary means for the support of schools, even without the aid which the State certainly will not refuse. Unfortunately there is something wanting which pecuniary means will not supply. There is a lack of sincere desire to attain the end. There have been schools enough in England, these thirty years, to have regenerated the people, if, wherever the means were found, the end had been desired. But it is not always where there are schools that there is a wish to educate. There may be a wish that children should learn to read the Bible, and, in the Church Schools, to repeat the Catechism. In most cases, there is little desire that they should be taught more; in many, a decided objection to it. Schoolmasters, like other public officers, are seldom inclined to do more than is exacted from them; but we believe that teaching the poor is almost the only public duty in which the payers are more a check than a stimulant to the zeal of their own agents. A teacher whose heart is in the work, and who attempts any enlargement of the instruction, often finds his greatest obstacle in the fears of the patrons and managers lest the poor should be 'over-educated;' and is driven to the most absolute evasions to obtain leave to teach the common rudiments of knowledge. The four rules of arithmetic are often only tolerated through ridiculous questions about Jacob's lambs, or the number of the Apostles or the Patriarchs; and geography can only be taught through maps of Palestine, to children who have yet to learn that the earth consists of

Europe, Asia, Africa, and America. A person must be beyond being argued with, who believes that this is the way to teach religion, or that a child will be made to understand the Bible by being taught to understand nothing else. We forbear to comment on the instances in which Church Schools have been opened, solely that through the influence of superiors the children might be drawn away from a Dissenting School already existing; and, as soon as that was shut up, the rival establishment, having attained its end, has been allowed to fall into disuse.

This spirit could never be tolerated by any person of honest intentions, who knew the value of even the commonest knowledge to the poor. We know not how the case may be in other countries, among a more quick-witted people; but in England, it would hardly be believed to what a degree all that is morally objectionable in the lowest class of the working people is nourished, if not engendered, by the low state of their understandings. Their infantine credulity to what they hear, when it is from their own class; their incapacity to observe what is before their eyes; their inability to comprehend or believe purposes in others which they have not been taught to expect, and are not conscious of in themselves – are the known characteristics of persons of low intellectual faculties in all classes. But what would not be equally credible without experience, is an amount of deficiency in the power of reasoning and calculation, which makes them insensible to their own direct personal interests. Few have considered how any one who could instil into these people the commonest worldly wisdom – who could render them capable of even selfish prudential calculations – would improve their conduct in every relation of life, and clear the soil for the growth of right feelings and worthy propensities.

To know what schools may do, we have but to think of what our Scottish Parochial Schools have formerly done. The progress of wealth and population has outgrown the machinery of these schools, and, in the towns especially, they no longer produce their full fruits: but what do not the peasantry of Scotland owe to them? For two centuries, the

Scottish peasant, compared with the same class in other situations, has been a reflecting, an observing, and therefore naturally a self-governing, a moral, and a successful human being – because he has been a reading and a discussing one; and this he owes, above all other causes, to the parish schools. What during the same period have the English peasantry been?

Let us be assured that too much opportunity cannot be given to the poor of exercising their faculties, nor too great a variety of ideas placed within their reach. We hail, therefore, the cheap Libraries, which are supplying even the poorest with matter more or less instructive, and, what is of equal importance, calculated to interest their minds. But it is not only, or even principally, books and book learning, that constitutes education for the working or for any other class. Schools for reading are but imperfect things, unless systematically united with schools of industry; not to improve them as workmen merely, but as human beings. It is by action that the faculties are called forth, more than by words – more at least than by words unaccompanied by action. We want schools in which the children of the poor should learn to use not only their hands, but their minds, for the guidance of their hands; in which they should be trained to the actual adaptation of means to ends; should become familiar with the accomplishment of the same object by various processes, and be made to apprehend with their intellects in what consists the difference between the right way of performing industrial operations and the wrong. Meanwhile they would acquire, not only manual dexterity, but habits of order and regularity, of the utmost use in after-life, and which have more to do with the formation of character than many persons are aware of. Mr Aubin's school at Norwood contains, if reports may be trusted, many features worthy of study and imitation; and there are others to which favourable testimony is borne by competent observers. But we are inculcating principles, not proposing models.[15] Such things would do much more than is usually believed towards converting these neglected creatures into rational beings – beings capable of foresight, accessible to reasons and motives addressed to their understanding; and therefore not governed by the utterly senseless modes of feeling and action, which so much astonish educated and observing persons who are brought into contact with them.

But when education, in this its narrow sense, has done its best, and even to enable it to do its best, an education of another sort is required, such as schools cannot give. What is taught to a child at school will be of little effect, if the circumstances which surround the grown man or woman contradict the lesson. You may cultivate his understanding, but what if he cannot employ it without becoming discontented with his position, and disaffected to the whole order of things in which he is cast? Society educates the poor, for good or for ill, by its conduct to them, even more than by direct teaching. A sense of this truth is the most valuable feature in the new philanthropic agitation; and the recognition of it is important, whatever mistakes may be at first made in practically applying it.

In the work before us, and in the best of the other writings which have appeared lately on the philanthropic side of the subject, a strong conviction is expressed, that there can be no healthful state of society, and no social or even physical welfare for the poor, where there is no relation between them and the rich except the payment of wages, and (we may add) the receipt of charity; no sense of co-operation and common interest between those natural associates who are now called the employers and the employed. In part of this we agree, though we think the case not a little overstated. A well-educated labouring class could, and we believe would, keep up its condition to a high standard of comfort, or at least at the great distance from physical destitution, by the exercise of the same degree of habitual prudence now commonly practised by the middle class; among whom the responsibilities of a family are rarely incurred without some prospect of being able to maintain it with the customary decencies of their station. We believe, too, that if this were the case, the poor could do very well without those incessant attentions on the part of the rich, which constitute the new whole duty of man to his poorer neighbour. Seeing no necessary reason why the poor should be hopelessly dependent, we do not look upon them as permanent subjects for the exercise of those peculiar virtues which are essentially intended to mitigate the humiliation and misery of dependence. But the need of greater fellow-feeling and community of interest between the mass of the people and those who are by courtesy considered to guide and govern them, does not require the aid of exaggeration. We yield to no one in our wish that 'cash payment' should be no longer 'the universal *nexus* between man and man;' that the employers and employed should have the feelings of friendly allies, not of hostile rivals whose gain is each other's loss. But while we agree, so far, with the new doctrines, it seems to us that some of those who preach them are looking in the wrong quarter for what they seek. The social relations of former times, and those of the present, not only are not, but cannot possibly be, the same. The essential requirements of human nature may be alike in all ages, but each age has its own appropriate means of satisfying them. Feudality, in whatever manner we may conceive it modified, is not the type on which institutions or habits can now be moulded. The age that produces railroads which, for a few shillings, will convey a labourer and his family fifty miles to find work; in which agricultural labourers read newspapers, and make speeches at public meetings called by themselves to discuss low wages – is not an age in which a man can feel loyal and dutiful to another because he has been born on his estate. Obedience in return for protection, is a bargain only made when protection can be had on no other terms. Men now make that bargain with society, not with an individual. The law protects them, and they give their obedience to that. Obedience in return for wages is a different matter. They will make that bargain too, if necessity drives them to it. But good-will and gratitude form no part of the conditions of such a contract. The deference which a man now pays to his 'brother of the earth,' merely because the one was born rich and the other poor, is either hypocrisy or servility. Real attachment, a genuine feeling of subordination, must now be the result of personal qualities, and requires them on both sides equally. When these are wanting, in proportion to the enforced observances will be the concealed enmity; not, perhaps, towards the individual, for there will seldom be the extremes either of hatred or of affection in a relation so merely transitory; but that *sourde* animosity which is universal in this country towards the whole class of employers, in the whole class of the employed.

As one of the correctives to this deep-seated alienation of feeling, much stress is laid on the importance of personal demeanour. In the *Claims of Labour* this is the point most insisted upon. The book contains numerous aphorisms on this subject, and they are such as might be expected from the author of 'Essays written in the Intervals of Business,' and 'Thoughts in the Cloister and the Crowd.' A person disposed to criticise might indeed object, that these earnest and thoughtful sayings are chiefly illustrative of the duty of every one to every one; and are applicable to the formation of our own character, and to human relations generally, rather than to the special relation between the rich and the poor. It is not as concerning the poor specially, that these lessons are needed. The faults of the rich to the poor are the universal faults. The demeanour fitting towards the poor, is that which is fitting towards every one. It is a just charge against the English nation, considered generally, that they do not know how to be kind, courteous, and considerate of the feelings of others. It is their character throughout Europe. They have much to learn from other nations in the arts not only of being serviceable and amiable with grace, but of being so at all. Whatever brings the habitual feelings of human beings to one another nearer to the Christian standard, will produce a better demeanour to every one, and therefore to the poor. But it is not peculiarly towards them that the deficiency manifests itself. On the contrary, speaking of the rich individually (as distinguished from collective conduct in public life), there is generally, we believe, a very sincere desire to be amiable to the poor.

Where there exists the quality, so rare in England, of genuine sociability, combined with as much knowledge of the feelings and ways of the working classes as can enable any one to show interest in them to any useful purpose, the effects obtained are even now very valuable. The author of the *Claims of Labour* has done a useful thing by giving additional publicity to the proceedings of a generous and right-minded mill-owner, whom he does not name, but who is known to be Mr Samuel Greg, from whose letters to Mr Leonard Horner he has quoted largely. Mr Greg proceeded partly in the obvious course, of building good cottages, granting garden allotments, establishing schools, and so forth. But the essence of his plan consisted in becoming personally acquainted with the operatives, showing interest in their pursuits, taking part in their social amusements, and giving to the *élite* of them – men, women, and young persons – periodical access to the society and intercourse of his own home. He has afforded a specimen and model of what can be done for the people under the calumniated Factory System. And in nothing is he more to be commended, than in the steadiness with which he upholds the one essential principle of all effectual philanthropy. 'The motto on our flag,' says he, 'is *Aide-toi, le ciel t'aidera.*' It is the principle I endeavour to keep constantly in view. It is the only principle on which it is safe to help anybody, or which can prevent benevolence from being poisoned into a fountain of moral mischief.' His experiment has, for many years, been well rewarded by success. But, for the cure of great social evils, too great stress must not be laid upon it. The originator of such a scheme is, most likely, a person peculiarly fitted by natural and acquired qualifications for winning the confidence and attachment of untutored minds. If the spirit should diffuse itself widely among the employers of labour, there might be, in every large neighbourhood, some such man; we could never expect that the majority would be such. Even Mr Greg had to begin, as he tells us, by *selecting* his labourers. He had to 'get rid of his aborigines.' He 'endeavoured, as far as possible, to find such families as we knew to be respectable, or thought likely to be so, and who, we hoped, if they were made comfortable, would remain and settle upon the place; thus finding and making themselves a home, and losing, by degrees that restless and migratory spirit which is one of the peculiar characteristics of the manufacturing population, and perhaps the greatest of all obstacles in the way of permanent improvement among them.' It is in the nature of things that employers so much beyond the average should gather round them better labourers than the average, and retain them, while so eligible a lot is not to be had elsewhere. But ordinary human nature is so poor a thing, that the same attachment and influence would not, with the same certainty, attend similar conduct, if it no longer formed a contrast with the indifference of other employers. The gratitude of men is for things unusual and unexpected. This does not take from the value of Mr Greg's exertions. Whoever succeeds in improving a certain number of the working people, does so much towards raising the class; and all such good influences have a tendency to spread. But, for creating a permanent tie between employers and employed, we must not count upon the results manifested in cases of exception, which would probably lose a part of their beneficial efficacy if they became the rule.

If, on a subject on which almost every thinker has his Utopia, we might be permitted to have ours; if we might point to the principle on which, at some distant date, we place our chief hope for healing the widening breach between those who toil and those who live on the produce of former toil; it would be that of raising the labourer from a receiver of hire – a mere bought instrument in the work of production, having no residuary interest in the work itself – to the position of being, in some sort, a partner in it. The plan of remunerating subordinates in whom trust must be reposed, by a commission on the return instead of only a fixed salary, is already familiar in mercantile concerns, on the ground of its utility to the employer. The wisdom, even in a worldly sense, of associating the interest of the agent with the end he is employed to attain, is so universally recognised in theory, that it is not chimerical to expect it may one day be more extensively exemplified in practice. In some form of this policy we see the only, or the most practicable, means of harmonizing the 'rights of industry' and those of property; of making the employers the real chiefs of the people, leading and guiding them in a work in which they also are interested – a work of co-operation, not of mere hiring and service; and justifying, by the superior capacity in which they contribute to the work, the higher remuneration which they receive for their share of it.*

But without carrying our view forward to changes of manners, or changes in the relation of the different orders of society to one another, let us consider what can be done immediately, and by the legislature, to improve either the bodily or mental condition of the labouring people.

And let it here be remembered that we have to do with a class, a large portion of which reads, discusses, and forms opinions on public interests. Let it be remembered also, that

* In the able and interesting 'Lettres Politiques' of M. Charles Duveyrier, some account is given of an attempt which has been successfully made to carry this principle into practice, on a small scale, by an employer of labour at Paris. The name of the individual is Leclaire, his occupation that of a house-painter, and he has made his proceedings public in a pamphlet, entitled 'Répartition des Bénéfices du Travail en 1842.' M. Leclaire pays his labourers, and other employés, by fixed salaries or weekly wages in the usual manner. He assigns also to himself a fixed allowance. When the year's accounts are made up the surplus profits are shared among all concerned, himself included, in the ratio of their fixed allowances. The result has been most prosperous both to himself and to his labourers, not one of whom, who worked as much as three hundred days, obtained, in the year of which he has published the accounts, less than 1500 francs (£60,) and some considerably more.

In the mining districts of Cornwall the working miners are invariably joint adventurers in the concern; and for intelligence, independence, and good conduct, as well as prosperous circumstances, no labouring population in the island is understood to be comparable to the Cornish miners.[16]

we live in a political age; in which the desire of political rights, or the abuse of political privileges by the possessors of them, are the foremost ideas in the minds of most reading men – an age, too, the whole spirit of which instigates every one to demand fair play for helping himself, rather than to seek or expect help from others. In such an age, and in the treatment of minds so predisposed, justice is the one needful thing rather than kindness. We may at least say that kindness will be little appreciated, will have very little of the effect of kindness upon the objects of it, so long as injustice, or what they cannot but deem to be injustice, is persevered in. Apply this to several of the laws maintained by our legislature. Apply it, for example, to the Corn-Laws. Will the poor thank you for giving them money in alms; for subscribing to build baths and lay out parks for them, or, as Lord John Manners proposes, playing at cricket with them, if you are at the same time taxing their bread to swell your rents? We entreat 'Young England' to believe, that as long as they vote for the Corn-Laws, people will never begin to take them and their professions *au sérieux*; they will be looked upon as they are now, as light-headed young men, momentarily more successful than other dandies in the line of peculiarity which they have chosen; but not as serious thinkers acting upon any consistent intellectual scheme, or from any real conscientious feeling.[17] We could understand persons who said – the people will not be better off whatever we do, and why should we sacrifice our rents or open our purses for so meagre a result. But we cannot understand men who give alms with one hand, and take away the bread of the labourer with the other. Can they wonder that the people say – Instead of doling out to us a small fragment of what is rightfully our own, why do you not disgorge your unjust gains? One of the evils of the matter is, that the gains are so enormously exaggerated. Those who have studied the question know that the landlords gain very little by the Corn-Laws; and would soon have even that little restored to them by the indirect consequences of the abrogation. The rankling sense of gross injustice, which renders any approximation of feeling between the classes impossible while even the remembrance of it lasts, is inflicted for a quite insignificant pecuniary advantage.

There are some other practices which, if the new doctrines are embraced in earnest, will require to be reconsidered. For example, it seems to us that mixing in the social assemblies of the country people, and joining in their sports, would square exceedingly ill with the preserving of game. If cricketing is to be taken in common by the rich and poor, why not shooting? We confess that when we read of enormous game preserves, kept up that great personages may slaughter hundreds of wild animals in a day's shooting, we are amazed at the puerility of taste which can call this a sport; as much as we lament the want of just feeling which, for the sake of sport, can keep open from generation to generation this source of crime and bitterness in the class which it is now so much the fashion to patronize.

We must needs think, also, that there is something out of joint, when so much is said of the value of refining and humanizing tastes to the labouring people – when it is proposed to plant parks and lay out gardens for them, that they may enjoy more freely nature's gift alike to rich and poor, of sun, sky, and vegetation; and along with this a counter-progress is going on, of stopping up paths and enclosing commons; nay, a bill annually introduced into Parliament, with the prospect of success, offering new and unheard-of facilities to the latter operation. Is not this another case of giving with one hand, and taking back more largely with the other? We look with the utmost jealousy upon any further enclosure of commons. In the greater part of this island, exclusive of the mountain and moor districts, there certainly is not more land remaining in a state of natural wildness than is desirable. Those who would make England resemble many parts of the Continent, where every foot of soil is hemmed in by fences and covered over with the traces of human labour, should remember that where this is done, it is done for the use and benefit, not of the rich, but of the poor; and that in the countries where there remain no commons, the rich have no parks. The common is the peasant's park. Every argument for ploughing it up to raise more produce, applies *a fortiori* to the park, which is generally far more fertile. The effect of either, when done in the manner proposed, is only to make the poor more numerous, not better off; and is particularly uncalled for in the face of a probable abolition of the Corn-Laws, rendering speculations upon the turning up of barren soils at this time especially precarious. But what ought to be said when, as so often happens, the common is taken from the poor, that the whole or great part of it may be added to the enclosed pleasure domain of the rich? Is the miserable compensation, and though miserable yet seldom granted, of a small scrap of the land to each of the cottagers who had a goose on the common, any equivalent to the poor generally, to the lovers of nature, or to future generations, for this legalized spoliation?

These are things to be avoided. Among things to be done, the most obvious is to remove every restriction, every artificial hindrance, which legal and fiscal systems oppose to the attempts of the labouring classes to forward their own improvement. These hindrances are sometimes to be found in quarters in which they may not be looked for; as a few instances will show.

Some years ago the Society for the Diffusion of Useful Knowledge, in a well-intended tract addressed to the working people, to correct the prejudices entertained by some of them against the 'claims of capital,' gave some advice to the labourers, which produced considerable comment at the time. It exhorted them to 'make themselves capitalists.' To most labouring people who read it, this exhortation probably appeared ironical. But some of the more intelligent of the class found a meaning in it. It did occur to them that there was a mode in which they could make themselves capitalists. Not, of course, individually; but by bringing their small means into a common fund, by forming a numerous partnership or joint stock, they could, as it seemed to them, become their own employers – dispense with the agency of receivers of profits, and share among themselves the entire produce of their labour. This was a most desirable experiment. It would have been an excellent thing to have ascertained whether any great industrial enterprise, a manufactory for example, could be successfully carried on upon this principle. If it succeeded, the benefit was obvious; if, after sufficient trial, it was found impracticable, its failure also would be a valuable lesson. It would prove to the operatives that the profits of the employer are but the necessary price paid for the superiority of management produced by the stimulus of individual interest; and that if the capitalist be the costliest part of the machinery of production, he more than repays his cost. But it was found that the defects of the law of partnership, as applicable to numerous associations, presented difficulties rendering it impracticable to give this experiment a fair trial. Here, then, is a thing which Parliament might do for the labouring classes. The framing of a good law of partnership, giving every attainable facility to the formation of large industrial capitals by the aggregation of small savings, would be a real boon. It would be the removal of no ideal grievance, but of one which we know to be felt, and felt deeply, by the most intelligent and right-thinking of the class – those who are most fitted to acquire, and best qualified to exercise, a beneficent influence over the rest.

Again, it is often complained of, as one of the saddest features of the constitution of society in the rural districts, that the class of yeomanry has died out; that there is no longer any intermediate connecting link between the mere labourer and the large farmer – no class somewhere above his own, into which, by industry and frugality, a labourer can hope to rise; that if he makes savings, they are less a benefit to him than a burden and an anxiety, from the absence of any local means of investment; unless indeed by becoming a shopkeeper in a town or village, where an additional shop is probably not wanted, where he has to form new habits, with great risk of failure, and, if he succeeds, does not remain an example and encouragement to others like himself. Is it not strange, then, that supposing him to have an opportunity of investing this money in a little patch of land, the Stamp-office would interfere and take a toll on the transaction? The tax, too, which the State levies on the transfer of small properties, is a trifling matter compared with the tax levied by the lawyers. The stamp-duty bears some proportion to the pecuniary amount; but the law charges are the same on the smallest transactions as on the greatest, and these are almost wholly occasioned by the defects of the law. There is no real reason why the transfer of land should be more difficult or costly than the transfer of three per cent stock, except that a trifle more of description is necessary to identify the subject-matter; all the rest is the consequence of mere technicalities, growing out of the obsolete incidents of the Feudal System.

A great part of the revenue of the country is raised by imports which stand directly between the labourers and their essential comforts. The window-tax operates to deprive them of light; the excise on soap is a tax on cleanliness; the duties on bricks and timber render building expensive, and directly counteract the attempt to improve the dwellings of the poor. The duty and port dues on coal, exacted by the corporation of London, aggravate, to the inhabitants of the metropolis and surrounding districts, the most distressing of the physical privations incident to poverty.[18]

Many of the removable causes of ill-health are in the power of Government; but there is no need to enlarge upon a subject to which official Reports have drawn so much attention. The more effectual performance by Government of any of its acknowledged duties; the more zealous prosecution of any scheme tending to the general advantage, is beneficial to the labouring classes. Of schemes destined specially to give them employment, or add to their comforts, it may be said, once for all, that there is a simple test by which to judge them. Is the assistance of such a kind, and given in such a manner, as to render them ultimately independent of the continuance of similar assistance? If not, the best that can be said of the plans is, that they are harmless. To make them useful, it is an indispensable condition that there be a reasonable prospect of their being at some future time self-supporting. Even upon the best supposition, it appears to us that too much importance is attached to them. Giving education and just laws, the poorer class would be as competent as any other class to take care of their own personal habits and acquirements.[19]

12 *Thornton on Labour and its Claims*

(*Fortnightly Review,* new series V, 1869; reprinted *Dissertations and Discussions,* Vol. IV, 1875.)

In a former article[20] it has been seen how Mr Thornton, in the first chapter of his First Book, disproved, on grounds of pure political economy, the supposed natural law by which, in the opinion of many, the price of labour is as strictly determined as the motion of the earth, and determined in a manner unalterable by the will or effort of either party to the transaction. But whatever in the affairs of mankind is not peremptorily decided for them by natural laws, falls under the jurisdiction of the moral law. Since there is a certain range, wider than has been generally believed, within which the price of labour is decided by a conflict of wills between employers and labourers, it is necessary, as in every other case of human voluntary action, to ascertain the moral principles by which this conflict ought to be regulated. The terms of the bargain not being a matter of necessity, but, within certain limits, of choice, it has to be considered how far either side can rightfully press its claims, and take advantage of its opportunities. Or, to express the same ideas in other phraseology, it has to be decided whether there are any *rights,* of labour on the one hand, or of capital on the other, which would be violated if the opposite party pushed its pretensions to the extreme limits of economic possibility.

To this Mr Thornton answers, – None. As a matter of mere right, both the employer and the labourer, while they abstain from force or fraud, are entitled to all that they can get, and to nothing more than what they can get. The terms of their contract, provided it is voluntary on both sides, are the sole rule of justice between them. No one being under any obligation of justice to employ labour at all, still less is any one bound in justice to pay for it any given price.

> 'Except under the terms of some mutual agreement, the employer is not bound to give anything. Before joining in the agreement he was under no obligation to furnish the labourer with occupation. Either he might not have required his or any one else's services, or he might have preferred to employ some one else. But if he was not bound to furnish employment at all, *a fortiori* he was not bound to furnish it on any particular terms. If, therefore, he did consent to furnish it, he had a right to dictate his own terms; and whatever else those terms might be, however harsh, illiberal, exorbitant, or what you will, they could not, at any rate or by any possibility, be unjust. For they could only be unjust in so far as they deviated from some particular terms which justice might have exacted. But, as we have seen, there were no such terms, and it is manifestly absurd to condemn a thing merely because its limits do not coincide with those of an abstraction incapable of being realised or defined, incapable, that is to say, of having any limits at all.' (Thornton, p. 111.)

The counter-theory, on which the labourer's side of the question is usually argued, 'that every man who has not by crime forfeited the right, and who has no other means of living, has a right to live by labour,' Mr Thornton entirely rejects.

> 'Although [he says] these pages have little other object than that of determining how the labouring classes may most easily and effectually obtain fully as much as they ever dreamt of asking, the writer is constrained, even in the interest of those classes, to protest against the theory set up in their behalf. No cause can be permanently maintained that is suffered to rest on fallacies;

and one pervading fallacy, beginning at the very first link, runs through the whole chain of reasoning of which the theory consists.

'The right of the poor to live by labour, affirmed as unhesitatingly as if it were a self-evident proposition beyond the possibility of dispute, is explained to mean not merely the right so to live if they can themselves find the means but to have the means supplied by others if they cannot themselves obtain them and to have them supplied, nominally by society at large, but really by the richer portion of it, the rich alone being in a position to furnish what is required. But right on the one side necessarily implies corresponding obligation on the other; and how can society, or how can the rich, have incurred the obligation of maintaining in the world those whom they were in no degree instrumental in bringing into it? Only, if at all, in one or other of two ways. Either mankind were placed in possession of the earth which they inhabit on condition expressed, or implied, that the wants of all the earth's human inhabitants should be provided for from its produce; or part of those inhabitants have, by some communal act or institution of the whole body, been dispossessed of the means of providing for themselves. But in the first of these hypotheses, in order that the supposed condition should be equitable, it would be necessary that the earth should be capable of producing enough for the wants of whatever number of inhabitants might obtain footing upon it; whereas it is demonstrable that population would infallibly everywhere speedily outrun subsistence, if the earth's produce were freely accessible to all who had need. Of the other supposition, it is to be remarked that the only institution that has ever been accused of producing the alleged effect is the institution of property; and very slight advocacy will suffice to absolve an institution from the charge of depriving people of that which, but for itself, could not have existed. Let it be admitted that the earth was bestowed by the Creator, not on any privileged class or classes, but on all mankind, and on all successive generations of men, so that no one generation can have more than a life interest in the soil, or be entitled to alienate the birthright of succeeding generations. Let this be admitted, and the admission is surely large enough to satisfy the most uncompromising champion of the natural rights of man. Still it is certain that those rights, if fully exercised, must inevitably have proved themselves to be so far worse than worthless, as to have prevented any but a very minute fraction of the existing number of claimants from being born to claim them. The earth, if unappropriated, must also have remained untilled, and consequently comparatively unproductive. Anything like the world's actual population could not possibly have been in existence, nor, if it had been, would a whole year's growth of the earth's natural produce have sufficed for the subsistence of the earth's inhabitants during a single day. The utmost of which the poor have been dispossessed by the institution of property is their fair proportion of what the earth could have produced if it had remained unappropriated. Compensation for this is the utmost which is due to them from society, and the debt is obviously so infinitesimally small, that the crumbs which habitually fall from the tables of the rich are amply sufficient to pay it.

'If these things be so, a strict debtor and creditor account between rich and poor would show no balance against the former. Society cannot properly be said to owe anything to the poor beyond what it is constantly and regularly paying. It is not bound in equity, whatever it may be in charity, to find food for the hungry because they are in need, nor to find occupation for the unemployed because they are out of work. By withholding aid, it is not guilty of the smallest injustice. For injustice implies violation of a right; and not only can there be no breach of right without disregard of a corresponding obligation, but that only can be a right the breach or denial of which constitutes a wrong. But wrong is committed only when some good which is due is withheld, or when some evil which is not due is inflicted. Applying this test, we shall find that the poor, as such, have no unliquidated claim against the rich. The latter are doing them no wrong, are guilty of no injustice towards them in merely abstaining from paying a debt which, whether due to the poor or not, is, at any rate, not due to them from the rich. It was not the rich who placed the poor on the earth, and it is not the rich who owe them the means of living here. How far the poor may be forgiven for complaining, as of a grievance, of having been placed here without adequate means of living, may possibly be a question for the theologian. But the political economist may fairly content himself with showing that the grievance is, at any rate, not one with which they can reproach any of their fellow-creatures, except their own parents. No other portion of society was a party to the transaction, and no other portion can justly be responsible for its consequences.'* (pp. 91-94.)

It is unnecessary to quote the application of these principles to the particular case of contracts for labour.

* That those who have not yet read Mr Thornton's book may not be even temporarily liable to the misunderstanding of his meaning, and of the whole spirit of his writings, which might be the effect of reading only the passage cited in the text, I will at once bring forward the other side of his opinion. Nothing, he says, can be further from his purpose 'than to exculpate the existing social system, or to suggest an excuse for continued acquiescence in its enormities. . . . To affirm that those evils of the existing social polity which constitute the peculiar grievance of the poor are not the result of human injustice, is perfectly consistent with the most vehement denunciation both of the evils themselves and of the heartless indifference that would perpetuate them. It is perfectly consistent, even with the admission that the rich are bound to do what they can to alleviate those evils—with this proviso, however, that they are so bound, not by their duty to others, but by their duty to themselves. The obligation is imposed upon them not by injunctions of justice, but by the force of sympathy and the exhortations of humanity and charity. The sacrifices which it may thus become incumbent on the rich to make, the poor are not in consequence entitled to demand.

Here, then, are two theories of justice arrayed against each other in order of battle: theories differing in their first principles, markedly opposed in their conclusions, and both of them doctrines *a priori*, claiming to command assent by their own light – to be evident by simple intuition: a pretension which, as the two are perfectly inconsistent, must, in the case of one or other of them, be unfounded, and may be so in the case of both. Such conflicts in the domain of ethics

If the sacrifices are withheld, the rich stand convicted indeed of brute selfishness, but they do not thereby lay themselves open to the additional charge of injustice. This distinction is not drawn for the sake of pedantic precision; it is one of immense practical importance. To all right reasoning, it is essential that things should be called by their right names; and that nothing, however bad, should receive a worse name than it deserves. The more glaring a sin, the less reason is there for exaggerating it; and, in the case before us, the use of an erroneous epithet has been a fruitful source of further error. Unless the present constitution of society had been arbitrarily assumed to be unjust, it would never have been proposed to correct its injustice by resorting to means which would otherwise have been at once perceived to be themselves utterly unjustifiable. On no other account could it ever have been supposed that liberty demanded for its own vindication the violation of liberty, and that the freedom of competition ought to be fettered or abolished. For freedom of competition means no more than that every one should be at liberty to do his best for himself, leaving all others equally at liberty to do their best for themselves. Of all the natural rights of man, there is not one more incontestable than this, nor with which interference would be more manifestly unrighteous. Yet this it is proposed to set aside as incompatible with the rights of labour, as if those could possibly be rights which cannot be maintained except by unrighteous means.' (pp. 94-5.)

The heartiness of Mr Thornton's devotion to the interest of the labouring classes (or, it should rather be said, to the interest of human nature as embodied in them), is manifested throughout the work; but nowhere so vividly as in the noble Introductory Chapter, where he depicts a state of things in which all the grosser and more palpable evils of their poverty might be extinct, and shows that with this they ought not, and we ought not, to be content. It is not enough that they should no longer be objects of pity. The conditions of a positively happy and dignified existence are what he demands for them, as well as for every other portion of the human race.

are highly instructive, but their value is chiefly negative; the principal use of each of the contrary theories is to destroy the other. Those who cherish any one of the numerous *a priori* systems of moral duty, may learn from such controversies how plausible a case may be made for other *a priori* systems repugnant to their own; and the adepts of each may discover, that while the maxims or axioms from which they severally set out are all of them good, each in its proper place, yet what that proper place is, can only be decided, not by mental intuition, but by the thoroughly practical consideration of consequences; in other words, by the general interest of society and mankind, mental and bodily, intellectual, emotional, and physical, taken together. Mr Thornton seems to admit the general happiness as the criterion of social virtue, but not of positive duty – not of justice and injustice in the strict sense: and he imagines that it is in making a distinction between these two ideas that his doctrine differs from that of utilitarian moralists. But this is not the case. Utilitarian morality fully recognizes the distinction between the province of positive duty and that of virtue, but maintains that the standard and rule of both is the general interest. From the utilitarian point of view, the distinction between them is the following: –There are many acts, and a still greater number of forbearances, the perpetual practice of which by all is so necessary to the general well-being, that people must be held to it compulsorily, either by law, or by social pressure. These acts and forbearances constitute duty. Outside these bounds there is the innumerable variety of modes in which the acts of human beings are either a cause, or a hindrance, of good to their fellow-creatures, but in regard to which it is, on the whole, for the general interest that they should be left free; being merely encouraged, by praise and honour, to the performance of such beneficial actions as are not sufficiently stimulated by benefits flowing from them to the agent himself. This larger sphere is that of Merit or Virtue.

The anxiety of moralists for some more definite standard of judgment than the happiness of mankind appears to them to be, or for some first principle which shall have a greater hold on the feeling of obligation than education has yet given to the idea of the good of our fellow-creatures, makes them eager to erect into an axiom of morals any one of the familiar corollaries from the principle of general utility, which, from the impressiveness of the cases to which it is applicable, has taken a deep root in the popular mind, and gathered round itself a considerable amount of human feeling. When they have made choice of any such maxim, they follow it out as if there were no others of equal authority by which its application ought to be limited; or with only as much regard to those limitations, as the amount of common sense possessed by the particular thinker peremptorily enforces upon him as a practical being. The two opposite theories of social justice set forth by Mr Thornton – the Rousseau or Proudhon theory, and his own – are cases of this description. The former of these, according to which all private appropriation of any of the instruments of production was a wrong from the beginning, and an injury to the rest of mankind, there is neither room, nor is it necessary, here to discuss. But I venture to think that, on intuitional grounds, there is quite as much to be said for it as for the rival theory. Mr Thornton must admit that the Rousseau doctrine, in its most absolute form, has charmed great numbers of human beings, including not merely those to whose apparent interests it was favourable, but many of those to whom it was hostile; that it has satisfied their highest conceptions of justice and moral right, and has the 'note' of intuitive truth as completely as the principles from which his own system is a deduction. Still more may this be said of the more moderate forms of the same theory. 'Justice is supposed' – erroneously in the author's opinion – 'to require that a labourer's remuneration should correspond with his wants and his merits' (p. 111). If justice is an affair of intuition – if we are guided to it by the immediate and spontaneous perceptions of the moral sense – what doctrines of justice are there, on which the human race would more instantaneously and with one accord put the stamp of its recognition, than these – that it is just that each should have what he deserves, and that, in the dispensation of good things, those whose wants are most urgent should have the preference? In conscience, can it be expected that any one, who has grounded his social theories on these maxims, should discard them in favour of what Mr Thornton tenders instead – viz., that no one is accountable for any evil which he has not produced by some violence, fraud, or breach of engagement of his own; and that, these things apart, no one has any ground of complaint for his lot on earth, against those who had no hand in placing him here? Mr Thornton himself concedes so much, as not positively to deny the justice of the maxims which he practically repudiates; but regards their violation as a grievance (if grievance at all) against the general order of the universe, and not against society, or the employers of labour. But if there be in the natural constitution of things something patently unjust – something contrary to sentiments of justice, which sentiments, being intuitive, are supposed to have been implanted in us by the same Creator who made the order of things that they protest against – do not these sentiments impose on us the duty of striving, by all human means, to correct the injustice? And if, on the contrary, we avail ourselves of it for our own personal advantage, do we not make ourselves participators in injustice – allies and auxiliaries of the Evil Principle?

While the author's intuitive theory of right and wrong has thus no advantage in point of intuitive evidence over the doctrine which it is brought to contradict, it illustrates an incurable defect of all these *a priori* theories – that their most important applications may be rebutted without denying their premises. To point out in what manner this consequence arises out of the inherent nature of such theories, would detain us too long; but the examples afforded of it by the author's theory are numerous and remarkable.

Take, for instance, what seems the strongest point in his principal argument – viz., that the institution of property in land does not deprive the poor of anything except 'their fair proportion of what the earth could have produced if it had remained unappropriated;' that is, little or nothing – since, if unappropriated, it would have been untilled, and its spontaneous produce would have yielded sustenance to only a very small number of human beings. This may be an answer to Rousseau, though even to him not a complete one;* but it is no answer to the Socialists of the present day. These are, in general, willing enough to admit that property in land was a necessary institution in early ages, and until mankind were sufficiently civilised to be capable of managing their affairs in common for the general benefit. But when this time has arrived – and according to them it has arrived – the legitimacy of private landed property, they contend, has ceased, and mankind at large ought now to re-enter on their inheritance. They deny the claim of the first possessors to impose fetters on all generations, and to prevent the species at large from resuming rights of which, for good but temporary reasons, it had suspended the exercise. Society made the concession, and society can at any moment take it back.

Again, the author, in his chapter on the Rights of Capital, very truly and forcibly argues, that these are a portion of the rights of labour. They are the rights of past labour, since labour is the source of all capital; and sacred, in the same sense, and in an equal degree, with those of present labour. From this he deduces the equal legitimacy of any contract for employment, which past labour may impose on the necessities of present labour, provided there is no taint of force or fraud. But is there no taint of force or fraud in the original title of many owners of past labour? The author states the case as if all property, from the beginning of time, had been honestly come by; either

* By no means a complete answer; for there is a medium between private appropriation of land and denial of protection to its fruits. Is there not such a thing as temporary appropriation? As a matter of fact, even in countries of the most improved agriculture, the tillage is usually performed by persons who have no property in the soil—often by mere tenants at will.

produced by the labour of the owner himself, or bestowed on him by gift or bequest from those whose labour did produce it. But how stands the fact? Landed property at least, in all the countries of modern Europe, derives its origin from force; the land was taken by military violence from former possessors, by those from whom it has been transmitted to its present owners. True, much of it has changed hands by purchase, and has come into the possession of persons who had earned the purchase-money by their labour; but the sellers could not impart to others a better title than they themselves possessed. Movable property, no doubt, has on the whole a purer origin, its first acquirers having mostly worked for it, at something useful to their fellow-citizens. But, looking at the question merely historically, and confining our attention to the larger masses, the doctrine that the rights of capital are those of past labour is liable even here to great abatements. Putting aside what has been acquired by fraud, or by the many modes of taking advantage of circumstances, which are deemed fair in commerce, though a person of a delicate conscience would scruple to use them in most of the other concerns of life – omitting all these considerations, how many of the great commercial fortunes have been, at least partly, built up by practices which in a better state of society would have been impossible – jobbing contracts, profligate loans, or other abuses of Government expenditure, improper use of public positions, monopolies, and other bad laws, or perhaps only by the manifold advantages which imperfect social institutions gave to those who are already rich, over their poorer fellow-citizens, in the general struggle of life? We may be told that there is such a thing as prescription, and that a bad title may become a good one by lapse of time. It may, and there are excellent reasons of general utility why it should; but there would be some difficulty in establishing this position from any *a priori* principle. It is of great importance to the good order and comfort of the world that an amnesty should be granted to all wrongs of so remote a date that the evidence necessary for the ascertainment of title is no longer accessible, or that the reversal of the wrong would cause greater insecurity and greater social disturbance than its condonation. This is true, but I believe that no person ever succeeded in reconciling himself to the conviction, without doing considerable violence to what is called the instinctive sentiment of justice. It is not at all conformable to intuitive morality that a wrong should cease to be a wrong because of what is really an aggravation, its durable character; that because crime has been successful for a certain limited period, society for its own convenience should guarantee its success for all time to come. Accordingly, those who construct their systems of society upon the natural rights of man, usually add to the word natural the world imprescriptible, and strenuously maintain that it is impossible to acquire a fee–simple in an injustice.

Yet one more example, to show the case with which conclusions that seem to follow absolutely from an *a priori* theory of justice can be defeated by other deductions from the same premises. According to the author, however inadequate the remuneration of labour may be, the labourer has no grievance against society, because society is not the cause of the insufficiency, nor did society ever bargain with him, or bind itself to him by any engagement, guaranteeing a particular amount of remuneration. And, this granted, the author assumes (at p. 394 and elsewhere) as a logical consequence, that proprietors must not be interfered with, out of regard to the interests of labour, in the perfectly free use of their property conformably to their own inclination. Now, if this point were being argued as a practical question, on utilitarian grounds, there probably would be little difference between Mr Thornton's conclusions and my own. I should stand up for the free disposal of property as strongly, and most likely with only the same limitations, as he would. But we are now on *a priori* ground, and while that is the case, I must insist upon having the consequences of principles carried out to the full. What matters it that, according to the author's theory, the employer does no wrong in making the use he does of his capital, if the same theory would justify the employed in compelling him by law to make a different use – if the labourers would in no way infringe the definition of justice by taking the matter into their own hands, and establishing by law any modification of the rights of property which in their opinion would increase the remuneration of their labour? And, on the author's principles, this right cannot be denied them. The existing social arrangements, and law itself, exist in virtue not only of the forbearance, but of the active support of the labouring classes. They could effect the most fundamental changes in the whole order of society by simply withholding their concurrence. Suppose that they, who being the numerical majority cannot be controlled except by their own tacit consent, should come to the conclusion (for example) that it is not essential to the benefits of the institution of property that wealth should be allowed to accumulate in large masses; and should consequently resolve to deny legal protection to all properties exceeding a certain amount. There are the strongest utilitarian reasons against their doing this; but on the author's principles, they have a right to do it. By this mere abstinence from doing what they have never promised nor in any way bound themselves to do, they could extort the consent of the rich to any modification of proprietary rights which they might consider to be for their advantage. They might bind the rich to take the whole burden of taxation upon themselves. They might bind them to give employment, at liberal wages, to a number of labourers in a direct ratio to the amount of their incomes. They might enforce on them a total abolition of inheritance and bequest. All this would be a very wrong use of their power of withholding protection; but only because the conditions imposed would be injurious, instead of beneficial, to the public weal. Nor do I see what arguments, except utilitarian ones, are open to the author for condemning them. Even the manifest obligation of making the changes with the least possible detriment to the interests and feelings of the existing generation of proprietors, it would be extremely difficult to deduce from the author's premises, without calling in other maxims of justice than his theory recognises.

It is almost needless for me to repeat that these things are said, not with a view to draw any practical conclusions respecting the rights of labour, but to show that no practical conclusions of any kind can be drawn from such premises; and because I think, with Mr Thornton, that when we are attempting to determine a question of social ethics, we should make sure of our ethical foundation. On the questions between employers and labourers, or on any other social questions, we can neither hope to find, nor do we need, any better criterion than the interest, immediate and ultimate, of the human race. But the author's treatment of the subject will have a useful effect if it leads any of those friends of democracy and equality, who disdain the prosaic consideration of consequences, and demand something more high-flown as the ground on which to rest the rights of the human race, to perceive how easy it is to frame a theory of justice that shall positively deny the rights considered by them as so transcendent, and which yet shall make as fair a claim as theirs to an intuitive character, and shall command by its *a priori* evidence the full conviction of as enlightened a thinker, and as warm a supporter of the principal claims of the labouring classes, as the author of the work before us.

The author's polemic against the doctrines commonly preached by the metaphysical theorists of the Cause of Labour, is not without other points of usefulness. Not only are those theorists entirely at sea on the notion of right, when they suppose that labour has, or can have, a right to anything, by any rule but the permanent interest of the human race; but they also have confused and erroneous notions of matters of fact, of which Mr Thornton points out the fallacy. For example, the working classes, or rather their champions, often look upon the whole wealth of the country as the produce of their labour, and imply, or even assert, that if everybody had his due the whole of it would belong to them. Apart from all question as to right, this doctrine rests on a misconception of fact. The wealth of the country is not wholly the produce of present labour. It is the joint product of present labour and of the labour of former years and generations, the fruits of which, having been preserved by the abstinence of those who had the power of consuming them, are now available for the support or aid of present labour which, but for that abstinence, could not have produced subsistence for a hundredth part the number of the present labourers. No merit is claimed for this abstinence; those to whose persevering frugality the labouring classes owe this enormous benefit, for the most part thought only of benefiting themselves and their descendants. But neither is there any merit in labouring, when a man has no other means of keeping alive. It is not a question of merit, but of the common interest. Capital is as indispensable to labour as labour to capital. It is true the labourers need only capital, not capitalists; it would be better for them if they had capital of their own. But while they have not, it is a great benefit to them that others have. Those who have capital did not take it from them, and do not prevent them from acquiring it. And, however badly off they may be under the conditions which they are able to make with capitalists, they would be still worse off if the earth were freely delivered over to them without capital, and their existing numbers had to be supported upon what they could in this way make it produce.

On the other hand, there is on the opposite side of the question a kind of goody morality, amounting to a cant, against which the author protests, and which it is imperative to clear our minds of. There are people who think it right to be always repeating, that the interest of labourers and employers (and, they add, of landlords and farmers, the upper classes and the lower, governments and subjects, &c.) is one and the same. It is not to be wondered at that this sort of thing should be irritating to those to whom it is intended as a warning. How is it possible that the buyer and the seller of a commodity should have exactly the same interest as to its price? It is the interest of both that there should be commodities to sell; and it is, in a certain general way, the interest both of labourers and employers that business should prosper, and that the returns to labour and capital should be large. But to say that they have the same interest as to the division, is to say that it is the same thing to a person's interest whether a sum of money belongs to him or to somebody else. The employer, we are gravely told, will expend in wages what he saves in wages; he will add it to his capital, which is a fine thing for the labouring classes. Suppose him to do so, what does the labourer gain by the increase of capital, if his wages must be kept from rising to admit of its taking place?

> 'Workmen are solemnly adjured, [says Mr Thornton (p. 260).] not to try to get their wages raised, because success in the attempt must be followed by a fall of profits which will bring wages down again. They are entreated not to better themselves, because any temporary bettering will be followed by a reaction which will leave them as ill off as before; not to try to raise the price of labour, because to raise the price is to lower the demand, and to lower the demand is to lower the price. As if a great demand for labour were of any other use to the labourer than that of raising the price of labour, or as if an end were to be sacrificed to means whose whole merit consists in their leading to that same end. If all the political economy opposed to trades' unions were like this, trades' unions would be quite right in opposing political economy.'

What is true, is that wages might be so high as to leave no profit to the capitalist, or not enough to compensate him for the anxieties and risks of trade; and in that case labourers would be killing the goose to get at the eggs. And, again, wages might be so low as to diminish the numbers or impair the working powers of the labourers, and in that case the capitalist also would generally be a loser. But between this and the doctrine, that the money which would come to the labourer by a rise of wages will be of as much use to him in the capitalist's pocket as in his own, there is a considerable difference.

Between the two limits just indicated – the highest wages

consistent with keeping up the capital of the country, and increasing it *pari passu* with the increase of people, and the lowest that will enable the labourers to keep up their numbers with an increase sufficient to provide labourers for the increase of employment – there is an intermediate region within which wages will range higher or lower according to what Adam Smith calls 'the higgling of the market.' In this higgling, the labourer in an isolated condition, unable to hold out even against a single employer, much more against the tacit combination of employers, will, as a rule, find his wages kept down at the lower limit. Labourers sufficiently organised in Unions may, under favourable circumstances, attain to the higher. This, however, supposes an organisation including all classes of labourers, manufacturing and agricultural as well as skilled. When the union is only partial, there is often a nearer limit – that which would destroy, or drive elsewhere, the particular branch of industry in which the rise takes place. Such are the limiting conditions of the strife for wages between the labourers and the capitalists. The superior limit is a difficult question of fact, and in its estimation serious errors may be, and have been, committed. But, having regard to the greatly superior numbers of the labouring class, and the inevitable scantiness of the remuneration afforded by even the highest rate of wages which, in the present state of the arts of production, could possibly become general; whoever does not wish that the labourers may prevail, and that the highest limit, whatever it be, may be attained, must have a standard of morals, and a conception of the most desirable state of society, widely different from those of either Mr Thornton or the present writer.

The remainder of the book is occupied in discussing the means adopted or which might be adopted by the operative classes, for obtaining all such advantages in respect of wages, and the other conditions of labour, as are within the reach of attainment: a subject comprehending all the questions respecting the objects and practices of Trades' Unionism, together with the whole theory and practice of co-operative industry. And here I am nearly at the end of my disagreements with Mr Thornton. His opinions are in every respect as favourable to the claims of the labouring classes as is consistent with the regard due to the permanent interest of the race. His conclusions leave me little to do but to make a *résumé* of them, though I may still dissent from some of his premises. For example, the same principles which lead him to acquit employers of wrong, however they may avail themselves of their advantage to keep down wages, make him equally exculpate Unionists from a similar charge, even when he deems them to be making a short-sighted and dangerous use of the power which combinations give them. But while I agree with the author that conduct may be 'grovelling and sordid' without being morally culpable, I must yet maintain that if there are (as it cannot be doubted that there are demands which employers might make from labourers, or labourers from employers, the enforcement of which, even by the most innocent means, would be contrary to the interests of civilisation and improvement – to make these demands, and to insist on them as conditions of giving and receiving employment, is morally wrong.

Again, the author most justly stigmatises the English law of conspiracy, that reserved weapon of arbitrary and *ex-post-facto* coercion, by which anything, that a court of law thinks ought not to be done, may be made a criminal offence if done in concert by more than one person – a law of which a most objectionable use has been made against Trades' Unions. But I cannot go entirely with him when he lays it down as an absolute and self-evident truth, that whatever is lawful when done by one person, ought not to be an offence when done by a combination of several. He forgets that the number of agents may materially alter the essential character of the act. Suppose, merely for the sake of illustration, that the state of opinion was such as to induce legislators to tolerate, within certain limits, the prosecution of quarrels and the redress of injuries by the party's own hands; as is the case practically, though not legally, in all countries where duelling prevails. If, under cover of this licence, instead of a combat between one and one, a band of assailants were to set upon a single person, and take his life, or inflict on him bodily harm, would it be allowable to apply to this case the maxim, that what is permitted to one person ought to be permitted to any number? The cases are not parallel; but if there be so much as one case of this character, it is discussable, and requires to be discussed, whether any given case is such a one; and we have a fresh proof how little even the most plausible of these absolute maxims of right and wrong are to be depended on, and how unsafe it is to lose sight, even for a moment, of the paramount principle – the good of the human race. The maxims may, as the rough results of experience, be regarded as *prima facie* presumptions that what they inculcate will be found conducive to the ultimate end; but not as conclusive on that point without examination, still less as carrying an authority independent of, and superior to, the end.

My difference with Mr Thornton is in this case only theoretical; for I do not know of anything that ought to be legally interdicted to workmen in combination, except what would be criminal if done by any of them individually, viz., physical violence or molestation, defamation of character, injury to property, or threats of any of these evils. We hear much invective against Trades' Unions on the score of being infringements of the liberty of those working men on whom a kind of social compulsion is exercised to induce them to join a Union, or to take part in a strike. I agree with Mr Thornton in attaching no importance whatever to this charge. An infringement of people's liberty it undoubtedly is, when they are induced, by dread of other people's reproaches, to do anything which they are not legally bound to do; but I do not suppose it will be maintained that disapprobation never ought to be expressed except of things which are offences by law. As soon as it is acknowledged that there are lawful, and even useful, purposes to be fulfilled by Trades' Unions, it must be admitted that the members of Unions may reasonably feel a genuine moral disapprobation of those who profit by the higher wages or other advantages that the

Unions procure for non-Unionists as well as for their own members, but refuse to take their share of the payments, and submit to the restrictions, by which those advantages are obtained. It is vain to say that if a strike is really for the good of the workmen, the whole body will join in it from a mere sense of the common interest. There is always a considerable number who will hope to share the benefit without submitting to the sacrifice; and to say that these are not to have it brought before them, in an impressive manner, what their fellow-workmen think of their conduct, is equivalent to saying that social pressure ought not to be put upon any one to consider the interests of others as well as his own. All that legislation is concerned with is, that the pressure shall stop at the expression of feeling, and the withholding of such good offices as may properly depend upon feeling, and shall not extend to an infringement, or a threat of infringement, of any of the rights which the law guarantees to all – security of person and property against violation, and of reputation against calumny. There are few cases in which the application of this distinction can give rise to any doubt. What is called picketing is just on the border which separates the two regions; but the sole difficulty in that case is one of fact and evidence – to ascertain whether the language or gestures used implied a threat of any such treatment as, between individual and individual, would be contrary to law. Hooting, and offensive language, are points on which a question may be raised; but these should be dealt with according to the general law of the country. No good reason can be given for subjecting them to special restriction on account of the occasion which gives rise to them, or to any legal restraint at all beyond that which public decency, or the safety of the public peace, may prescribe as a matter of police regulation.

Mr Thornton enters into a minute examination of the limits to the efficacy of Trades' Unions – the circumstances in which increased wages may be claimed with a prospect of success, and, if successful, of permanence. These discussions I must content myself with recommending to the attention of the reader, who will find in them much matter of great value. In the present article there is only room for the most general considerations, either of political economy or of morals. Under the former aspect, there is a view of the question, not overlooked by the author, but hardly, perhaps, made sufficiently prominent by him. From the necessity of the case, the only fund out of which an increase of wages can possibly be obtained by the labouring classes considered as a whole, is profits. This is contrary to the common opinion, both of the general public and of the workmen themselves, who think that there is a second source from which it is possible for the augmentation to come, namely, prices. The employer, they think, can, if foreign or other competition will let him, indemnify himself for the additional wages demanded of him, by charging an increased price to the consumer. And this may certainly happen in single trades, and even in large branches of trade under conditions which are carefully investigated by Mr Thornton. The building trade, in its numerous subdivisions, is one of the most salient instances. But though a rise of wages in a given trade may be compensated to the masters by a rise of the price of their commodity, a rise of general wages cannot be compensated to employers generally by a general rise of prices. This distinction is never understood by those who have not considered the subject, but there are few truths more obvious to all who have. There cannot be a general rise of prices unless there is more money expended. But the rise of wages does not cause more money to be expended. It takes from the incomes of the masters and adds to those of the workmen; the former have less to spend, the latter have more; but the general sum of the money incomes of the community remains what it was, and it is upon that sum that money prices depend. There cannot be more money expended on everything, when there is not more money to be expended altogether. In the second place, even if there did happen a rise of all prices, the only effect would be that money, having become of less value in the particular country, while it remained of its former value everywhere else, would be exported until prices were brought down to nearly or quite their former level. But thirdly: even on the impossible supposition that the rise of prices could be kept up, yet, being general, it would not compensate the employer; for though his money returns would be greater, his outgoings (except the fixed payments to those to whom he is in debt) would be increased in the same proportion. Finally, if when wages rose all prices rose in the same ratio, the labourers would be no better off with high wages than with low; their wages would not command more of any article of consumption; a real rise of wages, therefore, would be an impossibility.

It being obvious, from these accumulated considerations, that a real rise of general wages cannot be thrown on the consumer by a rise of prices; it follows also that a real rise even of partial wages – of wages in one or a few employments – when thrown on the consumer by an increased price of the articles produced, is generally a gain made, wholly or in part, at the expense of the remainder of the labouring classes. For, the aggregate incomes of the purchasing public not being increased, if more is spent on some articles of consumption, less will be spent on others. There are two possible suppositions. The public may either reduce its consumption of the articles which have risen, or it may retrench by preference in other articles. In the former case, if the consumption falls off in full proportion to the rise of price, there is no more money than before expended in the article, and no more, therefore, to be divided between the labourers and their employers; but the labourers may possibly retain their improved wages, at the expense of profits, until the employers, weary of having less profit than other people, withdraw part of their capital. But if the consumption does not fall off, or falls off in a less degree, so that more is really spent on the articles after than before the rise, the prices of some other things will fall from diminished demand; the producers of those other things will have less to divide, and either wages or profits must suffer. It will usually be wages; for as there will not be employment in those departments for so many labourers as before, some labourers will be thrown out of work. As Mr Thornton remarks, the general increase of the incomes of the community through the progress of wealth may make up to the other branches of the productive classes for what they thus lose, and convert it from an absolute loss, to the loss of a gain – the gain which as a body they would have derived from the general increase of wealth, but of which the whole, or more than the fair share, has been drawn off by a single branch. Still, the rise of wages in any department is necessarily at the expense either of wages in other departments or of profits, and in general both will contribute to it. So long, at least, as there are any classes of labourers who are not unionised, the successes of the Unions will generally be a cause of loss to the labourers in the non-unionist occupations.

From the recognition of this fact arises a serious question of right and wrong, as between Unionists and the remainder of the labouring classes. As between themselves and their employers, they are under no obligations but those of prudence. The employers are quite capable of taking care of themselves. Unionists are under no moral duty to their employers which the conditions they may seek to impose on them can possibly violate. But they owe moral duties to the remainder of the labouring classes, and moral duties to the community at large; and it behoves them to care that the conditions they make for their own separate interest do not conflict with either of these obligations.

However satisfactorily the question may admit of being answered, it still requires to be asked, whether Unionists are justified in seeking a rise of wages for themselves, which will in all probability produce a fall of wages, or loss of employment, to other labourers, their fellow-countrymen. Still more is this question raised by those restrictive rules, forbidding the employment of non-unionists, limiting the number of apprentices, &c., which many Unions maintain, and which are sometimes indispensable to the complete efficacy of Unionism. For (as Mr Thornton recognises) there is no keeping up wages without limiting the number of competitors for employment. And all such limitation inflicts distinct evil upon those whom it excludes – upon that great mass of labouring population which is outside the Unions; an evil not trifling, for if the system were rigorously enforced it would prevent unskilled labourers or their children from ever rising to the condition of skilled. In what manner is a system which thus operates, to be reconciled either with the obligations of general morality, or with the special regard professed by labouring men for the interest of the labouring class? To the justification of Unionism it is necessary not only that a mode of reconciliation should exist, but that Unionists should know it and consider it; for if there is ever so good a defence of their conduct, and they do not know or care about it, their case is morally the same as if there were none. Unionists who do not concern themselves with these scruples are, in intention, sacrificing the interests of their fellow-labourers, the majority of the labouring classes, to their own separate advantage; they are making themselves into an oligarchy of manual labourers, indirectly supported by a tax levied on the democracy.

There are, however, two considerations, either of which, in the mind of an upright and public spirited working man, may fairly legitimate his adhesion to Unionism. The first is, by considering the Unions of particular trades as a mere step towards an universal Union, including all labour, and as a means of educating the *élite* of the working classes for such a future. This is well put by Mr Thornton:

> 'Though, in the interests of universal labour, the formation of national and cosmopolitan unionism be clearly an end to be aimed at, the best, if not the only means to that end is the previous formation and bringing to maturity of separate trade unions. The thing is scarcely to be done, if done at all, in any other way. National unionism is only to be built up piecemeal. To begin by laying foundations coextensive with the area to be finally covered, would be a sure way of never getting beyond the founda-

tions. The only plan at all feasible, is for separate sections of labourers to organise themselves independently, and for each separate organisation to confine its attention to its own affairs, wherein it would long find abundant occupation without troubling itself about those of its neighbours, until it and they, having grown strong enough to stand alone, should perceive it to be for their mutual advantage to coalesce and stand together. This is the plan which, unconsciously perhaps for the most part, trades' unions are at present following, each in obedience to its own selfish instinct, seeking only to do the best for itself, yet each doing thereby the best for the others also. That this or any other plan will ever really eventuate in the formation of a confederacy embracing the entire working population, may to most people appear an utterly chimerical notion, and no doubt the chances are great against its realisation. But the thing, however improbable, is not more improbable than some of the actual phenomena of unionism would not long since have appeared. Half a century back, while the marvellous organising aptitude of working men lay dormant and unsuspected, it would have been quite as difficult for any one to look forward to the existing 'amalgamation' of little less than 50,000 engineers or 70,000 miners, as it is now to imagine that in another century or so – no very long period in a nation's life – a combination of these and of other associations may weld together the whole community of British workmen as one brotherhood. At the present rate of progress less than a hundred years would suffice for the operation.' (pp. 289-90.)

This prospect may appear too remote, and even visionary, to be an actuating motive with any considerable number of Unionists; but it is certainly not beyond the aspirations of the intelligent leaders of Unionism, and what is more, some great steps have already been made in the direction of its realisation. A generation ago all Unions were local, and in those days strikes were much more frequent, much oftener unreasonable, and much oftener attended with criminal excesses, than is the case at present. Since then, a number of the most important trades have been formed into Amalgated Societies extending to the whole country, and a central council decides with a view to the interests of the entire trade, what conditions shall be imposed on employers, and in what cases strikes shall take place. And it is admitted that the rules of these Amalgamated Societies are much less objectionable than those of the local unions previously were, and that the central body prevents many more strikes than it sanctions. The immediate motive to the amalgamations was, of course, the experience that attempts in one town to obtain a rise of wages, only caused the transfer of the business to another. Concert having been at length substituted for competition between different towns, the Unions now aim at effecting the same substitution between different countries: and within the last few years there is a commencement of International Congresses of working people, to prevent the efforts made in one country from being frustrated for want of a common understanding with other countries. And there can be little doubt that these attempts to lay the foundation of an alliance among the artisans of competing countries, have already produced some effect, and will acquire increasing importance.

There is, however, another, and a less elevated, but not fallacious point of view, from which the apparent injustice of Unionism to the non-united classes of labourers may be morally vindicated to the conscience of an intelligent Unionist. This is the Malthusian point of view, so blindly decried as hostile and odious, above all, to the labouring classes. The ignorant and untrained part of the poorer classes (such Unionists may say) will people up to the point which will keep their wages at that miserable rate which the low scale of their ideas and habits makes endurable to them. As long as their minds remain in their present state, our preventing them from competing with us for employment does them no real injury; it only saves ourselves from being brought down to their level. Those whom we exclude are a morally inferior class of labourers to us; their labour is worth less, and their want of prudence and self-restraint makes them much more active in adding to the population. We do them no wrong by intrenching ourselves behind a barrier, to exclude those whose competition would bring down our wages, without more than momentarily raising theirs, but only adding to the total numbers in existence. This is the practical justification, as things now are, of some of the exclusive regulations of Trades' Unions. If the majority of their members look upon this state of things, so far as the excluded labourers are concerned, with indifference, and think it enough for the Unions to take care of their own members, this is not more culpable in them than is the same indifference in classes far more powerful and more privileged by society. But it is a strong indication of a better spirit among them, that the operatives and artisans throughout the country form the main strength of the demand, rapidly becoming irresistible, for universal and compulsory education. The brutish ignorance of the lowest order of unskilled labourers has no more determined enemies, none more earnest in insisting that it be cured, than the comparatively educated workmen who direct the Unions.

The moral duties which Unionists owe to society at large – to the permanent interest of the nation and of the race – are still less regarded than the duties imposed by good feeling towards their own class. There is as little practical sense of such duties in the minds of workmen as in those of employers – and there can scarcely be less. Yet it is evident (for instance) that it cannot be right that a contest between two portions of society as to the terms on which they will co-operate, should be settled by impairing the efficacy of their joint action. There must be some better mode of sharing the fruits of human productive power than by diminishing their amount. Yet this is not only the effect, but the intention, of many of the conditions imposed by some Unions on workmen and on employers. All restrictions on the employment of machinery, or on arrangements for economising labour, deserve this censure. Some of the Unionist regulations go even further than to prohibit improvements; they are contrived for the express purpose of making work inefficient; they positively prohibit the workman from working hard and well, in order that it may be necessary to employ a greater number. Regulations that no one shall move bricks in a wheelbarrow, but only carry them in a hod, and then no more than eight at a time; that stones shall not be worked at the quarry while they are soft, but must be worked by the masons of the place where they are to be used; that plasterers shall not do the work of plasterers' labourers, nor labourers that of plasterers, but a plasterer and a labourer must both be employed when one would suffice; that bricks made on one side of a particular canal must lie there unused, while fresh bricks are made for work going on upon the other; that men shall not do so good a day's work as to 'best their mates;' that they shall not walk at more than a given pace to their work when the walk is counted 'in the master's time' – these and scores of similar examples which will be found in Mr Thornton's book, equally vexatious, and some of them more ridiculous, are all grave violations of the moral rule, that disputes between classes should not be so conducted as to make the world a worse place for both together, and ultimately for the whole of the community. I do not say that there are never cases which justify a resort to measures even thus bad in principle. A portion of society which cannot otherwise obtain just consideration from the rest, may be warranted in doing a mischief to society in order to extort what it considers its dues. But when thus acting, that portion of society is in a state of war with the rest; and such means are never justifiable but as weapons of war, like the devastation of a country and the slaughter of its innocent inhabitants – things abominable in themselves, but which may unhappily be the only means of forcing a powerful adversary to consent to just terms of accommodation. It is palpably for the good of society that its means of production, that the efficacy of its industry, should be as great as possible, and it cannot be necessary to an equitable division of the produce to make that efficacy less.

The true morality of the workmen would be to second zealously all means by which labour can be economised or made more efficient, but to demand their share of the benefit. In what shape they shall obtain it, is a matter of negociation between the parties, the difficulties of which may be greatly lightened by an impartial arbitration; and it is in such cases, above all others, that advantage might be expected from the Councils of Conciliation, which Mr Mundella and Mr Rupert Kettle have so forcibly advocated, and have carried so successfully into practice in their respective localities. The identification of the interest of the workmen with the efficiency, instead of the inefficiency of the work, is a happy result as yet only attained by co-operative industry in some one of its forms. And if it should prove, in the end, not to be attainable otherwise; if the claims of the workmen to share the benefit of whatever was beneficial to the general interest of the business, became an embarrassment to the masters from which no system of arbitration could sufficiently relieve them, and growing inconvenience to them from the opposition of interest between themselves and the workmen should stimulate the conversion of existing businesses into Industrial Partnerships, in which the whole body of workpeople have a direct interest in the profits of the enterprise; such a transformation would be the true euthanasia of Trades' Unionism, while it would train and prepare at least the superior portion of the working classes for a form of co-operation still more equal and complete.

It is to this feature in the futurity of labour that the whole of Mr Thornton's argument leads up: and to this he looks forward as the true solution of the great economic problem of modern life. Nowhere will be found so compact and comprehensive an account of the various forms of co-operative industry which have been tried in this and other countries with such remarkable success, either by combinations of operatives uniting their small savings, or by capitalist employers admitting their workmen to a participation in profits. I will not weaken these most interesting statements by abridgment, nor is it necessary to prolong this article by disserting on a subject which is every year commanding more of the attention of the best practical minds. The reader may be referred to Mr Thornton for a conclusive answer to the hesitations concerning the probabilities of success of this great movement, as well as for an inspiring picture of the blessings to human society which may rationally be expected from its progressive realisation. I will rather turn back to Unionism, and conclude with a passage embodying the author's ultimate moral judgment upon it. (pp. 333-6.)

'Sufficient note has not perhaps been taken of the educational office which unionism is silently and unconsciously performing, and of the softening and composing influence which it is insensibly exercising over its constituents. Mere union, quite irrespectively of any special object, is of itself beneficial discipline. The mere act of association is of itself a wholesome subordination of the individual to the general. Merely to combine for some common object, causes people to take pride and pleasure in that object, whatever it be, and renders them ready to make sacrifices for its furtherance. And if the object be mutual defence and mutual support, then, for the associates to take an interest in it and in each other, is one and the same thing. Among trades' unionists accustomed to look to each other for assistance in sickness, in distress, and in old age, the sense of mutual dependence begets mutual attachment. In their official intercourse they speak of each other as 'brothers,' and the word is not an empty sound, but indicates the sort of relationship which they at least desire should subsist between them, and which, because they do desire it, is sure to grow up. So far their sympathies have already widened, and it is characteristic of all moral expansion never to cease expanding. Those who, from caring for none but themselves, have got so far as to care for their fellow-workmen, will not stop till they have learned to care for all their fellowmen. Love of their class will prove to have been only an intermediate stage between self-love and love of their kind. Nor is it only indirectly that unionism is qualified to contribute towards this moral development. Certain of its arrangements are calculated to lead straight towards the same result. Hitherto, protection against material evil and acquisition of material good have been its chief care, but higher objects are beginning to claim attention, and intellectual and moral improvement are coming in for a share of solicitude. In the lodges of the London bricklayers, drunkenness and swearing are expressly interdicted. Under the auspices of the Amalgamated Carpenters, industrial schools are being established. These are straws on the surface, showing how the current of unionist opinion is flowing. The day may not be very distant when increasing *esprit de corps* will make Amalgamated Engineers and Carpenters as proud individually of their respective societies, as jealous of their honour, and as unwilling to disgrace them, as the officers of the old Bengal Engineers used to be of their connexion with that pre-eminently distinguished corps; and in proportion as those feelings become general among unionists, in the same proportion may unionism be expected to divest itself of its offensive attributes, exchanging eventually past violence and extravagance for as much moderation as its nature will admit of.

'Still, even when so modified and chastened, the necessity for its continuing to exist at all will continue to be an evil. The one constitutional vice, inherent in and inseparable from unionism, is its being a visible and a tangible embodiment of that antagonism between labour and capital, which has always been the curse of the one and a thorn in the flesh of the other . . . The utmost successes of which it is capable can never be such as well-wishers of their fellow-men, with any catholicity of sympathy, will be much disposed to rejoice over. Its highest achievements must always fall very short indeed of the consummation to which speculative philanthropy loves to look forward, when labour and capital, no longer needing to keep each other's aggressiveness in check, shall cordially combine for mutual co-operation . . . But until the alliance is effected, and as long as the antagonism subsists, trades' unionism will continue to be an indispensable auxiliary of labour, and the sooner it is so recognised, both by the legislature and by capitalists, the better for the public peace.'

13 *Chapters on Socialism*

(*Fortnightly Review,* new series XXV, 1879.)

The Difficulties of Socialism.[21]

Among those who call themselves Socialists, two kinds of persons may be distinguished. There are, in the first place, those whose plans for a new order of society, in which private property and individual competition are to be superseded and other motives to action substituted, are on the scale of a village community or township, and would be applied to an entire country by the multiplication of such self-acting units; of this character are the systems of Owen, of Fourier, and the more thoughtful and philosophic Socialists generally. The other class, who are more a product of the Continent than of Great Britain and may be called the revolutionary Socialists, propose to themselves a much bolder stroke. Their scheme is the management of the whole productive resources of the country by one central authority, the general government. And with this view some of them avow as their purpose that the working classes, or somebody in their behalf, should take possession of all the property of the country, and administer it for the general benefit.

Whatever be the difficulties of the first of these two forms of Socialism, the second must evidently involve the same difficulties and many more. The former, too, has the great advantage that it can be brought into operation progressively, and can prove its capabilities by trial. It can be tried first on a select population and extended to others as their education and cultivation permit. It need not, and in the natural order of things would not, become an engine of subversion until it had shown itself capable of being also a means of reconstruction. It is not so with the other: the aim of that is to substitute the new rule for the old at a single stroke, and to exchange the amount of good realised under the present system, and its large possibilities of improvement, for a plunge without any preparation into the most extreme form of the problem of carrying on the whole round of the operations of social life without the motive power which has always hitherto worked the social machinery. It must be acknowledged that those who would play this game on the strength of their own private opinion, unconfirmed as yet by any experimental verification – who would forcibly deprive all who have now a comfortable physical existence of their only present means of preserving it, and would brave the frightful bloodshed and misery that would ensue if the attempt was resisted – must have a serene confidence in their own wisdom on the one hand and a recklessness of other people's sufferings on the other, which Robespierre and St Just, hitherto the typical instances of those united attributes, scarcely came up to. Nevertheless this scheme has great elements of popularity which the more cautious and reasonable form of Socialism has not; because what it professes to do it promises to do quickly, and holds out hope to the enthusiastic of seeing the whole of their aspirations realised in their own time and at a blow.

The peculiarities, however, of the revolutionary form of Socialism will be most conveniently examined after the considerations common to both the forms have been duly weighed.

The produce of the world could not attain anything approaching to its present amount, nor support anything approaching to the present number of its inhabitants, except upon two conditions: abundant and costly machinery, buildings, and other instruments of production; and the power of undertaking long operations and waiting a considerable time for their fruits. In other words, there must be a large accumulation of capital, both fixed in the implements and buildings, and circulating, that is, employed in maintaining the labourers and their families during the time which elapses before the productive operations are completed and the products come in. This necessity depends on physical laws, and is inherent in the condition of human life; but these requisites of production, the capital, fixed and circulating, of the country (to which has to be added the land, and all that is contained in it), may either be the collective property of those who use it, or may belong to individuals; and the question is, which of these arrangements is most conducive to human happiness. What is characteristic of Socialism is the joint ownership by all the members of the community of the instruments and means of production; which carries with it the consequence that the division of the produce among the body of owners must be a public act, performed according to rules laid down by the community. Socialism by no means excludes private ownership of articles of consumption; the exclusive right of each to his or her share of the produce when received, either to enjoy, to give, or to exchange it. The land, for example, might be wholly the property of the community for agricultural and other productive purposes, and might be cultivated on their joint account, and yet the dwelling assigned to each individual or family as part of their remuneration might be as exclusively theirs, while they continue to fulfil their share of the common labours, as any one's house now is; and not the dwelling only, but any ornamental ground which the circumstances of the association allowed to be attached to the house for purposes of enjoyment. The distinctive feature of Socialism is not that all things are in common, but that production is only carried on upon the common account, and that the instruments of production are held as common property. The *practicability* then of Socialism, on the scale of Mr Owen's or M. Fourier's villages, admits of no dispute. The attempt to manage the whole production of a nation by one central organization is a totally different matter; but a mixed agricultural and manufacturing association of from two thousand to four thousand inhabitants under any tolerable circumstances of soil and climate would be easier to manage than many a joint stock company. The question to be considered is, whether this joint management is likely to be as efficient and successful as the managements of private industry by private capital. And this question has to be considered in a double aspect; the efficiency of the directing mind, or minds, and that of the simple workpeople. And in order to state this question in its simplest form, we will suppose the form of Socialism to be simple Communism, *i.e.* equal division of the produce among all the sharers, or, according to M. Louis Blanc's still higher standard of justice, apportionment of it according to difference of need, but without making any difference of reward according to the nature of the duty nor according to the supposed merits or services of the individual. There are other forms of Socialism, particularly Fourierism, which do, on considerations of justice or expediency, allow differences of remuneration for different kinds or degrees of service to the community; but the consideration of these may be for the present postponed.

The difference between the motive powers in the economy of society under private property and under Communism would be greatest in the case of the directing minds. Under the present system, the direction being entirely in the hands of the person or persons who own (or are personally responsible for) the capital, the whole benefit of the difference between the best administration and the worst under which the business can continue to be carried on accrues to the person or persons who control the administration: they reap the whole profit of good management except so far as their self-interest or liberality induce them to share it with their subordinates; and they suffer the whole detriment of mismanagement except so far as this may cripple their subsequent power of employing labour. This strong personal motive to do their very best and utmost for the efficiency and economy of the operations, would not exist under Communism; as the managers would only receive out of the produce the same equal dividend as the other members of the association. What would remain would be the interest common to all in so managing affairs as to make the dividend as large as possible; the incentives of public spirit, of conscience, and of the honour and credit of the managers. The force of these motives, especially when combined, is great. But it varies greatly in different persons, and is much greater for some purposes than for others. The verdict of experience, in the imperfect degree of moral cultivation which mankind have yet reached, is that the motive of conscience and that of credit and reputation, even when they are of some strength, are, in the majority of cases, much stronger as restraining than as impelling forces – are more to be depended on for preventing wrong, than for calling forth the fullest energies in the pursuit of ordinary occupations. In the case of most men the only inducement which has been found sufficiently constant and unflagging to overcome the ever-present influence of indolence and love of ease, and induce men to apply themselves unrelaxingly to work for the most part in itself dull and unexciting, is the prospect of bettering their own economic condition and that of their family; and the closer the connexion of every increase of exertion with a corresponding increase of its fruits, the more powerful is this motive. To suppose the contrary would be to imply that with men as they now are, duty and honour are more powerful principles of action than personal interest, not solely as to special acts and forbearances respecting which those sentiments have been exceptionally cultivated, but in the regulation of their whole lives; which no one, I suppose, will affirm. It may be said that this inferior efficacy of public and social feelings is not inevitable – is the result of imperfect education. This I am quite ready to admit, and also that there are even now many individual exceptions to the general infirmity. But before these exceptions can grow into a majority, or even into a very large minority, much time will be required. The education of human beings is one of the most difficult of all arts, and this is one of the points in which it has hitherto been least successful; moreover improvements in general education are necessarily very gradual, because the future generation is educated by the present, and the imperfections of the teachers set an invincible limit to the degree in which they can train their pupils to be better than themselves. We must therefore expect, unless we are operating upon a select portion of the population, that personal interest will for a long time be a more effective stimulus to the most vigorous and careful conduct of the industrial business of society than motives of a higher character. It will be said that at present the greed of personal gain by its very excess counteracts its own end by the stimulus it gives to reckless and often dishonest risks. This it does, and under Communism that source of evil would generally be absent. It is probable, indeed, that enterprise either of a bad or of a good kind would be a deficient element, and that business in general would fall very much under the dominion of routine; the rather, as the performance of duty in such communities has to be enforced by external sanctions, the more nearly each person's duty can be reduced to fixed rules, the easier it is to hold them to its performance. A circumstance which increases the probability of this result is the limited power which the managers would have of independent action. They would of course hold their authority from the choice of the community, by whom their function might at any time be withdrawn from them; and this would make it necessary for them, even if not so required by the constitution of the community, to obtain the general consent of the body before making any change in the established mode of carrying on the concern. The difficulty of persuading a numerous body to make a change in their accustomed mode of working, of which change the trouble is often great, and the risk more obvious to their minds than the advantage, would have a great tendency to keep things in their accustomed track. Against this it has to be set, that choice by the persons who are directly interested in the success of the work, and who have practical knowledge and opportunities of judgment, might be expected on the average to produce managers of greater skill than the chances of birth, which now so often determine who shall be the owner of the capital. This may be true; and though it may be replied that the capitalist by inheritance can also, like the community, appoint a manager more capable than himself, this would only place him on the same level of advantage as the community, not on a higher level. But it must be said on the other side that under the Communist system the persons most qualified for the management would be likely very often to hang back from undertaking it. At present the manager, even if he be a hired servant, has a very much larger remuneration than the other persons concerned in the business; and there are open to his ambition higher social positions to which his function of manager is a stepping-stone. On the Communist system none of these advantages would be possessed by him; he could obtain only the same dividend out of the produce of the community's labour as any other member of it; he would no longer have the chance of raising himself from a receiver of wages into the class of capitalists; and while he could be in no way better off than any other labourer, his responsibilities and anxieties would be so much greater that a large proportion of mankind would be likely to prefer the less onerous position. This difficulty was foreseen by Plato as an objection to the system proposed in his Republic of community of goods among a governing class; and the motive on which he relied for inducing the fit persons to take on themselves, in the absence of all the ordinary inducements, the cares and labours of government, was the fear of being governed by worse men. This, in truth, is the motive which would have to be in the main depended upon; the persons most competent to the management would be prompted to undertake the office to prevent it from falling into less competent hands. And the motive would probably be effectual at times when there was an impression that by incompetent management the affairs of the community were going to ruin, or even only decidedly deteriorating. But this motive could not, as a rule, expect to be called into action by the less stringent inducement of merely promoting improvement; unless in the case of inventors or schemers eager to try some device from which they hoped for great and immediate fruits; and persons of this kind are very often unfitted by over-sanguine temper and imperfect judgment for the general conduct of affairs, while even when fitted for it they are precisely the kind of persons against whom the average man is apt to entertain a prejudice, and they would often be unable to overcome the preliminary difficulty of persuading the community both to adopt their project and to accept them as managers. Communistic management would thus be, in all probability, less favourable than private management to that striking out of new paths and making immediate sacrifices with risk, is generally indispensable to great improvements in the economic condition of mankind, and even to keeping up the existing state in the face of a continual increase of the number of mouths to be fed.

We have thus far taken account only of the operation of motives upon the managing minds of the association. Let us now consider how the case stands in regard to the ordinary workers.

These, under Communism, would have no interest, except their share of the general interest, in doing their work honestly and energetically. But in this respect matters would be no worse than they now are in regard to the great majority of the producing classes. These, being paid by fixed wages, are so far from having any direct interest of their own in the efficiency of their work, that they have not even that share in the general interest which every worker would have in the Communistic organization. Accordingly, the inefficiency of hired labour, the imperfect manner in which it calls forth the real capabilities of the labourers, is matter of common remark. It is true that a character for being a good workman is far from being without its value, as it tends to give him a preference in employment, and sometimes obtains for him higher wages. There are also possibilities of rising to the position of foreman, or other subordinate administrative posts, which are not only more highly paid than ordinary labour, but sometimes open the way to ulterior advantages. But on the other side is to be set that under Communism the general sentiment of the community, composed of the comrades under whose eyes each person works, would be sure to be in favour of good and hard working, and unfavourable to laziness, carelessness, and waste. In the present system not only is this not the case, but the public opinion of the workman class often acts in the very opposite direction: the rules of some trade societies actually forbid their members to exceed a certain standard of efficiency, lest they should diminish the number of labourers required for the work; and for the same reason they often violently resist contrivances for economising labour. The change from this to a state in which every person would have an interest in rendering every other person as industrious, skilful, and careful as possible (which would be the case under Communism), would be a change very much for the better.

It is, however, to be considered that the principal defects of the present system in respect to the efficiency of labour may be corrected, and the chief advantages of Communism in that respect may be obtained, by arrangements compatible with private property and individual competition. Considerable improvement is already obtained by piece-work, in the kinds of labour which admit of it. By this the workman's personal interest is closely connected with the quality of work he turns out – not so much with its quality, the security for which still has to depend on the employer's vigilance; neither does piece-work carry with it the public opinion of the workman class, which is often, on the contrary, strongly opposed to it, as a means of (as they think) diminishing the market for labourers. And there is really good ground for their dislike of piece-work, if, as is alleged, it is a frequent practice of employers, after using piece-work to ascertain the utmost which a good workman can do, to fix the price of piece-work so low that by doing that utmost he is not able to earn more than they would be obliged to give him as day wages for ordinary work.

But there is a far more complete remedy than piece-work for the disadvantages of hired labour, viz. what is now called industrial partnership – the admission of the whole body of labourers to a participation in the profits, by distributing among all who share in the work, in the form of a percentage on their earnings, the whole or a fixed portion of the gains after a certain remuneration has been allowed to the capitalist. This plan has been found of admirable efficacy, both in this country and abroad. It has enlisted the sentiments of the workmen employed on the side of the most careful regard by all of them to the general interest of the concern; and by its joint effect in promoting zealous exertion and checking waste, it has very materially increased the remuneration of every description of labour in the concerns in which it has been adopted. It is evident that this system admits of indefinite extension and of an indefinite increase in the share of profits assigned to the labourers, short of that which would leave to the managers less than the needful degree of personal interest in the success of the concern. It is even likely that when such arrangements become common, many of these concerns would at some period or another on the death or retirement of the chiefs, pass, by arrangement, into the state of purely co-operative associations.

It thus appears that as far as concerns the motives to exertion in the general body, Communism has no advantage which may not be reached under private property, while as respects the managing heads it is at a considerable disadvantage. It has also some disadvantages which seem to be inherent in it, through the necessity under which it lies of deciding in a more or less arbitrary manner questions which, on the present system, decide themselves, often badly enough, but spontaneously.

It is a simple rule, and under certain aspects a just one, to give equal payment to all who share in the work. But this is a very imperfect justice unless the work also is apportioned equally. Now the many different kinds of work required in every society are very unequal in hardness and unpleasantness. To measure these against one another, so as to make quality equivalent to quantity, is so difficult that Communists generally propose that all should work by turns at every kind of labour. But this involves an almost complete sacrifice of the economic advantages of the division of employments, advantages which are indeed frequently over-estimated (or rather the counter-considerations are under-estimated) by political economists, but which are nevertheless, in the point of view of the productiveness of labour, very considerable, for the double reason that the co-operation of employment enables the work to distribute itself with some regard to the special capacities and qualifications of the worker, and also that every worker acquires greater skill and rapidity on one kind of work by confining himself to it. The arrangement, therefore, which is deemed indispensable to a just distribution would probably be a very considerable disadvantage in respect of production. But further, it is still a very imperfect standard of justice to demand the same amount of work from every one. People have unequal capacities of work, both mental and bodily, and what is a light task for one is an insupportable burthen to another. It is necessary, therefore, that there should be a dispensing power, an authority competent to grant exemptions from the ordinary amount of work, and to proportion tasks in some measure to capabilities. As long as there are any lazy or selfish persons who like better to be worked for by others than to work, there will be frequent attempts to obtain exemptions by favour or fraud, and the frustration of these attempts will be an affair of considerable difficulty, and will by no means be always successful. These inconveniences would be little felt, for some time at least, in communities composed of select persons, earnestly desirous of the success of the experiment; but plans for the regeneration of society must consider average human beings, and not only them but the large residuum of persons greatly below the average in the personal and social virtues. The squabbles and ill-blood which could not fail to be engendered by the distribution of work whenever such persons have to be dealt with, would be a great abatement from the harmony and unanimity which Communists hope would be found among the members of their association. That concord would, even in the most fortunate circumstances, be much more liable to disturbance than Communists suppose. The institution provides that there shall be no quarrelling about material interests; individualism is excluded from that department of affairs. But there are other departments from which no institutions can exclude it: there will still be rivalry for reputation and for personal power. When selfish ambition is excluded from the field in which, with most men, it chiefly exercises itself, that of riches and pecuniary interest, it would betake itself with greater intensity to the domain still open to it, and we may expect that the struggles for pre-eminence and for influence in the management would be of great bitterness when the personal passions, diverted from their ordinary channel, are driven to seek their principal gratification in that other direction. For these various reasons it is probable that a Communist association would frequently fail to exhibit the attractive picture of mutual love and unity of will and feeling which we are often told by Communists to expect, but would often be torn by dissension and not unfrequently broken up by it.

Other and numerous sources of discord are inherent in the necessity which the Communist principle involves, of deciding by the general voice questions of the utmost importance to every one, which on the present system can be and are left to individuals to decide, each for his own case. As an example, take the subject of education. All Socialists are strongly impressed with the all-importance of the training given to the young, not only for the reasons which apply universally, but because their demands being much greater than those of any other system upon the intelligence and morality of the individual citizen, they have even more at stake than any other societies on the excellence of their educational arrangements. Now under Communism these arrangements would have to be made for every citizen by the collective body, since individual parents, supposing them to prefer some other mode of educating their children, would have no private means of paying for it, and would be limited to what they could do by their own personal teaching and influence. But every adult member of the body would have an equal voice in determining the collective system designed for the benefit of all. Here, then, is a most fruitful source of discord in every association. All who had any opinion or preference as to the education they would desire for their own children, would have to rely for their chance of obtaining it upon the influence they could exercise in the joint decision of the community.

It is needless to specify a number of other important questions affecting the mode of employing the productive resources of the association, the conditions of social life, the relations of the body with other associations, &c., on which difference of opinion, often irreconcilable, would be likely to arise. But even the dissensions which might be expected would be a far less evil to the prospects of humanity than a delusive unanimity produced by the prostration of all individual opinions and wishes before the decree of the majority. The obstacles to human progression are always great, and require a concurrence of favourable circumstances to overcome them; but an indispensable condition of their being overcome is, that human nature should have freedom to expand spontaneously in various directions, both in thought and practice; that people should both think for themselves and try experiments for themselves, and should not resign into the hands of rulers, whether acting in the name of a few or of the majority, the business of thinking for them, and of prescribing how they shall act. But in Communist associations private life would be brought in a most unexampled degree within the dominion of public authority, and there would be less scope for the development of individual character and individual preferences than has hitherto existed among the full citizens of any state belonging to the progressive branches of the human family. Already in all societies the compression of individuality by the majority is a great and growing evil; it would probably be much greater under Communism, except so far as it might be in the power of individuals to set bounds to it by selecting to belong to a community of persons like-minded with themselves.

From these various considerations I do not seek to draw

any inference against the possibility that Communistic production is capable of being at some future time the form of society best adapted to the wants and circumstances of mankind. I think that this is, and will long be, an open question, upon which fresh light will continually be obtained, both by trial of the Communistic principle under favourable circumstances, and by the improvements which will be gradually effected in the working of the existing system, that of private ownership. The one certainty is, that Communism, to be successful, requires a high standard of both moral and intellectual education in all the members of the community – moral, to qualify them for doing their part honestly and energetically in the labour of life under no inducement but their share in the general interest of the association, and their feelings of duty and sympathy towards it; intellectual, to make them capable of estimating distant interests and entering into complex considerations, sufficiently at least to be able to discriminate, in these matters, good counsel from bad. Now I reject altogether the notion that it is impossible for education and cultivation such as is implied in these things to be made the inheritance of every person in the nation; but I am convinced that it is very difficult, and that the passage to it from our present condition can only be slow. I admit the plea that in the points of moral education on which the success of Communism depends, the present state of society is demoralising, and that only a Communistic association can effectually train mankind for Communism. It is for Communism, then, to prove, by practical experiment, its power of giving this training. Experiments alone can show whether there is as yet in any portion of the population a sufficiently high level of moral cultivation to make Communism succeed, and to give to the next generation among themselves the education necessary to keep up that high level permanently. If Communist associations show that they can be durable and prosperous, they will multiply, and will probably be adopted by successive portions of the population of the more advanced countries as they become morally fitted for that mode of life. But to force unprepared populations into Communist societies, even if a political revolution gave the power to make such an attempt, would end in disappointment.

If practical trial is necessary to test the capabilities of Communism, it is no less required for those other forms of Socialism which recognise the difficulties of Communism and contrive means to surmount them. The principal of these is Fouricrism, a system which, if only as a specimen of intellectual ingenuity, is highly worthy of the attention of any student, either of society or of the human mind. There is scarcely an objection or a difficulty which Fourier did not foresee, and against which he did not make provision beforehand by self-acting contrivances, grounded, however, upon a less high principle of distributive justice than that of Communism, since he admits inequalities of distribution and individual ownership of capital, but not the arbitrary disposal of it. The great problem which he grapples with is how to make labour attractive, since, if this could be done, the principal difficulty of Socialism would be overcome. He maintains that no kind of useful labour is necessarily or universally repugnant, unless either excessive in amount or devoid of the stimulus of companionship and emulation, or regarded by mankind with contempt. The workers in a Fourierist village are to class themselves spontaneously in groups, each group undertaking a different kind of work, and the same person may be a member not only of one group but of any number; a certain minimum having first been set apart for the subsistence of every member of the community, whether capable or not of labour, the society divides the remainder of the produce among the different groups, in such shares as it finds attract to each the amount of labour required, and no more; if there is too great a run upon particular groups it is a sign that those groups are over-remunerated relatively to others; if any are neglected their remuneration must be made higher. The share of produce assigned to each group is divided in fixed proportions among three elements – labour, capital, and talent; the part assigned to talent being awarded by the suffrages of the group itself, and it is hoped that among the variety of human capacities all, or nearly all, will be qualified to excel in some group or other. The remuneration for capital is to be such as is found sufficient to induce savings from individual consumption, in order to increase the common stock to such point as is desired. The number and ingenuity of the contrivances for meeting minor difficulties, and getting rid of minor inconveniences, is very remarkable. By means of these various provisions it is the expectation of Fourierists that the personal inducements to exertion for the public interest, instead of being taken away, would be made much greater than at present, since every increase of the service rendered would be much more certain of leading to increase of reward than it is now, when accidents of position have so much influence. The efficiency of labour, they therefore expect, would be unexampled, while the saving of labour would be prodigious, by diverting to useful occupations that which is now wasted on things useless or hurtful, and by dispensing with the vast number of superfluous distributors, the buying and selling for the whole community being managed by a single agency. The free choice of individuals, as to their manner of life would be no further interfered with than would be necessary for gaining the full advantages of co-operation in the industrial operations. Altogether, the picture of a Fourierist community is both attractive in itself and requires less from common humanity than any other known system of Socialism; and it is much to be desired that the scheme should have that fair trial which alone can test the workableness of any new scheme of social life.*

* The principles of Fourierism are clearly set forth and powerfully defended in the various writings of M. Victor Considérant, especially that entitled *La Destinée Sociale*; but the curious inquirer will do well to study them in the writings of Fourier himself; where he will find unmistakable proofs of genius, mixed, however, with the wildest and most unscientific fancies respecting the physical world, and much interesting but rash speculation on the past and future history of humanity. It is proper to add that on some important social questions, for

The result of our review of the various difficulties of Socialism has led us to the conclusion that the various schemes for managing the productive resources of the country by public instead of private agency have a case for a trial, and some of them may eventually establish their claims to preference over the existing order of things, but that they are at present workable only by the *élite* of mankind, and have yet to prove their power of training mankind at large to the state of improvement which they pre-suppose. Far more, of course, may this be said of the more ambitious plan which aims at taking possession of the whole land and capital of the country, and beginning at once to administer it on the public account. Apart from all consideration of injustice to the present possessors, the very idea of conducting the whole industry of a country by direction from a single centre is so obviously chimerical, that nobody ventures to propose any mode in which it should be done; and it can hardly be doubted that if the revolutionary Socialists attained their immediate object, and actually had the whole property of the country at their disposal, they would find no other practicable mode of exercising their power over it than that of dividing it into portions, each to be made over to the administration of a small Socialist community. The problem of management, which we have seen to be so difficult even to a select population well prepared beforehand, would be thrown down to be solved as best it could by aggregations united only by locality, or taken indiscriminately from the population, including all the malefactors, all the idlest and most vicious, the most incapable of steady industry, forethought, or self-control, and a majority who, though not equally degraded, are yet, in the opinion of Socialists themselves, as far as regards the qualities essential for the success of Socialism, profoundly demoralised by the existing state of society. It is saying but little to say that the introduction of Socialism under such conditions could have no effect but

instance on marriage, Fourier had peculiar opinions, which, however, as he himself declares, are quite independent of, and separable from, the principles of his industrial system.

disastrous failure, and its apostles could have only the consolation that the order of society as it now exists would have perished first, and all who benefit by it would be involved in the common ruin – a consolation which to some of them would probably be real, for if appearances can be trusted the animating principle of too many of the revolutionary Socialists is hate; a very excusable hatred of existing evils, which would vent itself by putting an end to the present system at all costs even to those who suffer by it, in the hope that out of chaos would arise a better Kosmos, and in the impatience of desperation respecting any more gradual improvement. They are unaware that chaos is the very most unfavourable position for setting out in the construction of a Kosmos, and that many ages of conflict, violence, and tyrannical oppression of the weak by the strong must intervene; they know not that they would plunge mankind into the state of nature so forcibly described by Hobbes (*Leviathan,* Part I. ch. xiii.), where every man is enemy to every man:

> 'In such condition there is no place for industry, because the fruit thereof is uncertain, and consequently no culture of the earth, no navigation, no use of the commodities that may be imported by sea, no commodious building, no instruments of moving and removing such things as require much force, no knowledge of the face of the earth, no account of time, no arts, no letters, no society; and, which is worst of all, continual fear and danger of violent death; and the life of man solitary, poor, nasty, brutish, and short.'

If the poorest and most wretched members of a so-called civilised society are in as bad a condition as every one would be in that worst form of barbarism produced by the dissolution of civilised life, it does not follow that the way to raise them would be to reduce all others to the same miserable state. On the contrary, it is by the aid of the first who have risen that so many others have escaped from the general lot, and it is only by better organization of the same process that it may be hoped in time to succeed in raising the remainder.

The Idea of Private Property Not Fixed But Variable

The preceding considerations appear sufficient to show that an entire renovation of the social fabric, such as is contemplated by Socialism, establishing the economic constitution of society upon an entirely new basis, other than that of private property and competition, however valuable as an ideal, and even as a prophecy of ultimate possibilities, is not available as a present resource, since it requires from those who are to carry on the new order of things qualities both moral and intellectual, which require to be tested in all, and to be created in most; and this cannot be done by an Act of Parliament, but must be, on the most favourable supposition, a work of considerable time. For a long period to come the principle of individual property will be in possession of the field; and even if in any country a popular movement were to place Socialists at the head of a revolutionary government, in however many ways they might violate private property, the institution itself would survive, and would either be accepted by them or brought back by their expulsion, for the plain reason that people will not lose their hold of what is at present their sole reliance for subsistence and security until a substitute for it has been got into working order. Even those, if any, who had shared among themselves what was the property of others would desire to keep what they had acquired, and to give back to property in the new hands the sacredness which they had not recognised in the old.

But though, for these reasons, individual property has presumably a long term before it, if only of provisional existence, we are not, therefore, to conclude that it must exist during that whole term unmodified, or that all the rights now regarded as appertaining to property belong to it inherently, and must endure while it endures. On the contrary, it is both the duty and the interest of those who derive the most direct benefit from the laws of property to give impartial consideration to all proposals for rendering those laws in any way less onerous to the majority. This, which would in any case be an obligation of justice, is an injunction of prudence also, in order to place themselves in the right against the attempts which are sure to be frequent to bring the Socialist forms of society prematurely into operation.

One of the mistakes oftenest committed, and which are the sources of the greatest practical errors in human affairs, is that of supposing that the same name always stands for the same aggregation of ideas. No word has been the subject of more of this kind of misunderstanding than the word property. It denotes in every state of society the largest powers of exclusive use or exclusive control over things (and sometimes, unfortunately, over persons) which the law accords, or which custom, in that state of society, recognises; but these powers of exclusive use and control are very various, and differ greatly in different countries and in different states of society.

For instance, in early states of society, the right of property did not include the right of bequest. The power of disposing of property by will was in most countries of Europe a rather late institution; and long after it was introduced it continued to be limited in favour of what were called natural heirs. Where bequest is not permitted, individual property is only a life interest. And in fact, as has been so well and fully set forth by Sir Henry Maine in his most instructive work on Ancient Law, the primitive idea of property was that it belonged to the family, not the individual. The head of the family had the management and was the person who really exercised the proprietary rights. As in other respects, so in this, he governed the family with nearly despotic power. But he was not free so to exercise his power as to defeat the co-proprietors of the other portions; he could not so dispose of the property as to deprive them of the joint enjoyment or of the succession. By the laws and customs of some nations the property could not be alienated without the consent of the male children; in other cases the child could by law demand a division of the property and the assignment to him of his share, as in the story of the Prodigal Son. If the association kept together after the death of the head, some other member of it, not always his son, but often the eldest of the family, the strongest, or the one selected by the rest, succeeded to the management and to the managing rights, all the others retaining theirs as before. If, on the other hand, the body broke up into separate families, each of these took away with it a part of the property. I say the property, not the inheritance, because the process was a mere continuance of existing rights, not a creation of new; the manager's share alone lapsed to the association.

Then, again, in regard to proprietary rights over immovables (the principal kind of property in a rude age) these rights were of very varying extent and duration. By the Jewish law property in immovables was only a temporary concession; on the Sabbatical year it returned to the common stock to be redistributed; though we may surmise that in the historical times of the Jewish state this rule may have been successfully evaded. In many countries of Asia, before European ideas intervened, nothing existed to which the expression property in land, as we understand the phrase, is strictly applicable. The ownership was broken up among several distinct parties, whose rights were determined rather by custom than by law. The government was part owner, having the right to a heavy rent. Ancient ideas and even ancient laws limited the government share to some particular fraction of the gross produce, but practically there was no fixed limit. The government might make over its share to an individual, who then became possessed of the right of collection and all the other rights of the state, but not those of any private person connected with the soil. These private rights were of various kinds. The actual cultivators, or such of them as had been long settled on the land, had a right to retain possession; it was held unlawful to evict them while they paid the rent – a rent not in general fixed by agreement, but by the custom of the neighbourhood. Between the actual cultivators and the state, or the substitute to whom the state had transferred its rights, there were intermediate persons with rights of various extent. There were officers of government who collected the state's share of the produce, sometimes for large districts, who, though bound to pay over to government all they collected, after deducting a percentage, were often hereditary officers. There were also, in many cases, village communities, consisting of the reputed descendants of the first settlers of a village, who shared among themselves either the land or its produce according to rules established by custom, either cultivating it themselves or employing others to cultivate it for them, and whose rights in the land approached nearer to those of a landed proprietor, as understood in England, than those of any other party concerned. But the proprietary right of the village was not individual, but collective; inalienable (the rights of individual sharers could only be sold or mortgaged with the consent of the community) and governed by fixed rules. In mediæval Europe almost all land was held from the sovereign on tenure of service, either military or agricultural; and in Great Britain even now, when the services as well as all the reserved rights of the sovereign have long since fallen into disuse or been commuted for taxation, the theory of the law does not acknowledge an absolute right of property in land in any individual; the fullest landed proprietor known to the law, the freeholder, is but a 'tenant' of the Crown. In Russia, even when the cultivators of the soil were serfs of the landed proprietor, his proprietary right in the land was limited by rights of theirs belonging to them as a collective body managing its own affairs, and with which he could not interfere. And in most of the countries of continental Europe when serfage was abolished or went out of use, those who had cultivated the land as serfs remained in possession of rights as well as subject to obligations. The great land reforms of Stein and his successors in Prussia consisted in abolishing both the rights and the obligations, and dividing the land bodily between the proprietor and the peasant, instead of leaving each of them with a limited right over the whole. In other cases, as in Tuscany, the *metayer* farmer is virtually co-proprietor with the landlord, since custom, though not law, guarantees to him a permanent possession and half the gross produce, so long as he fulfils the customary conditions of his tenure.

Again, if rights of property over the same things are of different extent in different countries, so also are they exercised over different things. In all countries at a former time, and in some countries still, the right of property extended and extends to the ownership of human beings. There has often been property in public trusts, as in judicial offices, and a vast multitude of others in France before the Revolution; there are still a few patent offices in Great Britain, though I believe they will cease by operation of law on the death of the present holders; and we are only now abolishing property in army rank. Public bodies, constituted and endowed for public purposes, still claim the same inviolable right of property in their estates which individuals have in theirs, and though a sound political morality does not acknowledge this claim, the law supports it. We thus see that the right of property is differently interpreted, and held to be of different extent, in different times and places; that the conception entertained of it is a varying conception, has been frequently revised, and may admit of still further revision. It is also to be noticed that the revisions which it has hitherto undergone in the progress of society have generally been improvements. When, therefore, it is maintained, rightly or wrongly, that some change or modification in the powers exercised over things by the persons legally recognised as their proprietors would be beneficial to the public and conducive to the general improvement, it is no good answer to this merely to say that the proposed change conflicts with the idea of property. The idea of property is not some one thing, identical throughout history and incapable of alteration, but is variable like all other creations of the human mind; at any given time it is a brief expression denoting the right over things conferred by the law or custom of some given society at that time; but neither on this point nor on any other has the law and custom of a given time and place a claim to be stereotyped for ever. A proposed reform in laws or customs is not necessarily objectionable because its adoption would imply, not the adaptation of all human affairs to the existing idea of property, but the adaptation of existing ideas of property to the growth and improvement of human affairs. This is said without prejudice to the equitable claim of proprietors to be compensated by the state for such legal rights of a proprietary nature as they may be dispossessed of for the public advantage. That equitable claim, the grounds and the just limits of it, are a subject by itself, and as such will be discussed hereafter. Under this condition, however, society is fully entitled to abrogate or alter any particular right of property which on sufficient consideration it judges to stand in the way of the public good. And assuredly the terrible case which, as we saw in a former chapter, Socialists are able to make out against the present economic order of society, demands a full consideration of all means by which the institution may have a chance of being made to work in a manner more beneficial to that large portion of society which at present enjoys the least share of its direct benefits.

PART V APPENDIX

Macaulay – 'Mill on Government'

(*Edinburgh Review*, XLIX, 1829.)

Essays on Government, Jurisprudence, the Liberty of the Press, Prisons and Prison Discipline, Colonies, the Law of Nations, and Education.

By JAMES MILL, Esq. author of the History of British India. Reprinted by permission from the Supplement to the Encyclopædia Britannica. (Not for sale.) London, 1828.

Of those philosophers who call themselves Utilitarians, and whom others generally call Benthamites, Mr Mill is, with the exception of the illustrious founder of the sect, by far the most distinguished. The little work now before us contains a summary of the opinions held by this gentleman and his brethren on several subjects most important to society. All the seven essays of which it consists abound in curious matter. But at present we intend to confine our remarks to the Treatise on Government, which stands first in the volume. On some future occasion, we may perhaps attempt to do justice to the rest.

It must be owned that to do justice to any composition of Mr Mill is not, in the opinion of his admirers, a very easy task. They do not, indeed, place him in the same rank with Mr Bentham; but the terms in which they extol the disciple, though feeble when compared with the hyperboles of adoration employed by them in speaking of the master, are as strong as any sober man would allow himself to use concerning Locke or Bacon. The essay before us is perhaps the most remarkable of the works to which Mr Mill owes his fame.

By the members of his sect, it is considered as perfect and unanswerable. Every part of it is an article of their faith; and the damnatory clauses, in which their creed abounds far beyond any theological symbol with which we are acquainted, are strong and full against all who reject any portion of what is so irrefragably established. No man, they maintain, who has understanding sufficient to carry him through the first proposition of Euclid, can read this master-piece of demonstration and honestly declare that he remains unconvinced.

We have formed a very different opinion of this work. We think that the theory of Mr Mill rests altogether on false principles, and that even on those false principles he does not reason logically. Nevertheless, we do not think it strange that his speculations should have filled the Utilitarians with admiration. We have been for some time past inclined to suspect that these people, whom some regard as the lights of the world and others as incarnate demons, are in general ordinary men, with narrow understandings and little information. The contempt which they express for elegant literature is evidently the contempt of ignorance. We apprehend that many of them are persons who, having read little or nothing, are delighted to be rescued from the sense of their own inferiority by some teacher who assures them that the studies which they have neglected are of no value, puts five or six phrases into their mouths, lends them an odd number of the *Westminster Review*, and in a month transforms them into philosophers. Mingled with these smatterers, whose attainments just suffice to elevate them from the insignificance of dunces to the dignity of bores, and to spread dismay among their pious aunts and grandmothers, there are, we well know, many well-meaning men who have really read and thought much; but whose reading and meditation have been almost exclusively confined to one class of subjects; and who, consequently, though they possess much valuable knowledge respecting those subjects, are by no means so well qualified to judge of a great system as if they had taken a more enlarged view of literature and society.

Nothing is more amusing or instructive than to observe

the manner in which people who think themselves wiser than all the rest of the world fall into snares which the simple good sense of their neighbours detects and avoids. It is one of the principal tenets of the Utilitarians that sentiment and eloquence serve only to impede the pursuit of truth. They therefore affect a quakerly plainness, or rather a cynical negligence and impurity, of style. The strongest arguments, when clothed in brilliant language, seem to them so much wordy nonsense. In the meantime they surrender their understandings, with a facility found in no other party, to the meanest and most abject sophisms, provided those sophisms come before them disguised with the externals of demonstration. They do not seem to know that logic has its illusions as well as rhetoric, – that a fallacy may lurk in a syllogism as well as in a metaphor.

Mr Mill is exactly the writer to please people of this description. His arguments are stated with the utmost affectation of precision; his divisions are awfully formal; and his style is generally as dry as that of Euclid's Elements. Whether this be a merit, we must be permitted to doubt. Thus much is certain: that the ages in which the true principles of philosophy were least understood were those in which the ceremonial of logic was most strictly observed, and that the time from which we date the rapid progress of the experimental sciences was also the time at which a less exact and formal way of writing came into use.

The style which the Utilitarians admire suits only those subjects on which it is possible to reason *a priori.* It grew up with the verbal sophistry which flourished during the dark ages. With that sophistry it fell before the Baconian philosophy in the day of the great deliverance of the human mind. The inductive method not only endured but required greater freedom of diction. It was impossible to reason from phenomena up to principles, to mark slight shades of difference in quality, or to estimate the comparative effect of two opposite considerations between which there was no common measure, by means of the naked and meagre jargon of the schoolroom. Of those schoolmen Mr Mill has inherited both the spirit and the style. He is an Aristotelian of the fifteenth century, born out of due season. We have here an elaborate treatise on Government, from which, but for two or three passing allusions, it would not appear that the author was aware that any governments actually existed among men. Certain propensities of human nature are assumed; and from these premises the whole science of politics is synthetically deduced! We can scarcely persuade ourselves that we are not reading a book written before the time of Bacon and Galileo, – a book written in those days in which physicians reasoned from the nature of heat to the treatment of fever, and astronomers proved syllogistically that the planets could have no independent motion, – because the heavens were incorruptible, and nature abhorred a vacuum!

The reason, too, which Mr Mill has assigned for taking this course strikes us as most extraordinary.

'Experience,' says he, 'if we look only at the outside of the facts, appears to be *divided* on this subject. Absolute monarchy, under Neros and Caligulas, under such men as the Emperors of Morocco and Sultans of Turkey, is the scourge of human nature. On the other side, the people of Denmark, tired out with the oppression of an aristocracy, resolved that their king should be absolute; and, under their absolute monarch, are as well governed as any people in Europe.'

This Mr Mill actually gives as a reason for pursuing the *a priori* method. But, in our judgment, the very circumstances which he mentions irresistibly prove that the *a priori* method is altogether unfit for investigations of this kind, and that the only way to arrive at the truth is by induction. *Experience* can never be divided, or even appear to be divided, except with reference to some hypothesis. When we say that one fact is inconsistent with another fact, we mean only that it is inconsistent with *the theory* which we have founded on that other fact. But, if the fact be certain, the unavoidable conclusion is that our theory is false; and, in order to correct it, we must reason back from an enlarged collection of facts to principles.

Now here we have two governments which, by Mr Mill's

own account, come under the same head in his *theoretical* classification. It is evident, therefore, that, by reasoning on that theoretical classification, we shall be brought to the conclusion that these two forms of government must produce the same effects. But Mr Mill himself tells us that they do not produce the same effects. Hence he infers that the only way to get at truth is to place implicit confidence in that chain of proof *a priori* from which it appears that they must produce the same effects! To believe at once in a theory and in a fact which contradicts it is an exercise of faith sufficiently hard: but to believe in a theory *because* a fact contradicts it is what neither philosopher nor pope ever before required. This, however, is what Mr Mill demands of us. He seems to think that, if all despots, without exception, governed ill, it would be unnecessary to prove, by a synthetical argument, what would then be sufficiently clear from experience. But, as some despots will be so perverse as to govern well, he finds himself compelled to prove the impossibility of their governing well by that synthetical argument which would have been superfluous had not the facts contradicted it. He reasons *a priori,* because the phenomena are not what, by reasoning *a priori,* he will prove them to be. In other words, he reasons *a priori,* because, by so reasoning, he is certain to arrive at a false conclusion!

In the course of the examination to which we propose to subject the speculations of Mr Mill we shall have to notice many other curious instances of that turn of mind which the passage above quoted indicates.

The first chapter of his Essay relates to the ends of government. The conception on this subject, he tells us, which exists in the minds of most men is vague and undistinguishing. He first assumes, justly enough, that the end of government is 'to increase to the utmost the pleasures, and diminish to the utmost the pains, which men derive from each other.' He then proceeds to show, with great form, that 'the greatest possible happiness of society is attained by insuring to every man the greatest possible quantity of the produce of his labour.' To effect this is, in his opinion, the end of government. It is remarkable that Mr Mill, with all his affected display of precision, has here given a description of the ends of government far less precise than that which is in the mouths of the vulgar. The first man with whom Mr Mill may travel in a stage coach will tell him that government exists for the protection of the *persons* and property of men. But Mr Mill seems to think that the preservation of property is the first and only object. It is true, doubtless, that many of the injuries which are offered to the persons of men proceed from a desire to possess their property. But the practice of vindictive assassination as it has existed in some parts of Europe – the practice of fighting wanton and sanguinary duels, like those of the sixteenth and seventeenth centuries, in which bands of seconds risked their lives as well as the principals; – these practices, and many others which might be named, are evidently injurious to society; and we do not see how a government which tolerated them could be said 'to diminish to the utmost the pains which men derive from each other.' Therefore, according to Mr Mill's very correct assumption, such a government would not perfectly accomplish the end of its institution. Yet such a government might, as far as we can perceive, 'insure to every man the greatest possible quantity of the produce of his labour.' Therefore, such a government might, according to Mr Mill's subsequent doctrine, perfectly accomplish the end of its institution. The matter is not of much consequence, except as an instance of that slovenliness of thinking which is often concealed beneath a peculiar ostentation of logical neatness.

Having determined the ends, Mr Mill proceeds to consider the means. For the preservation of property some portion of the community must be intrusted with power. This is Government; and the question is, how are those to whom the necessary power is intrusted to be prevented from abusing it?

Mr Mill first passes in review the simple forms of government. He allows that it would be inconvenient, if not physically impossible, that the whole community should meet in a mass; it follows, therefore, that the powers of government cannot be directly exercised by the people. But he sees no objection to pure and direct Democracy, except the difficulty which we have mentioned.

'The community,' says he, 'cannot have an interest opposite to its interests. To affirm this would be a contradiction in terms. The community within itself, and with respect to itself, can have no sinister interest. One community may intend the evil of another; never its own. This is an indubitable proposition, and one of great importance.'

Mr Mill then proceeds to demonstrate that a purely aristocratical form of government is necessarily bad.

> 'The reason for which government exists is, that one man, if stronger than another, will take from him whatever that other possesses and he desires. But if one man will do this, so will several. And if powers are put into the hands of a comparatively small number, called an aristocracy, – powers which make them stronger than the rest of the community, they will take from the rest of the community as much as they please of the objects of desire. They will thus defeat the very end for which government was instituted. The unfitness, therefore, of an aristocracy to be intrusted with the powers of government, rests on demonstration.'

In exactly the same manner Mr Mill proves absolute monarchy to be a bad form of government.

> 'If government is founded upon this as a law of human nature, that a man, if able, will take from others anything which they have and he desires, it is sufficiently evident that when a man is called a king he does not change his nature, so that when he has got power to enable him to take from every man what he pleases, he will take whatever he pleases. To suppose that he will not, is to affirm that government is unnecessary, and that human beings

will abstain from injuring one another of their own accord.

'It is very evident that this reasoning extends to every modification of the smaller number. Whenever the powers of government are placed in any hands other than those of the community, whether those of one man, of a few, or of several, those principles of human nature which imply that government is at all necessary, imply that those persons will make use of them to defeat the very end for which government exists.'

But is it not possible that a king or an aristocracy may soon be saturated with the object of their desires, and may then protect the community in the enjoyment of the rest? Mr Mill answers in the negative. He proves, with great pomp, that every man desires to have the actions of every other correspondent to his will. Others can be induced to conform to our will only by motives derived from pleasure or from pain. The infliction of pain is of course direct injury; and even if it take the milder course, in order to produce obedience by motives derived from pleasure, the government must confer favours. But as there is no limit to its desire of obedience, there will be no limit to its disposition to confer favours; and as it can confer favours only by plundering the people, there will be no limit to its disposition to plunder the people. 'It is therefore not true that there is in the mind of a king, or in the minds of an aristocracy, any point of saturation with the objects of desire.'

Mr Mill then proceeds to show that, as monarchical and oligarchical governments can influence men by motives drawn from pain, as well as by motives drawn from pleasure, they will carry their cruelty, as well as their rapacity, to a frightful extent. As he seems greatly to admire his own reasonings on the subject, we think it but fair to let him speak for himself.

'The chain of inference in this case is close and strong to a most unusual degree. A man desires that the actions of other men shall be instantly and accurately correspondent to his will. He desires that the actions of the greatest possible number shall be so. Terror is the grand instrument. Terror can work only through assurance that evil will follow any failure of conformity between the will and the actions willed. Every failure must therefore be punished. As there are no bounds to the mind's desire of its pleasure, there are, of course, no bounds to its desire of perfection in the instruments of that pleasure. There are, therefore, no bounds to its desire of exactness in the conformity between its will and the actions willed; and by consequence to the strength of that terror which is its procuring cause. Even the most minute failure must be visited with the heaviest infliction; and as failure in extreme exactness must frequently happen, the occasions of cruelty must be incessant.

'We have thus arrived at several conclusions of the highest possible importance. We have seen that the principle of human nature, upon which the necessity of government is founded, the propensity of one man to possess himself of the objects of desire at the cost of another, leads on, by infallible sequence, where power over a community is attained, and nothing checks, not only to that degree of plunder which leaves the members (excepting always the recipients and instruments of the plunder) the bare means of subsistence, but to that degree of cruelty which is necessary to keep in existence the most intense terrors.'

Now no man who has the least knowledge of the real state of the world, either in former ages or at the present moment, can possibly be convinced, though he may perhaps be bewildered, by arguments like these. During the last two centuries, some hundreds of absolute princes have reigned in Europe. Is it true, that their cruelty has kept in existence the most intense degree of terror; that their rapacity has left no more than the bare means of subsistence to any of their subjects, their ministers and soldiers excepted? Is this true of all of them? Of one half of them? Of one tenth part of them?

Of a single one? Is it true, in the full extent, even of Philip the Second, of Louis the Fifteenth, or of the Emperor Paul? But it is scarcely necessary to quote history. No man of common sense, however ignorant he may be of books, can be imposed on by Mr Mill's argument; because no man of common sense can live among his fellow-creatures for a day without seeing innumerable facts which contradict it. It is our business, however, to point out its fallacy; and happily the fallacy is not very recondite.

We grant that rulers will take as much as they can of the objects of their desires; and that, when the agency of other men is necessary to that end, they will attempt by all means in their power to enforce the prompt obedience of such men. But what are the objects of human desire? Physical pleasure, no doubt, in part. But the mere appetites which we have in common with the animals would be gratified, almost as cheaply and easily as those of the animals are gratified, if nothing were given to taste, to ostentation, or to the affections. How small a portion of the income of a gentleman in easy circumstances is laid out merely in giving pleasurable sensations to the body of the possessor! The greater part even of what is spent on his kitchen and his cellar goes, not to titillate his palate, but to keep up his character for hospitality, to save him from the reproach of meanness in housekeeping, and to cement the ties of good neighbourhood. It is clear that a king or an aristocracy may be supplied to satiety with mere corporal pleasures, at an expense which the rudest and poorest community would scarcely feel.

Those tastes and propensities which belong to us as reasoning and imaginative beings are not indeed so easily gratified. There is, we admit, no point of saturation with objects of desire which come under this head. And therefore the argument of Mr Mill will be just, unless there be something in the nature of the objects of desire themselves which is inconsistent with it. Now, of these objects there is none which men in general seem to desire more than the good opinion of others. The hatred and contempt of the public are generally felt to be intolerable. It is probable that our regard for the sentiments of our fellow-creatures springs, by association, from a sense of their ability to hurt or to serve us. But, be this as it may, it is notorious that, when the habit of mind of which we speak has once been formed, men feel extremely solicitous about the opinions of those by whom it is most improbable, nay absolutely impossible, that they should ever be in the slightest degree injured or benefited. The desire of posthumous fame and the dread of posthumous reproach and execration are feelings from the influence of which scarcely any man is perfectly free, and which in many men are powerful and constant motives of action. As we are afraid that, if we handle this part of the argument after our own manner, we shall incur the reproach of sentimentality, a word which, in the sacred language of the Benthamites, is synonymous with idiocy, we will quote what Mr Mill himself says on the subject, in his Treatise on Jurisprudence.

> 'Pains from the moral source are the pains derived from the unfavourable sentiments of mankind . . . These pains are capable of rising to a height with which hardly any other pains incident to our nature can be compared. There is a certain degree of unfavourableness in the sentiments of his fellow-creatures, under which hardly any man, not below the standard of humanity, can endure to live.
>
> 'The importance of this powerful agency, for the prevention of injurious acts, is too obvious to need to be illustrated. If sufficiently at command, it would almost supersede the use of other means. . . .
>
> 'To know how to direct the unfavourable sentiments of mankind, it is necessary to know in as complete, that is, in as comprehensive, a way as possible, what it is which gives them birth. Without entering into the metaphysics of the question, it is a sufficient practical answer, for the present purpose, to say that the unfavourable sentiments of man are excited by every thing which hurts them.'

It is strange that a writer who considers the pain derived from the unfavourable sentiments of others as so acute that, if sufficiently at command, it would supersede the use of the gallows and the tread-mill, should take no notice of this most important restraint when discussing the question of government. We will attempt to deduce a theory of politics in the mathematical form, in which Mr Mill delights, from the premises with which he has himself furnished us.

Proposition I. Theorem.

No rulers will do anything which may hurt the people.

This is the thesis to be maintained; and the following we humbly offer to Mr Mill, as its syllogistic demonstration.

No rulers will do that which produces pain to themselves.

But the unfavourable sentiments of the people will give pain to them.

Therefore no rulers will do anything which may excite the unfavourable sentiments of the people.

But the unfavourable sentiments of the people are excited by everything which hurts them.

Therefore no rulers will do anything which may hurt the people. Which was the thing to be proved.

Having thus, as we think, not unsuccessfully imitated Mr Mill's logic, we do not see why we should not imitate, what is at least equally perfect in its kind, his self-complacency, and proclaim our *Εὕρηκα* in his own words: 'The chain of inference, in this case, is close and strong to a most unusual degree.'

The fact is, that, when men, in treating of things which cannot be circumscribed by precise definitions, adopt this mode of reasoning, when once they begin to talk of power, happiness, misery, pain, pleasure, motives, objects of desire, as they talk of lines and numbers, there is no end to the contradictions and absurdities into which they fall. There is no proposition so monstrously untrue in morals or politics that we will not undertake to prove it, by something which shall sound like a logical demonstration, from admitted principles.

Mr Mill argues that, if men are not inclined to plunder each other, government is unnecessary; and that, if they are so inclined, the powers of government, when entrusted to a small number of them, will necessarily be abused. Surely it is not by propounding dilemmas of this sort that we are likely to arrive at sound conclusions in any moral science. The whole question is a question of degree. If all men preferred the moderate approbation of their neighbours to any degree of wealth or grandeur, or sensual pleasure, government would be unnecessary. If all men desired wealth so intensely as to be willing to brave the hatred of their fellow-creatures for sixpence, Mr Mill's argument against monarchies and aristocracies would be true to the full extent. But the fact is, that all men have some desires which impel them to injure their neighbours, and some desires which impel them to benefit their neighbours. Now, if there were a community consisting of two classes of men, one of which should be principally influenced by the one set of motives and the other by the other, government would clearly be necessary to restrain the class which was eager for plunder and careless of reputation: and yet the powers of government might be safely entrusted to the class which was chiefly actuated by the love of approbation. Now, it might with no small plausibility be maintained that, in many countries, *there are* two classes which, in some degree, answer to this description; that the poor compose the class which government is established to restrain, and the people of some property the class to which the powers of government may without danger be confided. It might be said that a man who can barely earn a livelihood by severe labour is under stronger temptations to pillage others than a man who enjoys many luxuries. It might be said that a man who is lost in the crowd is less likely to have the fear of public opinion before his eyes than a man whose station and mode of living render him conspicuous. We do not assert all this. We only say that it was Mr Mill's business to prove the contrary; and that, not having proved the contrary, he is not entitled to say, 'that those principles which imply that government is at all necessary, imply that an aristocracy will make use of its power to defeat the end for which governments exist.' This is not true, unless it be true that a rich man is as likely to covet the goods of his neighbours as a poor man, and that a poor man is as likely to be solicitous about the opinions of his neighbours as a rich man.

But we do not see that by reasoning *a priori* on such subjects as these, it is possible to advance one single step. We know that every man has some desires which he can gratify only by hurting his neighbours, and some which he can gratify only by pleasing them. Mr Mill has chosen to look only at one-half of human nature, and to reason on the motives which impel men to oppress and despoil others, as if they were the only motives by which men could possibly be influenced. We have already shown that, by taking the other half of the human character, and reasoning on it as if it were the whole, we can bring out a result diametrically opposite to that at which Mr Mill has arrived. We can, by such a process, easily prove that any form of government is good, or that all government is superfluous.

We must now accompany Mr Mill on the next stage of his argument. Does any combination of the three simple forms of government afford the requisite securities against the abuse of power? Mr Mill complains that those who maintain the affirmative generally beg the question; and proceeds to settle the point by proving, after his fashion, that no combination of the three simple forms, or of any two of them, can possibly exist.

> 'From the principles which we have already laid down it follows that, of the objects of human desire, and, speaking more definitely, of the means to the ends of human desire, namely, wealth and power, each party will endeavour to obtain as much as possible.
>
> 'If any expedient presents itself to any of the supposed parties effectual to this end, and not opposed to any pre-

ferred object of pursuit, we may infer with certainty that it will be adopted. One effectual expedient is not more effectual than obvious. Any two of the parties, by combining, may swallow up the third. That such combination will take place appears to be as certain as any thing which depends upon human will; because there are strong motives in favour of it, and none that can be conceived in opposition to it . . . The mixture of three of the kinds of government, it is thus evident, cannot possibly exist . . . It may be proper to inquire whether an union may not be possible of two of them . . .

'Let us first suppose, that monarchy is united with aristocracy. Their power is equal or not equal. If it is not equal, it follows, as a necessary consequence, from the principles which we have already established, that the stronger will take from the weaker till it engrosses the whole. The only question therefore is, What will happen when the power is equal?

'In the first place, it seems impossible that such equality should ever exist. How is it to be established? or, by what criterion is it to be ascertained? If there is no such criterion, it must in all cases, be the result of chance. If so, the chances against it are as infinity to one. The idea, therefore, is wholly chimerical and absurd . . .

'In this doctrine of the mixture of the simple forms of government is included the celebrated theory of the balance among the component parts of a government. By this it is supposed that, when a government is composed of monarchy, aristocracy, and democracy, they balance one another, and by mutual checks produce good government. A few words will suffice to show that, if any theory deserves the epithets of 'wild, visionary and chimerical,' it is that of the balance. If there are three powers, how is it possible to prevent two of them from combining to swallow up the third?

'The analysis which we have already performed will enable us to trace rapidly the concatenation of causes and effects in this imagined case.

'We have already seen that the interest of the community, considered in the aggregate, or in the democratical point of view, is, that each individual should receive protection; and that the powers which are constituted for that purpose should be employed exclusively for that purpose . . . We have also seen that the interest of the king and of the governing aristocracy is directly the reverse. It is to have unlimited power over the rest of the community, and to use it for their own advantage. In the supposed case of the balance of the monarchical, aristocratical, and democratical powers, it cannot be for the interest of either the monarchy or the aristocracy to combine with the democracy; because it is the interest of the democracy, or community at large, that neither the king nor the aristocracy should have one particle of power, or one particle of the wealth of the community, for their own advantage.

'The democracy or community have all possible motives to endeavour to prevent the monarchy and aristocracy from exercising power, or obtaining the wealth of the community for their own advantage. The monarchy and aristocracy have all possible motives for endeavouring to obtain unlimited power over the persons and property of the community. The consequence is inevitable: they have all possible motives for combining to obtain that power.'

If any part of this passage be more eminently absurd than another, it is, we think, the argument by which Mr Mill proves that there cannot be an union of monarchy and aristocracy. Their power, he says, must be equal or not equal. But of equality there is no criterion. Therefore the chances against its existence are as infinity to one. If the power be not equal, then it follows, from the principles of human nature, that the stronger will take from the weaker, till it has engrossed the whole.

Now, if there be no criterion of equality between two portions of power there can be no common measure of portions of power. Therefore it is utterly impossible to compare them together. But where two portions of power are of the same kind, there is no difficulty in ascertaining, sufficiently for all practical purposes, whether they are equal or unequal. It is easy to judge whether two men run equally fast, or can lift equal weights. Two arbitrators, whose joint decision is to be final, and neither of whom can do any thing without the assent of the other, possess equal power. Two electors, each of whom has a vote for a borough, possess, in that respect, equal power. If not, all Mr Mill's political theories fall to the ground at once. For, if it be impossible to ascertain whether two portions of power are equal, he never can show that, even under a system of universal suffrage, a minority might not carry everything their own way, against the wishes and interests of the majority.

Where there are two portions of power differing in kind, there is, we admit, no criterion of equality. But then, in such a case, it is absurd to talk, as Mr Mill does, about the stronger and the weaker. Popularly, indeed, and with reference to some particular objects, these words may very fairly be used. But to use them mathematically is altogether improper. If we are speaking of a boxing-match, we may say that some famous bruiser has greater bodily power than any man in England. If we are speaking of a pantomime, we may say the same of some very agile harlequin. But it would be talking nonsense to say, in general, that the power of Harlequin either exceeded that of the pugilist, or fell short of it.

If Mr Mill's argument be good as between different branches of a legislature, it is equally good as between sovereign powers. Every government, it may be said, will, if it can, take the objects of its desires from every other. If the French government can subdue Egland it will do so. If the English government can subdue France it will do so. But the power of England and France is either equal or not equal. The chance that it is not exactly equal is as infinity to one, and may safely be left out of the account; and then the stronger will infallibly take from the weaker till the weaker is altogether enslaved.

Surely the answer to all this hubbub of unmeaning words is the plainest possible. For some purposes France is stronger than England. For some purposes England is stronger than France. For some, neither has any power at all. France has the greater population, England the greater capital; France has the greater army, England the greater fleet. For an expedition to Rio de Janeiro or the Philippines, England has the greater power. For a war on the Po or the Danube, France has the greater power. But neither has power sufficient to keep the other in quiet subjection for a month. Invasion would be very perilous; the idea of complete conquest on either side utterly ridiculous. This is the manly and sensible way of discussing such questions. The *ergo*, or rather the *argal*, of Mr Mill cannot impose on a child. Yet we ought scarcely to say this; for we remember to have heard *a child* ask whether Bonaparte was stronger than an elephant!

Mr Mill reminds us of those philosophers of the sixteenth century who, having satisfied themselves *a priori* that the rapidity with which bodies descended to the earth varied exactly as their weights, refused to believe the contrary on the evidence of their own eyes and ears. The British constitution, according to Mr Mill's classification, is a mixture of monarchy and aristocracy; one House of Parliament being composed of hereditary nobles, and the other almost entirely chosen by a privileged class who possess the elective franchise on account of their property, or their connection with certain corporations. Mr Mill's argument proves that, from the time that these two powers were mingled in our government, that is, from the very first dawn of our history, one or the other must have been constantly encroaching. According to him, moreover, all the encroachments must have been on one side. For the first encroachment could only have been made by the stronger; and that first encroachment would have made the stronger stronger still. It is, therefore, matter of absolute demonstration, that either the Parliament was stronger than the Crown in the reign of Henry VIII, or that the Crown was stronger than the Parliament in 1641. 'Hippocrate dira cc que lui plaira,' says the girl in Molière; 'mais le cocher est mort.' Mr Mill may say what he pleases; but the English constitution is still alive. That since the Revolution the Parliament has possessed great power in the state, is what nobody will dispute. The King, on the other hand, can create new peers, and can dissolve Parliaments. William sustained severe mortifications from the House of Commons, and was, indeed, unjustifiably oppressed. Anne was desirous to change a ministry which had a majority in both Houses. She watched her moment for a dissolution, created twelve Tory peers, and succeeded. Thirty years later, the House of Commons drove Walpole from his seat. In 1784, George III was able to keep Mr Pitt in office in the face of a majority of the House of Commons. In 1804, the apprehension of a defeat in Parliament compelled the same King to part from his most favoured minister. But, in 1807, he was able to do exactly what Anne had done nearly a hundred years before. Now, had the power of the King increased during the intervening century, or had it remained stationary? Is it possible that the one lot among the infinite number should have fallen to us? If not, Mr Mill has proved that one of the two parties must have been constantly taking from the other. Many of the ablest men in England think that the influence of the Crown has, on the whole, increased since the reign of Anne. Others think that the Parliament has been growing in strength. But of this there is no doubt, that both sides possessed great power then, and possess great power now. Surely, if there were the least truth in the argument of Mr Mill, it could not possibly be a matter of doubt, at the end of a hundred and twenty years, whether the one side or the other had been the gainer.

But we ask pardon. We forgot that a fact, irreconcilable with Mr Mill's theory, furnishes, in his opinion, the strongest reason for adhering to the theory. To take up the question in another manner, is it not plain that there may be two bodies, each possessing a perfect and entire power, which cannot be taken from it without its own concurrence? What is the meaning of the words stronger and weaker, when applied to such bodies as these? The one may, indeed, by physical force, altogether destroy the other. But this is not the question. A third party, a general of their own, for example, may, by physical force, subjugate them both. Nor is there any form of government, Mr Mill's utopian democracy not excepted, secure from such an occurrence. We are speaking of the powers with which the constitution invests the two branches of the legislature; and we ask Mr Mill how, on his own principles, he can maintain that one of them will be able to encroach on the other, if the consent of the other be necessary to such encroachment?

Mr Mill tells us that, if a government be composed of the three simple forms, which he will not admit the British constitution to be, two of the component parts will inevitably join against the third. Now, if two of them combine and act as one, this case evidently resolves itself into the last; and all the observations which we have just made will fully apply to it. Mr Mill says, that 'any two of the parties, by combining, may swallow up the third;' and afterwards asks, 'How it is possible to prevent two of them from combining to swallow up the third?' Surely Mr Mill must be aware that in politics two is not always the double of one. If the concurrence of all the three branches of the legislature be necessary to every law, each branch will possess constitutional power sufficient to protect it against anything but that physical force from which no form of government is secure. Mr Mill reminds us of the Irishman, who could not be brought to understand how one juryman could possibly starve out eleven others.

But is it certain that two of the branches of the legislature will combine against the third? 'It appears to be as certain,' says Mr Mill, 'as anything which depends upon human will; because there are strong motives in favour of it, and none that can be conceived in opposition to it.' He subsequently sets forth what these motives are. The interest of the democracy is that each individual should receive protection. The interest of the King and the aristocracy is to have all the power that they can obtain, and to use it for their own ends. Therefore the King and the aristocracy have all possible motives for combining against the people. If our readers will look back to the passage quoted above, they will see that we represent Mr Mill's argument quite fairly.

Now we should have thought that, without the help of either history or experience, Mr Mill would have discovered, by the light of his own logic, the fallacy which lurks, and indeed scarcely lurks, under this pretended demonstration. The interest of the King may be opposed to that of the people. But is it identical with that of the aristocracy? In the very page which contains this argument, intended to prove that the King and the aristocracy will coalesce against the people, Mr Mill attempts to show that there is so strong an opposition of interest between the King and the aristocracy that if the powers of government are divided between them the one will inevitably usurp the power of the other. If so, he is not entitled to conclude that they will combine to destroy the power of the people merely because their interests may be at variance with those of the people. He is bound to show, not merely that in all communities the interest of a king must be opposed to that of the people, but also that, in all communities, it must be more directly opposed to the interest of the people than to the interest of the aristocracy. But he has not shown this. Therefore he has not proved his proposition on his own principles. To quote history would be a mere waste of time. Every schoolboy, whose studies have gone so far as the Abridgments of Goldsmith, can mention instances in which sovereigns have allied themselves with the people against the aristocracy, and in which the nobles have allied themselves with the people against the sovereign. In general, when there are three parties, every one of which has much to fear from the others, it is not found that two of them combine to plunder the third. If such a combination be formed, it scarcely ever effects its purpose. It soon becomes evident which member of the coalition is likely to be the greater gainer by the transaction. He becomes an object of jealousy to his ally, who, in all probability, changes sides, and compels him to restore what he has taken. Everybody knows how Henry VIII trimmed between Francis and the Emperor Charles. But it is idle to cite examples of the operation of a principle which is illustrated in almost every page of history, ancient or modern, and to which almost every state in Europe has, at one time or another, been indebted for its independence.

Mr Mill has now, as he conceives, demonstrated that the simple forms of government are bad, and that the mixed forms cannot possibly exist. There is still, however, it seems, a hope for mankind.

> 'In the grand discovery of modern times, the system of representation, the solution of all the difficulties, both speculative and practical, will perhaps be found. If it cannot, we seem to be forced upon the extraordinary conclusion, that good government is impossible. For, as there is no individual or combination of individuals, except the community itself, who would not have an interest in bad government if intrusted with its powers, and as the community itself is incapable of exercising those powers, and must intrust them to certain individuals, the conclusion is obvious: the community itself must check those individuals; else they will follow their interest and produce bad government. But how is it the community can check? The community can act only when assembled; and when assembled, it is incapable of acting. The community, however, can choose representatives.

The next question is – How must the representative body be constituted? Mr Mill lays down two principles, about which, he says, 'it is unlikely that there will be any dispute.'

'First, The checking body must have a degree of power sufficient for the business of checking.'

'Secondly, It must have an identity of interest with the community. Otherwise, it will make a mischievous use of its power.'

The first of these propositions certainly admits of no dispute. As to the second, we shall hereafter take occasion to make some remarks on the sense in which Mr Mill understands the words 'interest of the community.'

It does not appear very easy, on Mr Mill's principles, to find out any mode of making the interest of the representative body identical with that of the constituent body. The plan proposed by Mr Mill is simply that of very frequent election. 'As it appears,' says he, 'that limiting the duration of their power is a security against the sinister interest of the people's representatives, so it appears that it is the only security of which the nature of the case admits.' But all the arguments by which Mr Mill has proved monarchy and aristocracy to be pernicious will, as it appears to us, equally prove this security to be no security at all. Is it not clear that the representatives, as soon as they are elected, are an aristocracy, with an interest opposed to the interest of the community? Why should they not pass a law for extending the term of their power from one year to ten years, or declare themselves senators for life? If the whole legislative power is given to them, they will be constitutionally competent to do this. If part of the legislative power is withheld from them, to whom is that part given? Is the people to retain it, and to express its assent or dissent in primary assemblies? Mr Mill himself tells us that the community can only act when assembled, and that, when assembled, it is incapable of acting. Or is it to be provided, as in some of the American republics, that no change in the fundamental laws shall be made without the consent of a convention, specially elected for the purpose? Still the difficulty recurs: Why may not the members of the convention betray their trust, as well as the members of the ordinary legislature? When private men, they may have been zealous for the interests of the community. When candidates, they may have pledged themselves to the cause of the constitution. But, as soon as they are a convention, as soon as they are separated from the people, as soon as the supreme power is put into their hands, commences that interest opposite to the interest of the community which must, according to Mr Mill, produce measures opposite to the interests of the community. We must find some other means, therefore, of checking this check upon a check; some other prop to carry the tortoise, that carries the elephant, that carries the world.

We know well that there is no real danger in such a case. But there is no danger only because there is no truth in Mr Mill's principles. If men were what he represents them to be, the letter of the very constitution which he recommends would afford no safeguard against bad government. The real security is this, that legislators will be deterred by the fear of resistance and of infamy from acting in the manner which we have described. But restraints, exactly the same in kind, and differing only in degree, exist in all forms of government. That broad line of distinction which Mr Mill tries to point out between monarchies and aristocracies on the one side, and democracies on the other, has in fact no existence. In no form of government is there an absolute identity of interest between the people and their rulers. In every form of government, the rulers stand in some awe of the people. The fear of resistance and the sense of shame operate, in a certain degree, on the most absolute kings and the most illiberal oligarchies. And nothing but the fear of resistance and the sense of shame preserves the freedom of the most democratic communities from the encroachments of their annual and biennial delegates.

We have seen how Mr Mill proposes to render the interest of the representative body identical with that of the constituent body. The next question is, in what manner the interest of the constituent body is to be rendered identical with that of the community. Mr Mill shows that a minority of the community, consisting even of many thousands, would be a bad constituent body, and, indeed, merely a numerous aristocracy.

'The benefits of the representative system,' says he, 'are lost, in all cases in which the interests of the choosing body are not the same with those of the community. It is very evident, that if the community itself were the choosing body, the interest of the community and that of the choosing body would be the same.'

On these grounds Mr Mill recommends that all males of mature age, rich and poor, educated and ignorant, shall have votes. But why not the women too? This question has often been asked in parliamentary debate, and has never, to our knowledge, received a plausible answer. Mr Mill escapes from it as fast as he can. But we shall take the liberty to dwell a little on the words of the oracle. 'One thing,' says he, 'is pretty clear, that all those individuals whose interests are involved in those of other individuals, may be struck off without inconvenience. . . . In this light women may be regarded, the interest of almost all of whom is involved either in that of their fathers, or in that of their husbands.'

If we were to content ourselves with saying, in answer to all the arguments in Mr Mill's essay, that the interest of a king is involved in that of the community, we should be accused, and justly, of talking nonsense. Yet such an assertion would not, as far as we can perceive, be more unreasonable than that which Mr Mill has here ventured to make. Without adducing one fact, without taking the trouble to perplex the question by one sophism, he placidly dogmatises away the interest of one half of the human race. If there be a word of truth in history, women have always been, and still are, over the greater part of the globe, humble companions, playthings, captives, menials, beasts of burden. Except in a few happy and highly civilised communities, they are strictly in a state of personal slavery. Even in those countries where they are best treated, the laws are generally unfavourable to them, with respect to almost all the points in which they are most deeply interested.

Mr Mill is not legislating for England or the United States; but for mankind. Is then the interest of a Turk the same with that of the girls who compose his harem? Is the interest of a Chinese the same with that of the woman whom he harnesses to his plough? Is the interest of an Italian the same with that of the daughter whom he devotes to God? The interest of a respectable Englishman may be said, without any impropriety, to be identical with that of his wife. But why is it so? Because human nature is *not* what Mr Mill conceives it to be; because civilised men, pursuing their own happiness in a social state, are not Yahoos fighting for carrion; because there is a pleasure in being loved and esteemed, as well as in being feared and servilely obeyed. Why does not a gentleman restrict his wife to the bare maintenance which the law would compel him to allow her, that he may have more to spend on his personal pleasures? Because, if he loves her, he has pleasure in seeing her pleased; and because, even if he dislikes her, he is unwilling that the whole neighbourhood should cry shame on his meanness and ill-nature. Why does not the legislature, altogether composed of males, pass a law to deprive women of all civil privileges whatever, and reduce them to the state of slaves? By passing such a law they would gratify what Mr Mill tells us is an inseparable part of human nature, the desire to possess unlimited power of inflicting pain upon others. That they do not pass such a law, though they have the power to pass it, and that no man in England wishes to see such a law passed, proves that the desire to possess unlimited power of inflicting pain is not inseparable from human nature.

If there be in this country an identity of interest between the two sexes, it cannot possibly arise from any thing but the pleasure of being loved, and of communicating happiness. For, that it does not spring from the mere instinct of sex, the treatment which women experience over the greater part of the world abundantly proves. And, if it be said that our laws of marriage have produced it, this only removes the argument a step further; for those laws have been made by males. Now, if the kind feelings of one half of the species be a sufficient security for the happiness of the other why may not the kind feelings of a monarch or an aristocracy be sufficient at least to prevent them from grinding the people to the very utmost of their power?

If Mr Mill will examine why it is that women are better treated in England than in Persia, he may perhaps find out, in the course of his inquiries, why it is that the Danes are better governed than the subjects of Caligula.

We now come to the most important practical question in the whole essay. Is it desirable that all males arrived at years of discretion should vote for representatives, or should a pecuniary qualification be required? Mr Mill's opinion is, that the lower the qualification the better; and that the best system is that in which there is none at all.

> 'The qualification,' says he, 'must either be such as to embrace the majority of the population, or something less than the majority. Suppose, in the first place, that it embraces the majority, the question is, whether the majority would have an interest in oppressing those who, upon this supposition, would be deprived of political power? If we reduce the calculation to its elements, we shall see that the interest which they would have of this deplorable kind, though it would be something, would not be very great. Each man of the majority, if the majority were twice as great as the minority, each man of the majority would only have one half the benefit of oppressing a single man . . . Suppose, in the second place, that the qualification did not admit a body of electors so large as the majority, in that case taking again the calculation in its elements, we shall see that each man would have a benefit equal to that derived from the oppression of more than one man; and that, in proportion as the elective body constituted a smaller and smaller minority, the benefit of misrule to the selective body would be increased, and bad government would be insured.'

The first remark which we have to make on this argument is, that, by Mr Mill's own account, even a government in which every human being should vote would still be defective. For, under a system of universal suffrage, the majority of the electors return the representative, and the majority of the representatives make the law. The whole people may vote, therefore; but only the majority govern. So that, by Mr Mill's own confession, the most perfect system of government conceivable is one in which the interest of the ruling body to oppress, though not great, is something.

But is Mr Mill in the right when he says that such an interest could not be very great? We think not. If, indeed, every man in the community possessed an equal share of what Mr Mill calls the objects of desire, the majority would probably abstain from plundering the minority. A large minority would offer a vigorous resistance; and the property of a small minority would not repay the other members of the community for the trouble of dividing it. But it happens that in all civilised communities there is a small minority of rich men, and a great majority of poor men. If there were a thousand men with ten pounds apiece, it would not be worth while for nine hundred and ninety of them to rob ten, and it would be a bold attempt for six hundred of them to rob four hundred. But, if ten of them had a hundred thousand pounds apiece, the case would be very different. There would then be much to be got, and nothing to be feared.

'That one human being will desire to render the person and property of another subservient to his pleasures, notwithstanding the pain or loss of pleasure which it may occasion to that other individual, is,' according to Mr Mill, 'the foundation of government.' That the property of the rich minority can be made subservient to the pleasures of the poor majority will scarcely be denied. But Mr Mill proposes to give the poor majority power over the rich minority. Is it possible to doubt to what, on his own principles, such an arrangement must lead?

It may perhaps be said that, in the long run, it is for the interest of the people that property should be secure, and that therefore they will respect it. We answer thus: – It cannot be pretended that it is not for the immediate interest of the people to plunder the rich. Therefore, even if it were quite certain that, in the long run, the people would, as a body, lose by doing so, it would not necessarily follow that the fear of remote ill consequences would overcome the desire of immediate acquisitions. Every individual might flatter himself that the punishment would not fall on him. Mr Mill himself tells us, in his Essay on Jurisprudence, that no quantity of evil which is remote and uncertain will suffice to prevent crime.

But we are rather inclined to think that it would, on the whole, be for the interest of the majority to plunder the rich. If so, the Utilitarians will say, that the rich *ought* to be plundered. We deny the inference. For, in the first place, if the object of government be the greatest happiness of the greatest number, the intensity of the suffering which a measure inflicts must be taken into consideration, as well as the number of the sufferers. In the next place, we have to notice one most important distinction which Mr Mill has altogether overlooked. Throughout his essay, he confounds the community with the species. He talks of the greatest happiness of the greatest number: but, when we examine his reasonings, we find that he thinks only of the greatest number of a single generation.

Therefore, even if we were to concede that all those arguments of which we have exposed the fallacy are unanswerable, we might still deny the conclusion at which the essayist arrives. Even if we were to grant that he had found out the form of government which is best for the majority of the people now living on the face of the earth, we might still without inconsistency maintain that form of government to be pernicious to mankind. It would still be incumbent on Mr Mill to prove that the interest of every generation is identical with the interest of all succeeding generations. And how on his own principles he could do this we are at a loss to conceive.

The case, indeed, is strictly analogous to that of an aristocratic government. In an aristocracy, says Mr Mill, the few being invested with the powers of government, can take the objects of their desires from the people. In the same manner, every generation in turn can gratify itself at the expense of posterity, – priority of time, in the latter case, giving an advantage exactly corresponding to that which superiority of station gives in the former. That an aristocracy will abuse its advantage, is, according to Mr Mill, matter of demonstration. Is it not equally certain that the whole people will do the same; that, if they have the power, they will commit waste of every sort on the estate of mankind, and transmit it to posterity impoverished and desolated?

How is it possible for any person who holds the doctrines of Mr Mill to doubt that the rich, in a democracy such as that which he recommends, would be pillaged as unmercifully as under a Turkish Pacha? It is no doubt for the interest of the next generation, and it may be for the remote interest of the present generation, that property should be held sacred. And so no doubt it will be for the interest of the next Pacha, and even for that of the present Pacha, if he should hold office long, that the inhabitants of his Pachalik should be encouraged to accumulate wealth. Scarcely any despotic sovereign has plundered his subjects to a large extent without having reason before the end of his reign to regret it. Everybody knows how bitterly Louis the Fourteenth, towards the close of his life, lamented his former extravagance. If that magnificent prince had not expended millions on Marli and Versailles, and tens of millions on the aggrandisement of his grandson, he would not have been compelled at last to pay servile court to low-born money-lenders, to humble himself before men on whom, in the days of his pride, he would not have vouchsafed to look, for the means of supporting even his own household. Examples to the same effect might easily be multiplied. But despots, we see, do plunder their subjects, though history and experience tell them that, by prematurely exacting the means of profusion, they are in fact devouring the seed-corn from which the future harvest of revenue is to spring. Why then should we suppose that the people will be deterred from procuring immediate relief and enjoyment by the fear of distant calamities, of calamities which perhaps may not be fully felt till the times of their grand-children?

These conclusions are strictly drawn from Mr Mill's own principles: and, unlike most of the conclusions which he has himself drawn from those principles, they are not, as far as we know, contradicted by facts. The case of the United States is not in point. In a country where the necessaries of life are cheap and the wages of labour high, where a man who has no capital but his legs and arms may expect to become rich by industry and frugality, it is not very decidedly even for the immediate advantage of the poor to plunder the rich; and the punishment of doing so would very speedily follow the offence. But in countries in which the great majority live from hand to mouth, and in which vast masses of wealth have been accumulated by a comparatively small number, the case is widely different. The immediate want is, at particular seasons, craving, imperious, irresistible. In our own time it has steeled men to the fear of the gallows, and urged them on the point of the bayonet. And, if these men had at their command that gallows and those bayonets which now scarcely restrain them, what is to be expected? Nor is this state of things one which can exist only under a bad government. If there be the least truth in the doctrines of the school to which Mr Mill belongs, the increase of population will necessarily produce it everywhere. The increase of population is accelerated by good and cheap government. Therefore, the better the government, the greater is the inequality of conditions: and the greater the inequality of conditions, the stronger are the motives which impel the populace to spoliation. As for America, we appeal to the twentieth century.

It is scarcely necessary to discuss the effects which a general spoliation of the rich would produce. It may indeed happen that, where a legal and political system full of abuses is inseparably bound up with the institution of property, a nation may gain by a single convulsion, in which both perish together. The price is fearful. But, if, when the shock is over, a new order of things should arise under which property may enjoy security, the industry of individuals will soon repair the devastation. Thus we entertain no doubt that the Revolution was, on the whole, a most salutary event for France. But would France have gained if, ever since the year 1793, she had been governed by a democratic convention? If Mr Mill's principles be sound, we say that almost her whole capital would by this time have been annihilated. As soon as the first explosion was beginning to be forgotten, as soon as wealth again began to germinate, as soon as the poor again began to compare their cottages and salads with the hotels and banquets of the rich, there would have been another scramble for property, another maximum, another general confiscation, another reign of terror. Four or five such convulsions following each other, at intervals of ten or twelve years, would reduce the most flourishing countries of Europe to the state of Barbary or the Morea.

The civilised part of the world has now nothing to fear from the hostility of savage nations. Once the deluge of barbarism has passed over it, to destroy and to fertilise; and in the present state of mankind we enjoy a full security against that calamity. That flood will no more return to cover the earth. But is it possible that in the bosom of civilisation itself may be engendered the malady which shall destroy it? Is it possible that institutions may be established which, without the help of earthquake, of famine, of pestilence, or of the foreign sword, may undo the work of so many ages of wisdom and glory, and gradually sweep away taste, literature, science, commerce, manufactures, everything but the rude arts necessary to the support of animal life? Is it possible that, in two or three hundred years, a few lean and half-naked fishermen may divide with owls and foxes the ruins of the greatest European cities

– may wash their nets amidst the relics of her gigantic docks, and build their huts out of the capitals of her stately cathedrals? If the principles of Mr Mill be sound, we say, without hesitation, that the form of government which he recommends will assuredly produce all this. But, if these principles be unsound, if the reasonings by which we have opposed them be just, the higher and middling orders are the natural representatives of the human race. Their interest may be opposed in some things to that of their poorer contemporaries; but it is identical with that of the innumerable generations which are to follow.

Mr Mill concludes his essay, by answering an objection often made to the project of universal suffrage – that the people do not understand their own interests. We shall not go through his arguments on this subject, because, till he has proved that it is for the interest of the people to respect property, he only makes matters worse by proving that they understand their interests. But we cannot refrain from treating our readers with a delicious *bonne bouche* of wisdom, which he has kept for the last moment.

> 'The opinions of that class of the people who are below the middle rank are formed, and their minds are directed, by that intelligent, that virtuous rank, who come the most immediately in contact with them, who are in the constant habit of intimate communication with them, to whom they fly for advice and assistance in all their numerous difficulties, upon whom they feel an immediate and daily dependence in health and in sickness, in infancy and in old age, to whom their children look up as models for their imitation, whose opinions they hear daily repeated, and account it their honour to adopt. There can be no doubt that the middle rank, which gives to science, to art, and to legislation itself their most distinguished ornaments, and is the chief source of all that has exalted and refined human nature, is that portion of the community, of which, if the basis of representation were ever so far extended, the opinion would ultimately decide.

Of the people beneath them, a vast majority would be sure to be guided by their advice and example.'

This single paragraph is sufficient to upset Mr Mill's theory. Will the people not act against their own interest? Or will the middle rank act against its own interest? Or is the interest of the middle rank identical with the interest of the people? If the people act according to the directions of the middle rank, as Mr Mill says that they assuredly will, one of these three questions must be answered in the affirmative. But, if any one of the three be answered in the affirmative, his whole system falls to the ground. If the interest of the middle rank be identical with that of the people, why should not the powers of government be entrusted to that rank? If the powers of government were entrusted to that rank, there would evidently be an aristocracy of wealth; and 'to constitute an aristocracy of wealth, though it were a very numerous one, would,' according to Mr Mill, 'leave the community without protection, and exposed to all the evils of unbridled power.' Will not the same motives which induce the middle classes to abuse one kind of power induce them to abuse another? If their interest be the same with that of the people they will govern the people well. If it be opposite to that of the people they will advise the people ill. The system of universal suffrage, therefore, according to Mr Mill's own account, is only a device for doing circuitously what a representative system, with a pretty high qualification, would do directly.

So ends this celebrated Essay. And such is this philosophy for which the experience of three thousand years is to be discarded; this philosophy, the professors of which speak as if it had guided the world to the knowledge of navigation and alphabetical writing; as if, before its dawn, the inhabitants of Europe had lived in caverns and eaten each other! We are sick, it seems, like the children of Israel, of the objects of our old and legitimate worship. We pine for a new idolatry. All that is costly and all that is ornamental in our intellectual treasures must be delivered up, and cast into the furnace – and there comes out this Calf!

Our readers can scarcely mistake our object in writing this article. They will not suspect us of any disposition to advocate the cause of absolute monarchy, or of any narrow form of oligarchy, or to exaggerate the evils of popular government. Our object at present is, not so much to attack or defend any particular system of polity, as to expose the vices of a kind of reasoning utterly unfit for moral and political discussions; of a kind of reasoning which may so readily be turned to purposes of falsehood that it ought to receive no quarter, even when by accident it may be employed on the side of truth.

Our objection to the essay of Mr Mill is fundamental. We believe that it is utterly impossible to deduce the science of government from the principles of human nature.

What proposition is there respecting human nature which is absolutely and universally true? We know of only one: and that is not only true, but identical; that men always act from self-interest. This truism the Utilitarians proclaim with as much pride as if it were new, and as much zeal as if it were important. But in fact, when explained, it means only that men, if they can, will do as they choose. When we see the actions of a man we know with certainty what he thinks his interest to be. But it is impossible to reason with certainty from what *we* take to be his interest to his actions. One man goes without a dinner that he may add a shilling to a hundred thousand pounds: another runs in debt to give balls and masquerades. One man cuts his father's throat to get possession of his old clothes: another hazards his own life to save that of an enemy. One man volunteers on a forlorn hope: another is drummed out of a regiment for cowardice. Each of these men has, no doubt, acted from self-interest. But we gain nothing by knowing this, except the pleasure, if it be one, of multiplying useless words. In fact, this principle is just as recondite and just as important as the great truth that whatever is, is. If a philosopher were always to state facts in the following form – 'There is a shower: but whatever is, is;

therefore, there is a shower,' – his reasoning would be perfectly sound, but we do not apprehend that it would materially enlarge the circle of human knowledge. And it is equally idle to attribute any importance to a proposition which, when interpreted, means only that a man had rather do what he had rather do.

If the doctrine, that men always act from self-interest, be laid down in any other sense than this – if the meaning of the word self-interest be narrowed so as to exclude any one of the motives which may by possibility act on any human being, – the proposition ceases to be identical; but at the same time it ceases to be true.

What we have said of the word 'self-interest' applies to all the synonyms and circumlocutions which are employed to convey the same meaning; pain and pleasure, happiness and misery, objects of desire, and so forth.

The whole art of Mr Mill's essay consists in one simple trick of legerdemain. It consists in using words of the sort which we have been describing first in one sense and then in another. Men will take the objects of their desire if they can. Unquestionably: – but this is an identical proposition: for an object of desire means merely a thing which a man will procure if he can. Nothing can possibly be inferred from a maxim of this kind. When we see a man take something we shall know that it was an object of his desire. But till then we have no means of judging with certainty what he desires or what he will take. The general proposition, however, having been admitted, Mr Mill proceeds to reason as if men had no desires but those which can be gratified only by spoliation and oppression. It then becomes easy to deduce doctrines of vast importance from the original axiom. The only misfortune is, that by thus narrowing the meaning of the word desire the axiom becomes false, and all the doctrines consequent upon it are false likewise.

When we pass beyond those maxims which it is impossible to deny without a contradiction in terms, and which, therefore, do not enable us to advance a single step in practical knowledge, we do not believe that it is possible to lay down a single general rule respecting the motives which influence human actions. There is nothing which may not, by association or by comparison, become an object either of desire or of aversion. The fear of death is generally considered as one of the strongest of our feelings. It is the most formidable sanction which legislators have been able to devise. Yet it is notorious that, as Lord Bacon has observed, there is no passion by which that fear has not been often overcome. Physical pain is indisputably an evil; yet it has been often endured, and even welcomed. Innumerable martyrs have exulted in torments which made the spectators shudder; and, to use a more homely illustration, there are few wives who do not long to be mothers.

Is the love of approbation a stronger motive than the love of wealth? It is impossible to answer this question generally even in the case of an individual with whom we are very intimate. We often say, indeed, that a man loves fame more than money or money more than fame. But this is said in a loose and popular sense: for there is scarcely a man who would not endure a few sneers for a great sum of money, if he were in pecuniary distress; and scarcely a man, on the other hand, who, if he were in flourishing circumstances, would expose himself to the hatred and contempt of the public for a trifle. In order, therefore, to return a precise answer even about a single human being, we must know what is the amount of the sacrifice of reputation demanded and of the pecuniary advantage offered, and in what situation the person to whom the temptation is proposed stands at the time. But when the question is propounded generally about the whole species, the impossibility of answering is still more evident. Man differs from man; generation from generation; nation from nation. Education, station, sex, age, accidental associations, produce infinite shades of variety.

Now, the only mode in which we can conceive it possible to deduce a theory of government from the principles of human nature is this. We must find out what are the motives which, in a particular form of government, impel rulers to bad measures, and what are those which impel them to good measures. We must then compare the effect of the two classes of motives, and, according as we find the one or the other to prevail, we must pronounce the form of government in question good or bad.

Now let it be supposed that, in aristocratical and monarchical states, the desire of wealth and other desires of the same class always tend to produce misgovernment, and that the love of approbation and other kindred feelings always tend to produce good government. Then, if it be impossible, as we have shown that it is, to pronounce generally which of the two classes of motives is the more influential, it is impossible to find out, *a priori,* whether a monarchical or aristocratical form of government be good or bad.

Mr Mill has avoided the difficulty of making the comparison, by very coolly putting all the weights into one of the scales – by reasoning as if no human being had ever sympathised with the feelings, been gratified by the thanks, or been galled by the execrations, of another.

The case, as we have put it, is decisive against Mr Mill; and yet we have put it in a manner far too favourable to him. For, in fact, it is impossible to lay it down as a general rule that the love of wealth in a sovereign always produces misgovernment, or the love of approbation good government. A patient and far-sighted ruler, for example, who is less desirous of raising a great sum immediately than of securing an unencumbered and progressive revenue, will, by taking off restraints from trade and giving perfect security to property, encourage accumulation and entice capital from foreign countries. The commercial policy of Prussia, which is perhaps superior to that of any country in the world, and which puts to shame the absurdities of our republican brethren on the other side of the Atlantic, has probably sprung from the desire of an absolute ruler to enrich himself. On the other hand, when the popular estimate of virtues and vices is erroneous, which is too often the case, the love of approbation leads sovereigns to spend the wealth of the nation on useless shows, or to engage in wanton and destructive wars. If then we can neither compare the strength of two motives, nor determine with certainty to what descriptions of action either motive will lead, how can we possibly deduce a theory of government from the nature of man?

How, then, are we to arrive at just conclusions on a subject so important to the happiness of mankind? Surely by that method which, in every experimental science to which it has been applied, has signally increased the power and knowledge of our species, – by that method for which our new philosophers would substitute quibbles scarcely worthy of the barbarous respondents and opponents of the middle ages, – by the method of Induction; – by observing the present state of the world, – by assiduously studying the history of past ages, – by sifting the evidence of facts, – by carefully combining and contrasting those which are authentic – by generalising with judgment and diffidence, – by perpetually bringing the theory which we have constructed to the test of new facts, – by correcting, or altogether abandoning it, according as those new facts prove it to be partially or fundamentally unsound. Proceeding thus, – patiently, – diligently, – candidly, – we may hope to form a system as far inferior in pretension to that which we have been examining and as far superior to it in real utility as the prescriptions of a great physician, varying with every stage of every malady and with the constitution of every patient, to the pill of the advertising quack which is to cure all human beings, in all climates, of all diseases.

This is that noble Science of Politics, which is equally removed from the barren theories of the Utilitarian sophists, and from the petty craft, so often mistaken for statesmanship by minds grown narrow in habits of intrigue, jobbing, and official etiquette; – which of all science is the most important to the welfare of nations, – which of all sciences most tends to expand and invigorate the mind, – which draws nutriment and ornament from every part of philosophy and literature, and dispenses in return nutriment and ornament to all. We are sorry and surprised when we see men of good intentions and good natural abilities abandon this healthful and generous study to pore over speculations like those which we have been examining. And we should heartily rejoice to find that our remarks had induced any person of this description to employ, in researches of real utility, the talents and industry which are now wasted on verbal sophisms, wretched of their wretched kind.

As to the greater part of the sect, it is, we apprehend, of little consequence what they study or under whom. It would be more amusing, to be sure, and more reputable, if they would take up the old republican cant and declaim about Brutus and Timoleon, the duty of killing tyrants and the blessedness of dying for liberty. But, on the whole, they might have chosen worse. They may as well be Utilitarians as jockeys or dandies. And, though quibbling about self-interest and motives, and objects of desire, and the greatest happiness of the greatest number, is but a poor employment for a grown man, it certainly hurts the health less than hard drinking, and the fortune less than high play; it is not much more laughable than phrenology, and is immeasurably more humane than cock-fighting.

Textual Notes

1. Many changes took place between the first and the eighth edition. For a complete view of these revisions see J. S. Mill—*Collected Works* (University of Toronto Press) vol. VIII.

2. The extract printed here is part of a longer article reviewing Michelet's *Histoire de France,* 5 vols., Paris, 1835-42.

3. I have omitted a long footnote in which Mill quotes evidence to prove this point.

4. In *Dissertations and Discussions* (hereafter DD) vol. II, this reads 'Is he a disbeliever of revelation? a short sighted, narrow-minded . . .'

5. In DD vol. II, this reads 'and the laws of the outward world'.

6. This was published anonymously.

7. This was added in the second edition.

8. The article goes on: 'It now remains to exhibit the actual state of the law of this country, with respect to the liberty of the press.' I have omitted this section except for Mill's concluding paragraphs.

9. As the complete series of articles is too long to reprint here, I have included only very brief extracts, intended to convey something of Mill's views at this stage in his development.

10. The first section was extracted by Mill from an article 'Bailey's Rationale of Political Representation', *London Review,* I, 1835; the second section from his first review of

Tocqueville's book *Democracy in America, London Review,* II, 1835.

11. In DD vol. II Mill inserts here a passage, which reads: 'Crude and ill-considered legislation is the character of all governments whose laws are made and acts of administration performed *impromptu,* not in pursuance of a general design, but from the pressure of some present occasion; of all governments in which the ruling power is to any great extent exercised by persons not trained to government as a business. It is true that the governments which have been celebrated for their profound policy, have generally been aristocracies. But they have been very narrow aristocracies, consisting of so few members, that every member could personally participate in the business of administration. These are the governments which have a natural tendency to be administered steadily—that is, according to fixed principles. Every member of the governing body being trained to government as a profession, like other professions they respect precedent, transmit their experience from generation to generation, acquire and preserve a set of traditions, and all being competent judges of each other's merits, the ablest easily rises to his proper level. The governments of ancient Rome and modern Venice were of this character; and as all know, for ages conducted the affairs of those states with admirable constancy and skill, on fixed principles, often unworthy enough, but always emininently adapted to the ends of those governments. When the governing body, whether it consists of the many or of a privileged class, is so numerous, that the large majority of it do not and cannot make the practice of government the main occupation of their lives, it is impossible that there should be wisdom, foresight, and caution in the governing body itself. These qualities must be found, if found at all, not in the body, but in those whom the body trust. The opinion of a numerous ruling class is as fluctuating, as liable to be wholly given up to immediate impulses, as the opinion of the people. Witness the whole course of English history. All our laws have been made on temporary impulses. In no country has the course of legislation been less directed to any steady and consistent purpose.'

12. In DD vol. II Mill adds a long extract on the possibilities of correcting the weaknesses of democracy.

13. This reference to 'Young England' and *The Times,* was omitted in DD vol. II.

14. In DD vol. II, this became 'immediate'.

15. This sentence was omitted in DD vol. II.

16. This footnote was omitted in DD vol. II.

17. This sentence was omitted in DD vol. II.

18. This paragraph was omitted in DD vol. II.

19. The article goes on for several pages to review the allotment system; it was left out in DD vol. II; I also am omitting it.

20. Also in *Fortnightly Review,* n.s. V, 1869.

21. These instalments were published in *Fortnightly Review,* n.s. XXV, 1879. I have reprinted the third in full. The subheadings in the first two were: 'Introductory; Socialist Objections to the Present Order of Society'; 'The Socialist Objections to the Present Order of Society Examined'.

Chronological List of Contents

'Law of Libel and Liberty of the Press' 1825
'The Spirit of the Age' 1831
'Remarks on Bentham's Philosophy' 1833
'Democracy and Government' 1835
'M. de Tocqueville on Democracy in America' 1840
'On the Logic of the Moral Sciences' 1843
'Michelet's *History of France*' 1844
'Claims of Labour' 1845
On Liberty, chapter III 1859
Utilitarianism, chapter II 1861
'Thornton on Labour and its claims' 1869
'Chapters on Socialism' 1879

Appendix
Macaulay—'Mill on Government' 1829

Bibliography

For Mill's writings, excluding those published posthumously, there is a *Bibliography of the Published Writings of J. S. Mill* ed. MacMinn, Hainds, and McCrimmon (Northwestern University, Evanston, Illinois, 1945). The *Collected Works* is being published by the University of Toronto Press. For writings on Mill the most complete list appears in the *Mill News Letter* (University of Toronto Press) which began in 1965. Below is a selective guide to the main works by Mill (i) and on Mill (ii), grouped according to subject matter.

Biography

(i) *Autobiography,* London, 1873

(ii) BAIN, ALEXANDER, *J. S. Mill,* London, 1882.

COURTNEY, W. L., *Life of J. S. Mill,* London, 1889.

HAYEK, F. A., *J. S. Mill and Harriet Taylor,* London, 1951.

PACKE, M. ST J., *The Life of J. S. Mill,* London, 1954.

PAPPE, H. O., *J. S. Mill and the Harriet Taylor Myth,* London, 1960.

General and Philosophical

(i) *Auguste Comte and Positivism,* London, 1865.

An Examination of Sir William Hamilton's Philosophy, London, 1865.

Inaugural Address at St Andrews, London, 1867.

The Spirit of the Age, ed. F. A. Hayek, Chicago, 1942.

A System of Logic, London, 1843; eighth edition, 1872.

Three Essays on Religion, London, 1874.

Utilitarianism, London, 1863.

(ii) ANSCHUTZ, R. P., *The Philosophy of J. S. Mill,* Oxford, 1953.

BRITTON, K., *J. S. Mill,* London, 1953.

HALEVY, E., *The Growth of Philosophical Radicalism,* London, 1928.

ROBSON, J., *The Improvement of Mankind,* London, 1968.

STEPHEN, L., *The English Utilitarians,* 3 vols., London, 1900.

Democracy and Freedom

(i) 'Centralisation', *Edinburgh Review,* CXV, 1862.

Considerations on Representative Government, London, 1861.

'Law of Libel and Liberty of the Press', *Westminster Review* III, 1825.

On Liberty, London, 1859.

The Subjection of Women, London, 1869.

'Tocqueville on Democracy in America', *London and Westminster Review,* I and XXX, 1835; and *Edinburgh Review* LXXII, 1840.

A short extract from the first review was reprinted as part of the Appendix in *Dissertations and Discussions* vol. I, and the second review was reprinted in vol. II.

BERLIN, I., 'J. S. Mill and the Ends of Life' in *Four Essays on Liberty,* Oxford, 1969.

COWLING, M., *Mill and Liberalism,* Cambridge, 1963.

DEVLIN, P., *The Enforcement of Morals,* London, 1965.

HART, H. L. A., *Law, Liberty, and Morality,* London, 1963.

LETWIN, S., *The Pursuit of Certainty,* Cambridge, 1965.

RADCLIFF, P., (ed.) *Limits of Liberty,* California, 1966.

REES, J. C., *Mill and his Early Critics,* Leicester, 1956.
'A Re-reading of Mill on Liberty', *Political Studies* VIII, 1958, reprinted in Radcliff's collection.

STEPHEN, J. F., *Liberty, Equality, Fraternity,* London, 1873.

Parliamentary Reform

(i) 'Recent Writers on Reform', *Fraser's Magazine,* 1859; reprinted DD III.

'Reorganisation of the Reform Party', *London and Westminster Review,* 1839.

Thoughts on Parliamentary Reform, Pamphlet 1859; reprinted DD III.

(ii) BURNS, J. H., 'J. S. Mill and Democracy 1829-1861', *Political Studies* V, 1957.

Economics and Politics

(i) 'The Claims of Labour', *Edinburgh Review* LXXXI, 1845; reprinted DD II.
'Chapters on Socialism', *Fornightly Review*, n.s. XXV, 1879.
Essays on some Unsettled Questions of Political Economy, London, 1844.
Principles of Political Economy, 2 vols., London, 1848; 7th edition, 1871.
'Thornton on Labour and its Claims', *Fortnightly Review*, n.s. V 1869; reprinted DD IV.

Classical Political Thought

(i) There are three long reviews of Grote's work on the History of Greece, on Plato, and on Aristotle reprinted in *Dissertations and Discussions,* vols. II, III, and IV. Also, see: F. BORCHARDT (ed.) *Four Dialogues of Plato—J. S. Mill,* London 1946.

Contemporary Political Problems

(i) As can be seen from the following list of contents of the four volumes of *Dissertations and Discussions,* Mill wrote extensively on a wide range of topics:

Four volumes, London, 1859-1875. These contain a selection of Mill's writings, mainly from the *Westminster Review,* the *Edinburgh Review, Fraser's Magazine,* and the *Fortnightly Review;* vol. I 1859. State Interference with Corporation and Church Property; The Currency Jungle; A Few Observations on the French Revolution; Thoughts on Poetry and its Varieties; Sedgwick's Discourse; Civilisation; Aphorisms; Armand Carrel; A Prophecy; Alfred de Vigny; Bentham; Coleridge; Appendix.

vol. II 1859. Tocqueville on Democracy in America; Bailey on Berkeley; Michelet's History of France; The Claims of Labour; Guizot's Essays and Lectures on History; Early Grecian History and Legend; French Revolution 1848; Enfranchisement of Women; Whewell on Moral Philosophy; Grote's History of Greece; Appendix to French Revolution 1848.

vol. III 1867. Thoughts on Parliamentary Reform; Recent Writers on Reform; Bain's Psychology; A Few Words on Non-Intervention; The Contest in America; Austin on Jurisprudence; Plato.

vol. IV 1875. Endowments; Thornton on Labour and its Claims; Professor Leslie on the Land Question; Taine—De L'Intelligence; Treaty Obligations; Maine on Village Communities; Berkeley's Life and Writings; Grote's Aristotle; L'Avere de L'Imposta; Papers on Land Tenure.

(ii) HAMBURGER, J., *Intellectuals in Politics: J. S. Mill and the Philosophical Radicals,* 1965.

SEMMEL, B., *The Governor Eyre Controversy,* London, 1962.

Index

Edmund Burke
On Government, Politics and Society

Selected and Edited by B. W. Hill

Quoted more frequently than almost any other political writer, Edmund Burke has been cast in many roles – as arch-defender of established authority, radical critic of traditional orthodoxies, exponent of liberal values. Yet the historical Burke is a much more complex and fascinating thinker than any of these views allows.

The aim of this new selection is to reveal the range of Burke's outlook as politician, imaginative writer, and philosopher by drawing upon the extensive speeches and pamphlets on the American Colonies, the Monarchy and the Party system, and the Government of India, as well as the more widely known *Reflections on the Revolution in France*.

In his long introduction and editorial comments, Dr Hill presents Burke as an eclectic thinker, but a consistent advocate of social morality, a friend of good caring government, and an opponent of extremist politics whether of the Right or the Left.

'Almost alone in England, he brings thought to bear upon politics, he saturates politics with thought.' *Matthew Arnold*

'Burke *is* an extraordinary man. His stream of mind is perpetual.' *Samuel Johnson*

'No English writer has received, or has deserved, more splendid panegyrics than Burke.' *Leslie Stephen*

'There is no wise man in politics, with an important decision to make, who would not do well to refresh his mind by discussion with Burke's mind.' *Harold Laski*

Hitler: The Führer and the People

J. P. Stern

His life, his times, his policies, his strategies, his influence have often been analysed. But rarely is the most elementary question of all raised – how could it happen?

How could a predominantly sober, hard-working, and well-educated population have been persuaded to follow Hitler to the awful abyss of destruction? What was the source of his immense popularity? What was the image projected in his speeches, his writings, and his conversation?

Hitler: The Führer and the People is a compelling attempt to reconstruct the nature of Hitler's political ideology, its roots, logic, and function.

'Who really wants or needs another book on Hitler? The short answer is, when the book is as good and original and brief as Professor Stern's, that we all do.'

Donald G. MacRae, *New Statesman*

'Stern's book is, on all counts, a significant achievement.'

Geoffrey Barraclough, *New York Review of Books*

'. . . an excellent book, all the more so because it concerns itself, via Hitler, with the more general problems of the relationship between society and the individual leader, between ideas and action, between myth and reality.'

Douglas Johnson, *New Society*

'His short book is one of the most remarkable studies of Hitler and Nazism to have appeared.' Christopher Sykes, *Observer*